Schools Council/Rowntree Trust

World Studies 8–13

A Teacher's Handbook

Simon Fisher
World Studies Project of the One World Trust, London

David Hicks
Centre for Peace Studies, St. Martin's College, Lancaster

Oliver & Boyd
Edinburgh and New York

For Susannah, Abigail, Jonah, Naomi, Matthew and John-Mark

Oliver & Boyd
Robert Stevenson House
1–3 Baxter's Place
Leith Walk
Edinburgh EH1 3BB
A division of Longman Group Ltd

First published 1985

Distributed in the United States by Longman Inc., 1560 Broadway, New York, NY 10036.

British Library Cataloguing in Publication Data

Fisher, Simon
    World studies 8.13.
    1. International education — Great Britain
    I. Title II. Hicks, David III. Schools Council
    370.11′5   LC1090

    ISBN 0 05 003845 1

Library of Congress Cataloging in Publication Data

Fisher, Simon.
    World studies, 8–13.

    At head of title: Great Britain Schools Council.
    Bibliography: p.
    Includes index.
    1. History — Study and teaching (Elementary) — Great Britain.
    I. Hicks, David. II. Schools Council (Great Britain) III. Title.
    IV. Title: World studies, eight-thirteen.
    LB1582.G7F57   1984   372.8′9044   84–3663
    ISBN 0 05 003845 1

Printed in Hong Kong by
Sheck Wah Tong Printing Press Ltd

Acknowledgements

The publishers would like to thank the following for permission to reproduce cartoons, photographs or other copyright material. (Where relevant, detailed information on sources is given in captions in the text.)

The New Era, London (cartoon p. v); *Times Educational Supplement* (quotation p. v); Robin Richardson, *Change and Choice: Britain in an Independent World*, a study pack published by CWDE (The Galactic Traveller, p. 2); J. Allan Cash (Fig. 1.1); UNICEF/New Internationalist (Fig. 1.2); Steve Smith Graphics (Fig. 1.4); John Fien (Fig. 2.2); Robin Richardson (Fig. 2.3); Press Association (Fig. 2.4 photograph); *The Guardian* (Fig. 2.4 text); Stephen Scoffham (Figs. 2.5, 3.1, 3.6); Longman Group Ltd (Fig. 3.5); One World Trust (Figs. 3.2, 3.3, 4.2); Oxfam (Figs. 4.4, 4.5); Christian Aid (Fig. 4.9 and the play on pages 56–59); Len Munnik (Figs. 5.1, 5.12); EOC (Fig. 5.2); Ken Pyne (Fig. 5.9); Shell, Richard & Sally Greenhill, London Transport, J. Allan Cash (Fig. 5.13); CWDE (Fig. 6.1); Gillies McKinnon (Figs. 5.17, 7.3); Punch (Figs. 6.4, 6.13); New Internationalist (Figs. 6.7, 6.23, 6.24, 7.6, 7.10, 7.13); Ken Merrylees (Fig. 6.11 photographs); Bryan McAllister (Fig. 6.12); Zambia Tourist Office (Fig. 6.15 photograph); Keystone Press Agency (Fig. 6.20); University Tutorial Press (Fig. 6.23); Stefan Verney (Fig. 6.25); World Council of Churches (Fig. 7.5), Rachel Gardner (Fig. 7.4); UNICEF (Fig. 7.9); The National Federation of City Farms (Fig. 7.15); National Centre for Alternative Technology (Fig. 7.16); Bob Hart, Headteacher of the Pines School, Hertford (Fig. 7.17); Raymond Briggs (Fig. 7.18).

The publishers also thank those teachers and publishers who gave permission for quoted material to be reproduced in the book. Acknowledgement is given in the text.

Illustrated by Tim Smith, Stephen Gibson and Rob Norman.

Contents

Preface   v
Elephant Education: A Cautionary Tale   vi

Part 1   Curriculum Planning   **1**
1   World Studies and World Society   2
    An Interdependent World   2
    World Studies in Schools   5
    Why Teach World Studies?   8
    World Studies in Britain   9
    Further Reading   13
2   Teaching and Learning World Studies   14
    'Unteachable' Ideas   14
    Talking Together   15
    Integrated Approaches   19
    Subject-based Approaches   22
    Further Reading   23
3   World Studies and Curriculum Planning   24
    Aims and Objectives   24
    Attitudes and Skills   27
    Planning with Concepts   28
    Reflection and Action   29
    Conclusion   32
    Further Reading   32

Part 2   Classroom Activities   **33**
Introduction   34
4   Here is the World   37
    Introduction   37
    Looking at Ourselves   38
    Exploring the Neighbourhood   48
    Unequal Trade   54
    Starting Points   63
    Selected Resources   64

5   Getting on with Others   66
    Introduction   66
    Working Together   69
    Resolving Conflicts   80
    Sex-role Stereotyping   89
    Starting Points   97
    Selected Resources   98
6   Other Worlds   100
    Introduction   100
    Images and Assumptions   100
    Too Much or Too Little   103
    Minorities   109
    Starting Points   119
    Selected Resources   129
7   The World Tomorrow   130
    Introduction   132
    What Will the World be Like?   132
    What Should the World be Like?   135
    Making Changes   141
    Starting Points   150
    Selected Resources   158
        159

Part 3   In-service Ideas   **161**
8   Teachers Together   162
    The Whole School   162
    Planning Workshops and Courses   162
    Some In-service Approaches   163
    A School Case Study   179
    Further Reading   181
Appendix 1   182
Appendix 2   183
Appendix 3   184
Notes   185

Eating alone
is a disappointment,
but not eating
matters more, is
hollow and green, has
thorns like a chain of
fish hooks trailing
from the heart,
clawing
at your insides.

Hunger feels like
pincers, like the bite
of crabs, it burns,
burns and has no fire.
Hunger is a cold fire.
Let us sit down soon
to eat with all those
who haven't eaten;
let us spread great
tablecloths, put salt
in the lakes of the
world, set up
planetary bakeries,
stables with
strawberries in snow,
and a plate like
the moon itself from
which we can all eat.

For now I ask
no more than the
justice of eating.

Pablo Neruda
'The Great Tablecloth'

Preface

The modern world is increasingly one world, a single world society in which we are all involved. Its future and our personal futures are inextricably linked. What should we teach children in schools about world society and the changes taking place in it? And how should we teach? How can we tackle controversial issues in a fair and interesting way?

This book is a practical resource to help teachers answer these questions. It contains over eighty activities to stimulate and develop young people's interest in the wider world and their relationship to it. The activities are also designed to foster basic language and social skills. They are enjoyable and often amusing.

The book also offers a framework for curriculum planning, including a set of objectives and key concepts, and suggests strategies for running workshops and in-service courses with a world dimension. There is, further, a selective guide to resources for teachers and pupils in the middle years of schooling.

This book arose out of the work of the Schools Council/Rowntree Project *World Studies 8–13* (1980–3) a project jointly run by the One World Trust, a Westminster based educational charity, and the Centre for Peace Studies at St Martin's College in Lancaster. This project is now operating in some thirty Local Education Authorities in England and Wales.

In the course of writing this book we have been supported and encouraged by countless people, among them many of the local project co-ordinators and participating teachers. In particular, however, we would like to express our thanks to Patrick Armstrong and the One World Trust who have initiated and guided much curriculum development in world studies since 1973, including the *World Studies 8–13* Project and its predecessor at secondary level, the World Studies Project (1973–80).

The latter project, directed by Robin Richardson, has been one of the most influential in the field of world studies. We are particularly indebted to Robin for his wisdom, insight and encouragement over a number of years, including the period of this project. Several of the activities in the book have been influenced by his thinking. For the selected resources sections that go with each chapter in Part 2

we are grateful to Gillian Klein. Her labours were invaluable and we feel privileged to have benefited from her wide experience.

For their friendly advice and shrewd criticism we would like to thank Pat Whitaker, John Huckle, Margot Brown, Ann Baker, Janet Caton, John Burns, Nick Clough and Steven Barnes. Further helpful support came from members of our Schools Council Monitoring Group and the One World Trust's Guiding Group. To them also go our thanks.

For the funding to make the work and this book possible we are indebted to the Schools Council and the Joseph Rowntree Charitable Trust. In particular the latter generously continued to support the project after Schools Council funding had ended.

Throughout the progress of this book we have been fortunate in having Diana Hayden, Dianne Plahuta and Sylvia McCulloch to interpret and re-type the many drafts.

Simon Fisher, Bristol
David Hicks, Lancaster

No comment

'The world. What does our world and universe look like and how did it get here?'
Twenty-minute essay topic for a 13-year-old's religious education homework.

Robin Richardson
Elephant Education: A Cautionary Tale

'The world we live in contains elephants. The classrooms of our schools should therefore reflect our need to know about and to understand elephants. Resources should be allocated urgently to more and better elephant education.'

'Elephant education!' exclaimed the people when they heard this recommendation. 'We are not entirely sure what that is.' Six blind people went forth to find out.

The first blind person went to the Ivory Coast, in West Africa, since this is a country actually named after elephants, albeit only partially. This first blind person looked at the records and record of the Parti Democratique de la Côte d'Ivoire, its struggle for independence, its life in and out of the French community, its affair with de Gaulle, its use of pressure, power and resources over forty years: and concluded that elephant education is another phrase for political education.

The second blind person went to a film called The Elephant Man, and looked at elephantiasis, the swelling of limbs, obstructions in the flow of lymph, overgrowth of subcutaneous tissue: and in looking thus at sickly growth and wrong progress, and comparing it with healthy growth and right progress, this second blind person concluded that elephant education is another phrase for development education.

The third blind person looked at the diverse ways in which human beings relate to elephants. We corral them in keddahs, hump them with howdahs, train them for traction, parade them in processions, circle them in circuses. The third blind person saw not only diversity but also conflicts of interest, discrimination, prejudice, bars and barriers, and concluded that elephant education is another phrase for multicultural education.

The fourth blind person looked at the escalation of the arms race which was occasioned in 220 B.C. by Hannibal of Carthage, when he resolved to use elephants in his war of liberation against the Pax Romana. Seeing thus both direct and structural violence, this fourth blind person concluded that elephant education is another phrase for peace education.

The fifth blind person went to a place of consumption, read on the menu there of Jumbo burgers, Jumbo sandwiches, Jumbo pizzas; saw the waitresses, the pretty little maids there all in a row; saw beyond them the prairies and boardrooms, men doing there what men have to do; saw behind every good man Kirche and Küche, temple and table, synagogue and sink, shrine and shine, mosque and mop, church and chore. Reading thus between as well as along the lines of the menu, the fifth blind person concluded that elephant education is another phrase for equal opportunities and anti-sexist education.

The sixth blind person looked at a distinctive literary form, slightly reminiscent of Old Testament poetry, in which statements about elephants are frequently expressed. It consists of a litany of interrogatives and responses. Question: Why do elephants paint the soles of their feet yellow? – Answer: So that they can float upside-down in the custard without being seen. Question: How can you tell when you're in bed with an elephant? Answer: Because he has an 'E' embroidered on his pyjama jacket. Studying this literary form, the sixth blind person realised that elephants must suffer from a negative self-image and inadequate social skills, and concluded that elephant education is another phrase for personal and social education.

The six blind people went their separate ways, and polished separately their respective conclusions. Indeed they damn near perfected them. They applied separately for money from charitable trusts and from central and local government; set up working parties, standing conferences, associations, networks; formulated aims and objectives, and devised syllabuses and schemes of work; sent deputations to examination boards; made bids for the attention and commitment of influential teachers, lobbied and jockeyed for time and space in each individual school.

They failed however, completely, to achieve any of the values which they wished to promote; and failed also to avert any of the threats to which they wished to respond. They failed even to live out the short span of their own lives with integrity and love.

Robin Richardson, formerly Director of the World Studies Project, London, is now Adviser for Multicultural Education, Berkshire.

PART ONE

Curriculum Planning

1. World Studies and World Society

An Interdependent World

The Galactic Traveller

There is a tale told of a certain galactic traveller who visited Earth and collected various samples of sea water in order to carry out research on the oceans. Before returning to his own rim of the galaxy, however, he happened to find himself at a football match, an event which he watched with amazement. How, he wondered, could he possibly make sense of what was going on?

He decided to do the same for football as he had for the oceans: he would take a sample. He thus trained the zoom lens of his movie camera onto just one footballer and recorded every single movement the player made, in fact every step and leap and breath he took. Occasionally a round object came close to the player's feet, and the player would kick it, occasionally the player would appear to collide with another player. All these events were recorded faithfully on film.

The galactic traveller returned in due course to his own planet and his own laboratory where he analysed the samples of sea water, and published a book on the composition of the Earth's oceans. He also developed his film of the football player, examined it frame by frame, and as a result evolved an elaborate and elegant theory about, so he thought, the basic nature of football. He published his findings and – it is said – won many awards for his distinguished contribution to galactic science.[1]

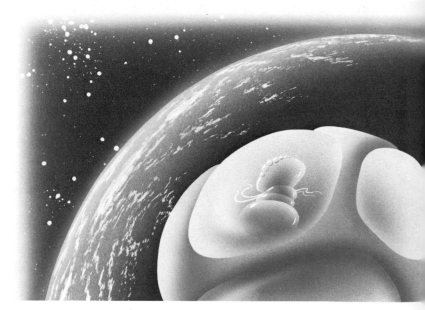

Local and Global Connections

If the galactic traveller had asked, someone would have told him that looking at the behaviour of one individual player is not the way to study and understand football. To understand each player's actions it is necessary to look at that player's relationship with others, and that player's part within the whole game, the whole system. The two goalkeepers, for example, seldom have direct contact with each other and their actions appear to be quite unrelated unless considered in the context of the game as a whole.

The same is true of a town in Britain and one in, say, Japan or Kenya. They may or may not directly affect each other, through the exchange of goods, or through the interchange of people and ideas, or through less direct economic and political relationships, but both are parts of one global system, and so are the individuals who live there, as is demonstrated in our own everyday lives.

This morning, for example, you may have been woken by an alarm clock. After washing and dressing you probably had breakfast: perhaps a bowl of cornflakes, a slice of bread and marmalade, a cup of tea. There may even have been time for a quick glance at the newspaper before leaving for school.

While this may seem an unsurprising start to the day, it is nevertheless one which is permeated by connections with the wider world. As likely as not, the clock was made by a Japanese firm from parts made in Mexico, Germany and Japan, shipped from the assembly plant in Brazil to Britain in a Greek-owned ship built in South Korea. Your soap was probably made by the multinational firm Unilever. Your clothes include cotton grown in the United States and wool from New Zealand. The cornflakes and the bread contain wheat from Canada. The marmalade was made with Spanish oranges and sugar grown in Barbados. Your tea came from Sri Lanka. Timber from Scandinavian forests was used to make the newspaper, which contains news of many world events. The bus or car you took to school included Zambian copper, iron ore from the United States, lead from Australia, chrome from Zimbabwe, and a wealth of other materials from many countries. In fact, we cannot make a move without being hooked into the global network in some way.[2]

In a similar way prominent events and issues on the world stage are also inescapably local ones, with connections between innumerable towns and neighbourhoods. Thus, for example, a North American space venture would be impossible without the knowledge of scientists from many different countries; a new intercontinental gas pipeline requires components made by firms on the other side of the globe; controversy over the status and role of women in the Islamic world raises critical questions about equal opportunities for women in Western Europe; acid rain over Scandinavia can be attributed to sulphurous fumes from industry in various parts of Britain; a war in the Middle East can only be fought with weapons and equipment made in a host of different places, perhaps even incorporating parts manufactured in our own town.

Connections of this nature affect almost every person and locality in the world, linking humankind firmly together, whether we like it or not, in a global web of interaction. More fundamental still are the ties which arise from our mutual dependence on the planet itself for survival, and our shared need to preserve and enhance its natural life-support systems. Especially since the advent of industrialisation, some humans have treated the earth as a store of materials to be exploited and mined, and as a recipient for all kinds of waste, however toxic. It is now evident that the conse-

quent depletion of resources and damage to the environment are causing many plant and animal species to disappear and threatening our own long-term future, this resulting in a reawakening of ecological awareness and concern.

Interdependence is one overall term which is often used to describe this state of affairs. Other similar phrases include global community, the biosphere, one world, village earth, global ecosystem.

The kind of world which these terms recall came into being over many centuries, at first gradually, and then increasingly rapidly since the early nineteenth century, mainly as a result of the development and spread of capitalist enterprise. Large-scale changes have taken place in technology and economic relationships, especially in the field of communications and transport, in the distribution of political power between countries, and in peoples' lifestyles.

New developments in information technology are currently increasing the speed of change and reducing still further the isolating effects of distance. For example, it is standard practice now for an American Express credit card used by a customer in a British high street to be checked in a matter of minutes through a computer link thousands of miles away in Arizona, USA.

The cumulative effect of these changes has been to force on us a new frame of reference: many of the problems which individual countries are faced with can no longer be properly understood, let alone solved, unless they are seen in the context of economic and social changes which have affected the world as a whole. Most obviously this is the case with the rich world/poor world divide, hunger, population growth, human rights, unemployment, the arms race, environmental damage, raw materials and energy supplies. The list could go on.

In this global system, action on a particular issue in one continent or country is often not only ineffective it; it may frequently make matters worse elsewhere, and exacerbate other problems. Some brief, and necessarily simplified, examples can illustrate the point:

● In their efforts during the 1970s to reduce unemployment at home, some governments of industrialised countries imposed restrictions on the import of textiles, and consequently reduced the exports and increased the unemployment of other countries, particularly in the 'third world'. The resulting drop in purchasing power in the poorer countries served to increase still further the gap between rich North and poor South. It also meant they were less able to buy goods manufactured in the North, thus helping to raise unemployment there too.

Alternatively, with the same aim in mind, these governments might have chosen to respond to the lobbying of conservationists, and given increased grants for house insulation. A side-effect of this, all things being equal, might have been a small reduction in the world demand and price for oil, which might in turn have assisted development programmes in the poorer countries.

● As a result of the labour shortage in Britain during the 1950s many firms encouraged people from the Caribbean to leave their homes and settle in this country. They came expecting to be welcomed but were given a reception that was often less than friendly. For many, good jobs and houses proved difficult to come by. The children of these people were born here and grew up in British society. They, however, were less willing than their parents to put up with the prejudice and discrimination that they often met. One result of this frustration was that many of them felt impelled to join in disturbances in inner cities as the only way left to vent their feelings.

● The destruction of Native American culture over the last hundred years by white settlers has arguably brought few benefits to the original inhabitants of America. Their education, health, living conditions, employment and life chances generally are the worst for any minority group in the USA. Some of their land has been appropriated for mining and industrial purposes causing the Indians to turn to the courts for legal redress.[3]

Repeated on a global scale, this destruction of indigenous 'native peoples' is eliminating a way of life which has been sustained for thousands of years. It is resulting in an irreversible loss of knowledge about the natural world, and about patterns of social and political organisation, at a time when many people in 'advanced' societies are urgently turning to these same peoples for clues to more ecologically aware styles of living.

● The current drive towards rapid economic development by governments of many 'third world' countries seems likely to result in the destruction

Figure 1.1 Deforestation in the Amazon

of half of the world's tropical forests by the turn of the century, with the rest to follow in a few decades. The aim of these governments, who are themselves often at the mercy of multinational corporations, is to acquire more land for the cultivation of cash crops, although after a few years such cleared areas are likely to become desert. The global cost of this process includes the progressive elimination of the earth's main and still largely unclassified store of medicinal and drug-yielding plants, the destruction of a vast source of new food and energy supplies, and potentially serious worldwide climatic changes, all aspects of life crucial to the future of humankind.[4]

World issues and events inevitably have an effect on individual people, and are in turn influenced for good or ill by them, as this hypothetical but quite plausible sequence indicates:

The increase in oil prices by OPEC in 1974 led to a Japanese export drive, which led to unemployment in certain British industries. This led to a depressive illness in John Smith when he lost his job; which led to his divorce; which led to John Smith and his wife and his children losing all interest in the wider world as they struggled to cope with life one day at a time; which led to them refusing to support the World Disarmament Campaign, the failure of this campaign being one factor which led to the outbreak of the Third World War.[5]

For many people the present state of our 'one world' is clearly not a cosy or a comfortable one. There are, unfortunately, opportunities for the powerful to exploit the weak and for the rich to benefit at the expense of the poor and of the earth itself.

Certainly there have been encouraging developments in recent years. For example, literacy rates have improved in many areas; food production has generally kept pace with population growth; the advent of a global network of satellite communication has meant that major events are more quickly known about and responded to; life expectancy and the quality of life have increased for many people.

But human invention and ingenuity for good are matched by worldwide manifestations of imbalance, inequality and injustice. Despite adequate food supplies, one in four of the world's people is hungry or starving; while tropical forests and arable land shrink, the deserts continue to grow; one in five of all species of living plants and animals are expected to be lost by the turn of the century; spending on the military increases steadily, at incalculable human and material cost, bringing the possibility of large-scale destruction through nuclear war ever nearer.

World Studies in Schools

For young people in schools now the future must seem at the same time exciting, alarming and bewildering. The outlook is certainly much more uncertain than we would often give them to understand.

But teachers too are in a difficult position: committed to helping young people equip themselves for a life which will be spent largely in the twenty-first century, yet having little clear idea of what conditions will be like and facing conflicting views on which attitudes and trends should be supported and which resisted.

Much thinking has, of course, gone on in many countries about how the school curriculum should reflect this 'world of change' and a variety of terms have been coined to describe the responses. These include: education for international understanding, world studies, multicultural education, development education, education for peace, personal and social education, political education.

While each of these fields has different origins, many of their concerns often overlap. Thus, although this book uses the term 'world studies', it will be of value and use to practitioners in *all* these fields.

Some Classroom Examples

World studies encompasses a wide range of issues and activities, as the following classroom glimpses indicate.

● In one classroom, a class of thirty pupils are playing a game called The Global Cake.[6] They are sitting in groups representing continents, with the size of each group corresponding to the appropriate percentage of world population. The groups are trading scissors, rulers, pencils and other items which they need to make their prescribed symbols for the 'ingredients': for example, sheaves of corn (for flour), chickens (for eggs), cows (for milk) and so on. At the end of an hour or so, when the symbols have all been fixed to a class mural representing the global cake, the teacher gives every group one or more real pieces of cake according to the actual level of consumption of food in the world. Not surprisingly, Asia's nine players are less than happy with their one and a half pieces, especially when they see North America's two players getting fat on eight and a half pieces.

● In another classroom there is silence. The pupils, seated in groups at tables, are pushing pieces of differently shaped card between each other. Each pupil is trying to make a square: if all are to succeed, each square must be the same size. The pupils may not ask for the pieces they need, nor take them. They are each depending on the co-operation and sensitivity of their fellow group members to achieve their task. One has formed a large square for herself, using some of the pieces that others need; can she bring herself to dismantle her square? Is the activity seen as a race to be won by whoever can, or as a common problem, to be solved by all the participants together?

● In a third, the classroom is empty. Having spent some time considering the needs of the area, the class are on one of their regular visits to the local city farm, planting and tending a variety of

Figure 1.2

6

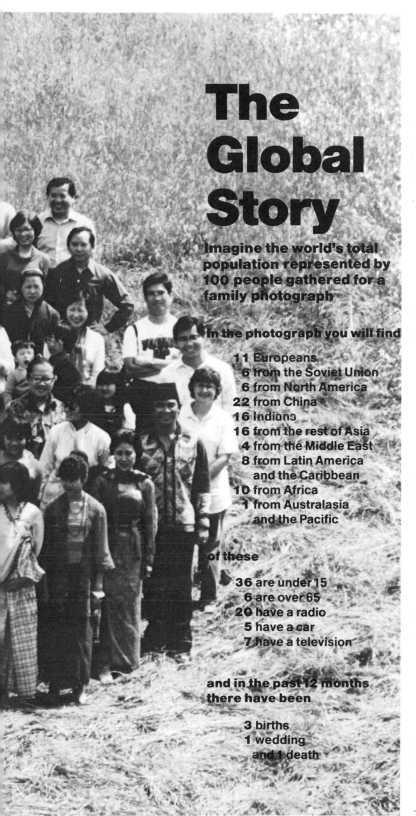

The Global Story

Imagine the world's total population represented by 100 people gathered for a family photograph

In the photograph you will find

11 Europeans
6 from the Soviet Union
6 from North America
22 from China
16 Indians
16 from the rest of Asia
4 from the Middle East
8 from Latin America
and the Caribbean
10 from Africa
1 from Australasia
and the Pacific

of these

36 are under 15
6 are over 65
20 have a radio
5 have a car
7 have a television

**and in the past 12 months
there have been**

3 births
1 wedding
and 1 death

vegetables and assisting with the overall development of the farm. In parallel the pupils are studying the life and work of people in an Indian village. What are the common basic needs and aspirations? How are these met? What are the differences?

● In another, a number of pupils were struck by a television programme about deforestation in the Amazon Basin. As a result the class and their teacher thought a great deal about what they could do to reverse this global process. Looking at the barrenness of their own school playing field they decided to fence off a small part of it in order to create a conservation area. So far they have dug a pond, planted over fifty trees and bushes, and are planning to install a weather station.[7]

● In yet another classroom the pupils are studying and discussing work. Specifically, what will it be like in twenty years time? They are doing this as part of a course on the future which includes a general review of some major global issues, more detailed consideration of housing, nuclear energy and appropriate technology, equal opportunities for women, and an exploration of the pupils' hopes for their personal futures in a multicultural society.

Each of these classrooms illustrates an aspect of world studies teaching. Although they are diverse in their subject matter, the activities described have a number of things in common. They all concern children of primary or lower secondary school age. They involve, explicitly or implicitly, an approach to teaching and learning which begins from, though is certainly not limited to, children's own experience and interests. Active teaching methods such as role-play, discussion exercises or games are used in order to explore more graphically problems of perception, communication and action. Children are being stimulated and challenged; they are being invited to express their own opinions, and their views are taken seriously. They are reflecting both on their own world and other people's worlds, and learning from each about both. Although the activities may seem demanding for this age level, the pupils are, in fact, also often achieving more than they would normally be expected to.

A Definition

These activities, and world studies generally, are based on the premise that the school curriculum needs to be permeated by a world perspective which emphasises the interdependence of all humanity. Effective responsible citizens in modern society need to know how their world works, how and why it doesn't work, and how it can be made to work more effectively. They need to know about the groups which human beings belong to and the countries or territories which they occupy. In particular they need to have a knowledge of, and sensitivity towards, cultures and societies other than their own if they are to pursue their own interests wisely and without harming the legitimate interests of others.

World studies can thus be defined as *studies which promote the knowledge, attitudes and skills that are relevant to living responsibly in a multicultural and interdependent world.*

World studies is, by its very nature, for all pupils, whatever their ability and age, and for all schools, whether rural or urban, whether multi-ethnic or not. It is a shorthand term which describes a dimension in the whole curriculum of a school and may sometimes also describe a distinct topic, course or subject. In either case world studies includes

(*a*) studying cultures and countries other than one's own, and the ways in which they are different from, and similar to, one's own;

(*b*) studying major issues which face different countries and cultures, for example those to do with peace and conflict, development, human rights and the environment;

(*c*) studying the ways in which everyday life and experience affect, and are affected by, the wider world.

If one inescapable focus for world studies is the world – its people, their aspirations and problems – the other, equally important, is the individual child. As with any other part of the curriculum, world studies teaching begins with, and must make a significant contribution to, the overall learning and development of those who experience it. And it must do so in a way which is consistent with the needs of young people facing an uncertain future, in particular by fostering the ability to co-operate with others, to think critically about their own assumptions and actions, and to make decisions independently and wisely.

The central question posed in this book brings these two areas of focus together: how can teachers help children build on their everyday experience and interests so that they develop an increasingly informed, critical awareness of the modern world, and the ability to participate in it?

Why Teach World Studies?

Some Important Reasons

One of the main arguments for introducing or strengthening world studies in a school has just been outlined: the state of our world in the late twentieth century – interdependent yet divided, beset by difficulties which threaten the very continuation of life – *requires* that young people learn about it in school.

There are several other important reasons.

Immediate interest in the wider world

Children are naturally interested in, and often quite knowledgeable about, world events and trends. They therefore tend to work hard at world studies and achieve a high standard. The satisfaction and self-confidence which they derive from this often improves their overall interest and achievement in other aspects of the curriculum, particularly in basic skills such as spoken language, literacy and numeracy.

Active teaching methods

As the activities described in the main part of this book show, world studies lends itself to a variety of active teaching approaches: discussion exercises, co-operative games, visits, visiting speakers, role-play, enquiry-based project work. Pupils and teachers alike tend to find these refreshing and stimulating.

Learning about others

The study of 'other' people – that is, in countries and cultures other than our own, or at times in history other than our own – helps pupils avoid making false generalisations. These frequently arise from an 'ethnocentric' world view in which people judge others exclusively by their own cultural norms. Learning about others can also help pupils learn about human nature – that is, about themselves.

Trade and prosperity

Parents, governors and employers are often strong supporters of world studies, on the grounds that a country whose prosperity depends on trade needs citizens with a sound understanding of the wider world and the ability both to see things from other people's points of view and to see themselves as others see them.

Politics and people

Change in our own society, and in the world as a whole, cannot be understood without some grasp of differing political and economic systems. World studies helps children understand major trends and events by enabling them to think in terms of systems and structures, as well as of individuals and groups.

Children's futures

Most of the lives of children now in school will be spent in the twenty-first century, about which we know very little except that it will be quite different from today. It is important that they are encouraged from an early age to think positively and imaginatively about the future and to respond creatively to uncertainty and change.

It would be facile to suggest that educating young children about world issues for these, or any other reasons, will help to manage or solve them in anything but the long term. Education, however, must be concerned with the long term, as well as with the immediate present.

Laying the Foundations

In the past, world studies teaching has tended to be concentrated in the upper years of secondary school. It has, however, become increasingly evident in recent years that children need to begin studying the wider world much earlier than this.

This realisation has come about partly because of the observation that, whatever schools may do, children are aware of world events at an early age, through television programmes such as *John Craven's Newsround*, *Blue Peter* and others. The large audiences for these and similar programmes indicate the great and continuing interest that children have in people, places and the issues which bring them into the news. If schools do not deal with these matters, children will have to form their opinions largely on the basis of the media and, perhaps, some discussion at home.

Given this powerful curiosity, it is not surprising that children begin to form their ideas about race, gender, other countries and world affairs at quite an early age. It is probable that, whatever their apparent behaviour, the children in a typical lower junior school class will be well aware of racial differences and have an elementary pecking order of racial groups in their minds.[8] They are also likely to have some simple ideas about war, for example, though probably less so about peace.[9]

Crucially, it is now understood that children often tend to develop attitudes in these fields before they have any appreciable knowledge. It is an aspect of world studies teaching which needs to be recognised clearly: we are at this level concerned very much, though not exclusively, with attitudes and awareness.

In the middle years children are potentially more flexible in their attitudes towards people of cultures other than their own than they are likely to be later in adolescence. The evidence suggests that a peak of tolerance is reached around the age of eleven or twelve, after which, unless there is a sound basis for reflection and understanding, attitudes tend to harden and tolerance decreases.[10] The message thus seems to be unequivocal: if we want children to acquire a thoughtful rational approach to the wider world, with all its contentious issues, we need to lay the foundations systematically from an early age.

The suggestions made in this book for curriculum planning, and the many classroom activities, all aim to assist in laying these foundations.

World Studies in Britain

Official Support

It is important to recall that there has for some time been consistent support in Britain for world studies.

In 1974, for example, the British Government, along with many others, signed the UNESCO *Recommendation Concerning Education for International Understanding, Co-operation and Peace and Education Relating to Human Rights and Fundamental Freedoms*.[11]

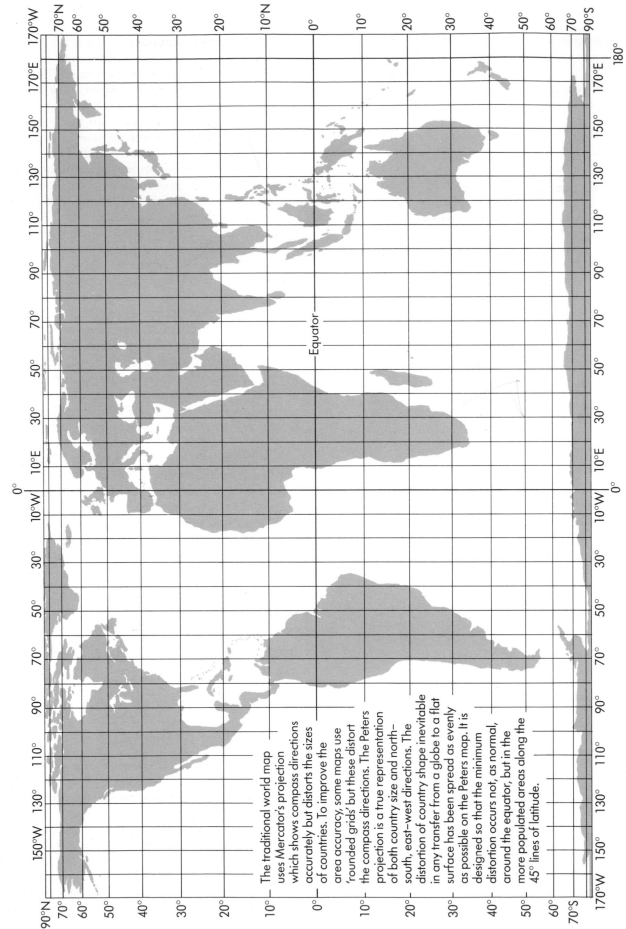

The traditional world map uses Mercator's projection which shows compass directions accurately but distorts the sizes of countries. To improve the area accuracy, some maps use 'rounded grids' but these distort the compass directions. The Peters projection is a true representation of both country size and north–south, east–west directions. The distortion of country shape inevitable in any transfer from a globe to a flat surface has been spread as evenly as possible on the Peters map. It is designed so that the minimum distortion occurs at, as normal, around the equator, but in the more populated areas along the 45° lines of latitude.

Figure 1.3 The Peters projection world map

Among other things its signatories agreed:

- to increase efforts to develop an 'international and intercultural dimension' in schools;
- to encourage teaching about human rights, injustice, inequality, war, disarmament and the environment;
- that 'education should bring every person to understand and assume his or her responsibilities for the maintenance of peace'.

More recently the Department of Education and Science (DES) report on *The School Curriculum*, published in 1981, included these suggested aims for schools:

- to help pupils to understand the world in which they live, and the interdependence of individuals, groups and nations;
- to instil respect for religious and moral values, and tolerance of other races, religions and ways of life.

Looking particularly at primary schools, the report stated:

- children should be encouraged, in the context of the multicultural aspect of Britain today and of our membership of the European Community, to develop an understanding of the world, of their own place in it and of how people live and work.

And, if evidence of the *need* for this kind of education is required, a report in 1979 by the Ministry of Overseas Development summarised the findings of a specially commissioned national survey in this way:

The Survey gives a picture of two thirds of the nation with parochial and introverted attitudes, unsympathetic to a world perspective, clinging to the past and untutored to approach the future constructively. Attitudes towards the underdeveloped countries in particular are confused by stereotyped images, post colonial guilt, racial and cultural prejudices, limited, unbalanced knowledge . . . [12]

There is little reason to suggest that the situation has changed in the 1980s.

Recent Developments

World studies has a distinct lineage of its own. It had its beginnings in the United States in the 1960s in phrases such as global studies, global education and world order studies. In Britain, during the 1970s the concerns of world studies became increasingly recognised as the result of a wide range of initiatives from many different sources.

The One World Trust's World Studies Project (1973–80), which was funded by the Department of Education and Science, the Leverhulme Trust and the Ministry of Overseas Development, played a key role with its workshops and publications for both teachers and pupils.[13] Subsequently the Schools Council/Rowntree project *World Studies 8–13* strengthened and legitimated the field still further as did various projects at Jordanhill College in Glasgow: the Jordanhill Project on International Understanding; International Understanding in the Primary School in Scotland; and the International and Multicultural Education Project.[14]

Two important journals in the field have been, and are, *The New Era* and the *World Studies Journal*. These, together with two books, Derek Heater's *World Studies: Education for International Understanding in Britain* and *Teaching World Studies: An Introduction to Global Perspectives in the Curriculum*, edited by David Hicks and Charles Townley, have greatly widened the interest in these concerns. Also of note here are the World Studies Network and the World Studies Teacher Training Centre at York University.

Common Concerns

Many people have contributed to the growth of interest in world studies during the 1970s and 1980s, though they may not have made explicit use of the term. This is particularly true of those working in the fields of multicultural education, development education and peace education.

Important activities and projects include the educational work of overseas agencies such as Oxfam and Christian Aid; the resources made available through the Council for Education in World Citizenship and the Centre for World Development Education; the brief but fruitful existence in the late 1970s of the Development Education Fund of the Ministry of Overseas Development, and the establishment of a national network of Development Education Centres with its own central organisation, the National Association of Development Education Centres.

The UNESCO Associated Schools Project, administered by the Council for Education in World Citizenship, operates in a range of schools and colleges to promote the study of the United Nations and, more generally, of different cultures and countries. The Standing Conference on Education for International Understanding is now well established, with the help of some initial government funding.

Many vital initiatives have occurred too in the field of multicultural education as the original concern with English language teaching has broadened to include the need to challenge intolerant and racist attitudes. For example, multicultural education centres in several areas have actively encouraged local schools and colleges to adopt a global perspective.

Within peace education there has been the creation of the Centre for Peace Studies at St Martins College, Lancaster, and the growth of many Teachers for Peace groups and the setting up of the Peace Education Network.

Overall, in secondary schools, the world dimension has come to be an important part of many geography, history, social studies, humanities and moral education courses, as teachers have sought to extend the boundaries of their subjects: for example, modern language teachers wishing to teach European studies, historians to teach world history, scientists to teach about the local and global implications of modern science and technology. In particular, interest has grown in studying world faiths at both primary and secondary levels. Some schools have introduced separate world studies courses for examination at CSE and O Level.

In primary and middle schools the growth of world studies, though it has come later, shows signs of being equally, perhaps even more strongly, sustained.

> If the Earth
> were only a few feet in
> diameter, floating a few feet above
> a field somewhere, people would come
> from everywhere to marvel at it. People would
> walk around it, marvelling at its big pools of water,
> its little pools and the water flowing between the pools.
> People would marvel at the bumps on it, and the holes in it,
> and they would marvel at the very thin layer of gas surrounding
> it and the water suspended in the gas. The people would
> marvel at all the creatures walking around the surface of the ball,
> and at the creatures in the water. The people would declare it
> as sacred because it was the only one, and they would protect
> it so that it would not be hurt. The ball would be the
> greatest wonder known, and people would come to
> pray to it, to be healed, to gain knowledge, to know
> beauty and to wonder how it could be. People
> would love it, and defend it with their lives
> because they would somehow know that
> their lives, their own roundness, could
> be nothing without it. If the
> Earth were only a few
> feet in diameter.

Figure 1.4 (source: a poster distributed by Steve Smith Graphics, 16 Old Palace Road, Norwich)

An unmistakable tide of conviction has given this impetus to world studies and carried it forward, even at a time when schools have been preoccupied with falling rolls and maintaining standards of provision, and thus might have been expected to reject or at least postpone its introduction.

The crucial issue has been, and remains: how can a teacher's enthusiasm for world studies be translated into educationally worthwhile activity? The following two chapters suggest that some possible answers can be found, first by examining the whole area of teaching method and second by adopting an appropriate framework for curriculum planning.

Further Reading

World Society

Allen, R., *How to Save the World: Strategy for World Conservation*, Corgi Books, 1982 (based on the World Conservation Strategy).

Barney, G., *Global 2,000 Report to the President of the United States: Entering the Twenty-First Century*, Penguin, 1982.

Hayter, T., *The Creation of World Poverty: An Alternative View to the Brandt Report*, Pluto Press, 1981.

Independent Commission on International Development Issues, *North–South: A Programme for Survival*, Pan, 1980.

Independent Commission on International Development Issues, *Common Crisis North–South: Co-operation for World Recovery*, Pan, 1983.

Kidron, M. and Segal, R., *The State of the World Atlas*, Pluto Press, 1981.

Leger Sivard, R., *World Military and Social Expenditure*, World Priorities, 1983 (updated annually).

Robertson, J., *The Sane Alternative: A Choice of Futures*, 1983, available from 9 New Road, Ironbridge, Shropshire TF8 7AU.

World Studies and Multicultural Education

More detailed information and discussion about world studies can be obtained from the following.

Becker, J. (ed.), *Schooling for a Global Age*, McGraw-Hill, 1979.

Fisher, S., Magee, R. and Wetz, J., *Ideas into Action: Curriculum for a Changing World*, World Studies Project of the One World Trust, 1980.

Fyson, N. L., *The Development Puzzle*, Hodder, 1984.

Heater, D. W., *World Studies: Education for International Understanding in Britain*, Harrap, 1980.

Hicks, D. and Townley, C. (eds.), *Teaching World Studies: An Introduction to Global Perspectives in the Curriculum*, Longman, 1982.

Lynch, J., *The Multicultural Curriculum*, Batsford, 1983.

Milner, D., *Children and Race: Ten Years On*, Ward Lock Educational, 1983.

O'Connor, E., *World Studies in the European Classroom*, Council for Europe, Strasbourg, 1980.

Richardson, R., *Learning for Change in World Society: Methods, Activities, Resources*, World Studies Project of the One World Trust, 1979 (second edition).

Tierney, J., *Race, Migration and Schooling*, Holt, 1982.

Twitchin, J. and Demuth, C., *Multicultural Education: Views From the Classroom*, BBC, 1981.

World Studies Teacher Training Centre, *World Studies Journal* (published quarterly), University of York.

2. Teaching and Learning World Studies

'Unteachable' Ideas

'Isn't world studies too *controversial*?' 'Aren't there dangers of *indoctrination*?' 'Can my pupils *really* cope with these ideas?' 'What is the *point* anyway?'

Questions such as these come to many teachers' minds as they begin to consider introducing world studies to their pupils. They are questions which concern, ultimately, the nature of education itself and the role of schools and teachers within it, and within our society.

Answers to them are being worked out every day, at a practical and down to earth level, as Part 2 of this book illustrates. After observing pupils in several schools, one of the evaluators for the *World Studies 8–13* project, remarked that teachers were handling 'unteachable' ideas in their classrooms. Quite young pupils were, to his surprise, exploring world issues confidently and competently, with a remarkable level of sophistication. The fact that they were able to do so was due in large part to the style, approach and skill of their teachers, underpinned, crucially, by a high expectation of what the children might achieve.[1]

It has often proved to be the case that children who are not *expected* to do well at a given task tend not to do well. Conversely when teachers have high expectations, or at least no negative expectations, children achieve more than they would otherwise have done. If we recall our own childhood perhaps we should be less surprised at this than we sometimes are. Faith in people is essentially a self-fulfilling prophecy.

Such faith is based on a deep respect for the humanity of each individual person, whether adult or child. It manifests itself in a genuine interest in everything that they have to communicate and contribute in any given situation. Thus 'in every educational exchange, it is first of all the teacher who has something to learn. The teacher must approach asking: "Who is this child? What does he

Figure 2.1 'In every educational exchange, it is first of all the teacher who has something to learn.'

or she bring into the world? What have I to discover here that no one has ever known before?"'[2]

It is a faith based on a recognition of the capacity of others to think and learn for themselves. Since children are essentially active and questioning it generally turns out to be well placed.

A further reason why the pupils mentioned above were able to explore quite complex ideas is that the teachers had recognised the impossibility of defining today exactly what knowledge will be essential for the 1990s and beyond. As a result they had adopted a conceptual approach to learning, helping children to understand and use some of the key concepts relating to world society and world studies. To do this involved the children in a continual process of thinking about both their own experience and that of others.

With this view of people, learning about the modern world becomes a shared responsibility. The teacher's task is to create a classroom climate of mutual interest and support in which the pupils themselves accept a share of the responsibility. Learning from each other may become as important as learning from the teacher or from written materials. The focus is on learning *how* to learn far more than on acquiring information. This requires self-discipline on the part of the learner and leads to a growing awareness of self, helped by one's peers and the teacher.

From this standpoint the key to education is enquiry, rather than knowledge itself. Teachers are not just those who know, but those who know how, and those who know how to ask. Education is thus no longer something that children have 'done' to them, but a venture in which teacher and learner participate together.

The important goals of world studies teaching accordingly focus on learning to learn, solving problems, clarifying values and making decisions. At the heart of these is the prime importance of enquiry, not just of asking questions but of creating situations in which pupils can formulate questions and find answers for themselves. Not only is this necessary for handling the subject matter of world studies, it is also the most appropriate education we can offer to young people in a world where information becomes obsolete so rapidly.

Extremely important elements in any enquiry-orientated classroom are the attitudes and skills of the teacher. It has been suggested that in enquiry-based learning the teachers displays the following characteristics.[3] He or she:

(**a**) rarely tells pupils what they 'ought' to know;
(**b**) is mainly interested in helping pupils learn to learn;
(**c**) stresses, by example, that education is a process of finding answers;
(**d**) uses questioning as a basic strategy with pupils;
(**e**) encourages openness to alternative perspectives, explanations and ideologies and rarely accepts one viewpoint as the single answer;
(**f**) encourages pupil–pupil interaction as opposed to solely pupil–teacher interaction;
(**g**) develops lessons from the interests and responses of pupils and not necessarily from a previously determined plan of how enquiry should proceed.

It can be instructive and amusing to look at one's own behaviour in the classroom from this standpoint. The checklist in Figure 2.2, 'Am I An Enquiry Teacher?', offers one practical way of doing this.

Everybody has an interest in education, but what is the *child's* interest – independent of all adult intervention and influence? Does that seem an impossible question to answer? Very likely it does. As impossible as it once seemed likely it does. As impossible as it once seemed to say what a woman's interest was in life independent of her husband or her father. As impossible as it once seemed to say what the interest of slaves might be in life independent of their masters. There are those who live in such ingrained, seemingly 'natural' conditions of subjugation that we cannot begin to imagine what autonomous interest they have in the world. Children are in that category, more so than any other social dependant. Yet, they have their own interest; it is the interest that each of us discovers, if only in moments of unaccustomed exhilaration or strange absorption, when we become our own person, caught up in our own work, our own salvation. In such moments, we find an autonomy and an adventure that alone deserves to be called life. That is the child's interest, and it needs to be defended from nothing so much as the terrible 'practicalities' that are always foremost in the adult mind.

Theodore Roszak, *Person/Planet*, Granada, 1981

Talking Together

Discussion Exercises

Creating opportunities for pupils to talk together, to communicate with each other, to voice opinions reasonably, to respond sensitively to others and to evaluate what they hear, also offers a context for them to construct and reconstruct their views of the world.

Many pupils, not surprisingly, are loath to voice their opinions in front of the whole class. Indeed many adults have a fear of speaking out in front of a group. It is therefore often a good idea for a class to talk about an issue in pairs or small groups. Discussion can then more easily occur in the class as a whole because pupils have had the opportunity to formulate and voice their opinions more privately first. But, for talking to be purposeful and productive in large or small groups,

Are you an enquiry teacher?

How often do you display these behaviours? Are you an enquiry teacher? Here is a self-evaluation checklist. Tick the spaces that correspond with the frequency with which you display the following behaviours.

_____

So, are you an enquiry teacher? Here is a very unscientific scoring system–but one that will provide a fairly accurate answer to the question. Total the number of responses of each frequency. Enter the results in the table below. Calculate your sub-totals by using the designated multiplier (for example, your 'very frequently' score is to be multiplied by 4). Finally calculate your total score (out of 80).

Responses	Number	Multiplier	Sub-total
Very frequently		x 4 =	
Frequently		x 3 =	
Sometimes		x 2 =	
Rarely		x 1 =	
		Total	

Are you an enquiry teacher? Here is another unscientific guide:

If you scored 65-80
Yes you are. You are consciously looking for ways to promote student enquiry and are aware of your role in maintaining an atmosphere of enquiry in your classroom.

45-64
You are convinced of the value of enquiry teaching and use it where and when appropriate issues and materials are available. You could try a little harder to create more such opportunities.

35-44
Maybe you should try a lot harder–but I am convinced that all is not lost. . . .

Less than 34
Well now . . . !

	Very frequently	Frequently	Sometimes	Rarely
1. I opt for flexible seating, student movement and the maximum interaction between students.				
2. I make available a wide range of resources and materials for student use.				
3. My introductory lessons on a unit of work present a problem, issue, question or contradiction to simulate student thinking.				
4. In doing so, I encourage students to react freely with little direction from me. The course of the enquiry becomes theirs to plan.				
5. The students talk more than I do during classroom enquiry work.				
6. When I talk, I question, not 'tell'.				
7. I consciously use the ideas raised by students and base my next questions on them.				
8. I redirect student questions in such a way that students are encouraged to seek their own answers.				
9. My questions encourage students to test the validity of their ideas in the broad context of experience.				
10. Class dialogue is conducted in a fashion that emphasises courtesy and openness to divergent views.				
11. Skills are developed and practised as they are required during an enquiry, not as a separate set of activities.				
12. I encourage a rigorous questioning of the grounds upon which statements are made.				
13. I encourage students to explore the implications of holding alternative value and policy positions.				
14. I make students aware of personal, social and political bases for diversity in attitude, values and policies.				
15. I encourage students to arrive at value and policy positions of their own that they can understand and defend.				
16. I use evaluation in the classroom as a means to improve learning and not to judge people.				
17. The results of evaluation help me make amendments to existing enquiry procedures with students.				
18. I evaluate students on growth in many aspects of the learning experience, rather than simply on the knowledge acquired.				
19. I share the results of evaluation with students, identifying strengths as well as areas where we both need to improve.				
20. I make my students aware that I am involved in my own geographical enquiries, and that learning need not stop when one leaves school.				

Figure 2.2 (source: Fien, J., 'Am I an enquiry teacher?', Geography 16–19 Curriculum Development *Project News*, No. 11, July 1980. Copyright Schools Council 1979)

it needs to be carefully planned. Fruitful small-group discussion is not, it is worth recalling, the same as saying to the class 'Discuss this for a minute with your neighbour'. Neither is the use of small groups a mere convenience. It has, rather, a specific purpose in a specific situation.

For the pupil, discussion activities provide an opportunity to test personal statements, to extend or qualify ideas, and to be supportive of others. Indeed, mutual support is essential for many if that basic self-confidence which underlies frank discussion is to be developed and maintained.

In small-group discussion exercises, pupils clarify and develop their own understanding of an issue as they talk with one another. Everyone is encouraged to participate and a small, but significant, experience of co-operation is provided. Discussion exercises need to involve distinct steps, each only taking a few minutes, with specific outcomes and decisions to be reached. Alternatively, the purpose may be to explore an issue rather than coming to a conclusion. Whichever of these aims is paramount, it is often useful at the planning stage to have in mind a checklist of 'practical tips' (See Figure 2.3).

The approach and style of the teacher is, of

Discussion exercises: some practical tips

Things to handle
Arrange for pupils to have things which are literally tangible – objects, pictures, slips of paper, which they can move around with their hands.

Precise tasks
Give precise instructions about what is to be done. For example: 'Here are pictures of six different people. Choose the two people you would most like to meet. For each of them, write down the one question you would most like to ask.'

Co-operation
Choose discussion tasks which require pupils to listen to each other and to help each other. For example use 'jigsaw games', which can only be completed if everyone takes part.

Small groups
The smaller the group, the more pupils feel secure. Also, the more they're able to talk. Often arrange for them to work in pairs or in threes. The maximum for most group work is six.

Controversy
Choose subjects on which pupils are likely to have conflicting opinions. Or build controversy into a discussion by requiring some of the participants to play specific roles.

Nonverbal materials
Use material which communicates ideas symbolically and nonverbally rather than through words alone – photographs, cartoons, posters, statistical diagrams.

Comparing, contrasting, selecting, justifying
Provide a collection of things to be compared and contrasted with each other; require pupils to arrange them or to select from them; and to explain their arrangement or selection.

Activity then reflection
Give pupils an activity to perform, or require them to watch an activity – for example a nonverbal game or exercise. Then invite discussion and clarification of what happened, and of how they felt, and of what can be learnt.

Not too easy, not too hard
Definitely try to stretch pupils with discussion tasks you set. But don't depress them or annoy them by providing things which are too difficult. When you fail (as you sometimes will) to get the balance right, invite discussion of how people feel.

Figure 2.3 (source: Richardson, R., 'Talking about equality: the use and importance of discussion in multicultural education', *Cambridge Journal of Education*, Vol. 12, No. 2, 1982)

course, critical. The success of group discussion will depend, in part, on how the teacher *normally* treats pupils' contributions to lessons; if these are not taken seriously, and responded to with interest, then pupils may doubt the value of discussion exercises. At the same time the choice of small-group discussion as a technique is an important way of showing that the teacher sees young people as capable of creating meaning for themselves. The temptation to take over must be resisted if the pupil's own autonomy is to be asserted, and it is best for the teacher to be quietly supportive, without being obtrusive.

Small-group discussion is perhaps most commonly used in tutorial work and for developing communication skills. However, it can be argued that learning to participate effectively in small-group discussion needs to be a part of *all* that goes on in an enquiring classroom. There are four main advantages of such an approach. It leads to (i) an increased ability to use language effectively; (ii) the development of social skills in negotiating one's relationship with others; (iii) valuing others as a result of paying heed to their views, seeing them as people like oneself and not just 'objects' to react to; (iv) continually challenging and developing one's own views, particularly, in the case of world studies, in relation to the wider world.

Questions and Values

Talking together encourages pupils and teachers to ask questions. Questions, however, vary in the extent to which they may lead to genuine enquiry.

Broadly speaking there are two main categories of questions: closed and open. It is interesting to note that the Oracle Project, which looked closely at teacher–pupil interaction in classrooms, found that most of the questions asked by teachers were closed ones, i.e. those that require fairly simple recall, asking what, who, why and where?[4] They are the sort of questions that encourage sequencing, ordering and classifying. Requiring straightforward predictable answers, they are important in establishing basic information, and as a basis for developing higher-order skills.

Open questions, on the other hand, do not have a single or predetermined answer. They are:

enabling questions, not guess-what-I'm thinking questions . . . [The teacher] is suspicious of the single cause and the 'right answer', and thinks instead of reaso*n*s, cause*s*, and meaning*s*. He

does not rush to summarise what other people have said or learned, for fear of closing the door to further thought or imposing his own interpretation. He constantly questions his own questions. Do they increase people's will to learn as well as their capacity? Do they increase people's confidence in their ability to know? Do they encourage them to weigh alternatives, look at similarities and contradictions, and classify, reason or decide? Do they generate questions of which the hearers were previously unaware?[5]

Open questioning thus specifically encourages the development of higher-order skills such as making hypotheses and testing them, drawing conclusions from evidence, speculating and assessing the limitations of evidence. It also leads naturally to the exploration of values.

There can, of course, be no such thing as value-free lessons or schools. What we choose to include in the curriculum or leave out, how we choose to teach, how we relate to pupils and colleagues, our feelings about the purposes of education itself are all value-laden processes. They all involve choices on the part of the teacher, whether conscious or unconscious, choices which are determined by our priorities, which in turn, are influenced by various factors, including our age, gender, race and social class.

If pupils are to grow more aware of their own values and priorities they need to be helped carefully to do so. As they tackle a particular issue or dilemma it is useful to have in mind the following steps in clarifying their own values.[6] They should be provided with opportunities in which they can *choose*, *prize* and *act*, that is:

(**a**) choose freely;
(**b**) choose from alternatives;
(**c**) choose after thoughtful consideration of the consequences of each alternative;
(**d**) cherish and be happy with their choice;
(**e**) be willing to affirm their choice in front of others;
(**f**) do something as a result of their choice;
(**g**) do this repeatedly, as part of their everyday life.

The following questions are the sort that need to be asked when choosing between different courses of action or analysing a particular event.
Who gains and who loses?
Is it wise or unwise?
Is it just or unjust?

The first question is arguably the crucial one since the answers to the others will often depend on whose viewpoint is considered. Thus, for example, in looking at the takeover of peasant small holdings by a large-scale ranching enterprise one would ask:

Who gains and who loses from such a takeover?
How will this affect the local environment?
Is the takeover sensible, and, if so, for whom?
Is the takeover right or wrong?

Processes such as these are vital in an enquiry classroom, for it is through exploring dilemmas, clarifying and freely choosing from alternatives that the ability comes to detect bias and indoctrination. It is when pupils are left *unaware* of differing value positions and perspectives that they become susceptible to false authority.

As one primary headteacher has commented:

In my view teachers ought not to accept aims of education based upon the transmission of any prescribed values, when those values are presented to children as having a timeless and unquestionable existence. Teachers should help children to understand the nature of their situation in the world and the need to question, though not necessarily reject, existing values in formulating their own.[7]

The approaches touched on in this chapter so far are essential characteristics of good world studies teaching, but certainly not unique to it. We need now to look a little more closely at some of the other ways in which world studies can find a place in children's overall learning.

Integrated Approaches

Basic Skills

World studies contributes to language proficiency and numeracy by offering a context which stimulates pupils' interest and involvement.

In terms first of content there is an inexhaustible supply of interesting subject matter, about ourselves, about the lifestyles of other people, about events in the news, our hopes for the future and so on. Many examples will be found later in this book. Secondly, world studies teaching can contribute to the choice of method for language

work with approaches that require active involvement on the part of children. The direct experience of an activity such as Our Word House (page 42), can help develop observation and spoken language skills, for instance.

World studies can also greatly assist the development of reading ability in that a conscious effort is made to introduce children to books from, and books about, peoples and cultures other than their own, as well as those concerning contemporary issues. This can also lead to an awareness of the nature of bias – both racist and sexist – in teaching materials and elsewhere, an issue which is discussed in more detail on pages 100–29.

The same advantages apply to number work as apply to language development. The subject matter of world studies, events and issues, will often provide suitable and motivating material: for example, figures on wealth, or population, or the arms trade. These and similar statistics can be used in many interesting ways. It is worth recalling that children generally perform better on basic skills when they are provided with a broad and rich curriculum.[8]

World studies also contributes to personal and social education in that global links can often be shown with the children's own immediate environment and circumstances. And the broader context of personal and social education is, after all, the world. Detailed examples of this can be found in Chapter 4.

A strong case can also be made for considering survival as a further basic skill, living as we do at a particularly dangerous time, when science and technology, directed largely by military, commercial and industrial interests, may solve but yet also produce major crises.

Different problems, of course, seem more acute in different parts of the world. Worrying about a nuclear holocaust may be an urgent matter for the rich one-third of the world's population, but many of the other two-thirds, in the so-called 'third world', are already barely surviving because of lack of food and other essentials.

But, whatever the perceived priorities, world studies can help children understand and cope with global issues which threaten survival, and develop 'local' survival skills such as the ability to counter despair, to co-operate for common goals, to empathise, to think critically and flexibly, and to resolve conflicts non-violently in everyday life. It is skills such as these, developed in our own communities, which may contribute to human survival on a world scale.

Figure 2.4 (source: Graham Wade, *The Guardian*, 6 July 1982)

Lives cost more than anything in the world. I wouldn't like to be in a war.

Graham Wade asks a class of fourth year juniors in a North London school for their views on the Falklands conflict and its aftermath.

Toslin: "I think Britain was in the right because Argentina claimed that the Falklands were theirs and they set up new rules like having to talk Spanish and renaming the place to Las Malvinas. The people didn't agree with the rules and they wanted to live under British control. It was about the cause of freedom.

"I wouldn't mind risking my life or going there, but to kill someone else is another matter. War is supposed to be about winning with the loss of as few lives as possible. I don't think all those deaths were worth it – it's just a little thing on a map and all those people died for a little thing. Maybe it should have been done by talking. The Argentinians might have given up by talking . . ."

Josie: "I don't think it is worth fighting for. I don't know why one country has to say the Falklands is theirs – but I still support the British. The owners of the islands probably will make some money somehow – did they find oil on it or something like that? . . .

"It's all these politicians that send out young boys of 18 and let them get killed – and the politicians just stay here at home. There might be more war over it soon. I don't think that land is more important than people's lives."

Nicola: "A bit of both sides were right really – I'm not quite sure whether the British or the Argentinians should have the islands. Most of the people who lived there agreed with us.

"I would have gone there to fight, but then again I don't understand why people will risk their lives just to get an island. It would have been better for them to have had a vote on it – that would have saved a lot of people's lives.

"I don't feel that all those lost lives were worth it. The Falklands were not worth all of that trouble. The British and the Argentinians should come to some sort of agreement to share the island. Wars are definitely bad things."

Topics and Projects

Certain themes studied in topic and project work tend to come up again and again. A survey of all primary schools in Britain would probably find that animals, other countries, the local environment, autumn, Christmas and dinosaurs were the most popular. Other favourites would include: home and houses, time, ourselves, farms, polar regions, energy, North American Indians, conservation, and the earth.

A world studies approach to planning topics is likely both to raise questions about existing work, including traditional themes such as these, and to suggest many new ideas for innovation in this key area of the primary curriculum. Part 2 of this book is made up largely of suggestions related to teaching method and content, much of which may be introduced into existing programmes of work in response to questions such as: Are local themes shown to be linked with the wider world? Are distant themes shown to be linked with our everyday lives? What images are being given of other people: do they involve racial or sexual stereotyping, for example? Are we limiting children's learning by our own expectations, or are we creating situations for them which lead to new insights?

Social Studies

The HMI Survey *Primary Education in England* reported a lack of structure in both topic work and the social studies as well as a general underestimation of children's capacities. The framework for planning offered in this present book can go a long way to rectifying these deficiencies.

Social studies in the primary school focusses on the children's social environment and the social relationships which occur around them. At the secondary level, integrated studies in the first two years may fulfil a similar, if broader, role. Both the Schools Council project *History, Geography and Social Science* and the Inner London Education Authority (ILEA) project *Social Studies in the Primary School* use a conceptual and enquiry-based approach to learning similar to the one suggested in Chapter 3. As the first of these projects noted, a global perspective can make an important contribution to the middle years of schooling. However, while that project considered this to be part of a geographical contribution to the social studies, it can be argued that *all* subjects require their own global dimension and can in turn contribute to that dimension across the whole curriculum.

The Local Environment

World studies is sometimes seen as being in opposition to local studies and to the need for children to understand and explore their local environment. The reverse, however, is the case: the two levels are complementary and inextricably linked. A world studies approach invites the teacher to draw out the links between a particular town or village and the wider world, and insists that to leave this wider dimension out is to present pupils with a parochial and distorted picture. A study of Bristol, for example, which ignored its long-standing involvement in international trade – including slaves, tobacco, wine and armaments – and the prominent everyday indications of an international dimension such as the well-established West Indian and Asian populations, the statues of explorers, the street names (Whiteladies Road, Blackboy Hill, Blackmoors Lane) would be difficult to sustain and demonstrably the poorer.

The local area is also the place where children can most easily begin to participate in the 'real' world. It is here, in particular, that children learn to be ecologically responsive and responsible, and they can, for example, become practically involved in conservation projects as they learn about damage to the environment on a wider scale.

Figure 2.5

Subject-based Approaches

World studies should not necessarily be seen as in conflict with the more traditional subjects on the timetable; it can contribute to virtually all subjects at all levels in the curriculum.

Below are some suggestions, listed under individual subjects for ease of reference. Taken as a whole they are relevant to *all* levels of schooling, though of course primary schools generally do not specifically refer to subjects in this way, and some of the subjects are found only at secondary level.

English
International and intercultural issues and events in world literature
Appreciation of the literature of other countries including folk tales
Comprehension and writing, and development of discussion skills, with regard to themes such as change, conflict, justice, environment
Studies of the mass media
Recognition of dialect and other non-standard forms, where used appropriately, being as valid as standard English

Mathematics
Origins of mathematics, algebra and geometry
Mathematics as a universal activity
Counting in other countries
Mathematical concepts illustrated with regard to certain current issues, for example world trade
Use of statistics on food, population, inequality, the arms race

Science
The role of scientific research and achievement in world history
Scientific concepts illustrated with regard to, for example, contemporary issues in agriculture, technology, industrial development
Non-European inventions
Social responsibility in science
Environmental issues
Science as a world enterprise and an international language
Comparative study of the human species with other forms

Religious education
Religious beliefs and practice, and the quest for meaning in a variety of cultures
Major world religions
The teachings of Christianity and of other world religions with regard to conflict, justice, care of the environment
Religion as a universal practice

History
The historical background to global interdependence, to the North–South and East–West divides, and to this country's current place in world society
Concepts such as conflict, conflict management, law, democracy
Pre-colonial history
Non-European civilisations
Colonialism
Reappraisal of national and local history

Geography
'Developing' and 'developed' countries
Minority cultures and groups
Trade and economic interdependence and dependence
Agriculture and modernisation
Hunger and maldistribution of food
Mapping levels of human welfare
Multinational companies
The ecological basis of life
Human responses to different environments

Cookery and home economics
Comparisons between countries and cultures over food and nutrition
Sex roles
Aspects of the world food situation
The consumer's needs and responsibilities in a world economy and market
Different forms of child care

Art
Artists' treatment of conflict and change
Appreciation of a variety of artistic traditions, including those of ethnic minority groups
Painting and drawing in a variety of styles, and with world issues as stimuli
Art as a product of culture

Craft, design and technology

Designing and making as universal human activities

Comparison over time, and between countries

Appreciation of traditional forms

The role of intermediate/appropriate technology in both developed and developing countries, and issues raised by this

Modern languages

Language as a distinctive human ability

The history and variety of language

Appreciation of French, Indian (or whatever) cultures

Francophone Africa

Latin America

World issues in French, Spanish or another language

The role of France, Germany (or wherever) studied in the world

PE and games

Sport as a basic human activity

International sport

Differing cultural attitudes to fitness, sport, winning and losing

Competition and co-operation

New Games

Non-European games

Music

Music as a vital element in all societies, past and present

Appreciation and performance of a wide variety of styles and forms

Lives of composers and musicians, both classical and popular

Music as a worldwide language

Economics

Links between the local economy and the world economy

Causes of world poverty and action to overcome it

Aid and its effects

The costs of the arms race

Conversion of military production to civilian uses

Multinational companies

Trade in basic commodities

The economics of pollution and its control

Unemployment on a global scale

Further Reading

Baldwin, J. and Wells, H. (eds.), *Active Tutorial Work*, Books 1–5, Basil Blackwell/Lancashire County Council, 1979/81.

Barnes, D. and Todd, F. *Communication and Learning in Small Groups*, Routledge & Kegan Paul, 1977.

Bridges, D. *Education, Democracy and Discussion*, National Foundation for Educational Research (NFER) Publishing Co., 1979.

Button, L. *Group Tutoring for the Form Teacher: Lower Secondary School*, Hodder & Stoughton, 1981.

Macy, J. R. *Despair and Personal Power in the Nuclear Age*, New Society Publishers, Philadelphia, 1983.

Purpel, D. and Ryan, K. *Moral Education*, McCutchan Publishing Corporation, 1976.

Rogers, C. *Freedom to Learn in the 1980s*, C. E. Merrill, 1983.

Roszak, T. *Person/Planet: The Creative Disintegration of Industrial Society*, Paladin/Granada, 1981, Chapter 7.

Wolsk, D. *An Experience-Centred Curriculum: Exercises in Perception, Communication and Action*, Educational Studies and Documents No. 17, UNESCO, 1975.

Wren, B. *Education for Justice*, Student Christian Movement (SCM) Press, 1977.

3. World Studies and Curriculum Planning

Aims and Objectives

The Purpose and Aim of World Studies

The middle years are a period of rapid growth for children in terms of their cognitive, social and moral development. It was suggested earlier, however, that we often underestimate what they are capable of, and that we limit children's thinking by our own.[1]

By the age of eight, children have begun to develop all sorts of attitudes and values, for example in relation to race, gender and class. They are on 'voyages of reconnaissance', drawing on their existing but often distorted maps of experience, yet continually seeking to expand and refine them. The classroom activities described in Part 2 of this book can assist such exploration by providing specific experiences for children to become involved in, posing problems for them to investigate, and encouraging open-ended questioning. But each activity, each topic or unit of work, requires careful planning for the anticipated outcomes to occur. How then can we *plan* the curriculum effectively for such world studies teaching and learning? The first step must be to consider our aims.

Figure 3.1

On the basis of the definition given on page 8 the overall aim of world studies teaching is *to help children develop the knowledge, attitudes and skills which are relevant to living in a multicultural society and an interdependent world.*

Such an overall aim is necessarily broad. It provides immediately an outline map of the field. It reminds us of the key idea of interdependence, between countries, within them, and between people and planet. It reminds us that our own society, as most societies, is made up of many cultures and subcultures, and that to understand it fully we need to view it in a world context. Further it recalls that children need positively to gain information, acquire attitudes and develop skills which will enable them to pursue their own interests wisely in this worldwide society. Such a process does not occur by chance.

From this overall aim we are able to sketch in more details on our outline map and to gain some idea of the features of the landscape by identifying possible objectives.

Objectives for World Studies

Part of the debate about the value of specifying precise objectives for classroom teaching has arisen from the assumption that worthwhile learning can only be judged by measurable changes in pupil behaviour. As one writer found, this is sometimes taken to extremes:

> I was once asked to review sets of behavioural objectives produced by some special education teachers . . . One group had developed a set of forty-one chained objectives on use of the toilet, starting with objective 1 'can lower trousers' to objective 41 'can raise trousers' with thirty-nine unspeakable steps in between. 'How did the programme work out in practice?', I asked innocently. Not too well, I was told, as all the children could use the toilet perfectly well already. All that trouser raising and lowering practice probably just confused them.[2]

Objectives for world studies

Knowledge

Ourselves and others
Pupils should know about their own society and culture and their place in it. They should also know about certain societies and cultures other than their own, including minority cultures within their own society. They should understand the nature of interdependence, and the economic and cultural influence – both helpful and harmful – of other people on their own way of life.

Rich and poor
Pupils should know about major inequalities of wealth and power in the world, both between and within other countries and in their own. They should understand why such inequalities persist and about efforts being made to reduce them.

Peace and conflict
Pupils should know about the main conflicts currently in the news and in the recent past, and about attempts to resolve such conflicts. They should also know about the ways of resolving conflicts in everyday life.

Our environment
Pupils should know about the basic geography, history and ecology of the earth. They should understand the interdependence of people and planet and should know about measures being taken to protect the environment both locally and globally.

The world tomorrow
Pupils should know how to investigate and reflect on a variety of possible futures: personal, local, national and for the world as a whole. They should also be aware of ways in which they may act to influence the future.

Attitudes

Human dignity
Pupils should have a sense of their own worth as individuals, and that of others, and of the worth of their own particular social, cultural and family background.

Curiosity
Pupils should be interested to find out more about issues related to living in a multicultural society and an interdependent world.

Appreciation of other cultures
Pupils should be ready to find aspects of other cultures of value to themselves and to learn from them.

Empathy
Pupils should be willing to imagine the feelings and viewpoints of other people, particularly people in cultures and situations different from their own.

Justice and fairness
Pupils should value genuinely democratic principles and processes at local, national and international levels and be ready to work for a more just world.

Skills

Enquiry
Pupils should be able to find out and record information about world issues from a variety of sources, including printed and audio-visual, and through interviews with people.

Communication skills
Pupils should be able to describe and explain their ideas about the world in a variety of ways: in writing, in discussion and in various art forms; and with a variety of other people, including members of other groups and cultures.

Grasping concepts
Pupils should be able to understand certain basic concepts relating to world society, to use these concepts to make generalisations and to support and test these.

Critical thinking
Pupils should be able to approach issues with an open and critical mind and to change their ideas as they learn more.

Political skills
Pupils should be developing the ability to influence decision making at local, national and international levels.

Figure 3.2 (source: developed from an original model contributed by Robin Richardson in *Ideas into Action: Curriculum for a Changing World*, World Studies Project of the One World Trust, 1980)

By contrast, the objectives set out in Figure 3.2 are deliberately general and open-ended. They arose out of a lengthy period of discussion and consultation with teachers who had used them in their own curriculum planning. They are intended primarily as a checklist which can be used at any time – before, during and after a unit of work takes place – to stimulate thinking and to review progress. They are intended either as a basis for planning specifically world studies work or as a means of introducing a world dimension into almost any topic or subject. In either case they can help a teacher to ensure that, over a certain period, pupils are introduced to the main aspects of world studies in a way which will encourage and enable them to continue learning. In many cases, of course, teachers will want to use this list as a starting point for writing their own list to suit their individual circumstances.

As well as their more obvious relevance at classroom level, these objectives can be used by a whole staff or a working party to review the entire curriculum and climate of the school. To what extent does each of these objectives feature in the life and work of a particular school? What changes need to be made for the school to reflect the wider world more fully? They might also be presented to pupils for their own consideration.

Figure 3.3 provides a visual summary of the objectives for world studies. The familiar categories of knowledge, attitudes and skills – thinking, feeling and doing – are not as distinct as the separate boxes suggest. Their close interrelationship is indicated by the arrows; for example, attitudes are affected by knowledge and also by skills. Skills are affected both by attitudes and knowledge. No one category can be treated in isolation.

Objectives for world studies: a summary

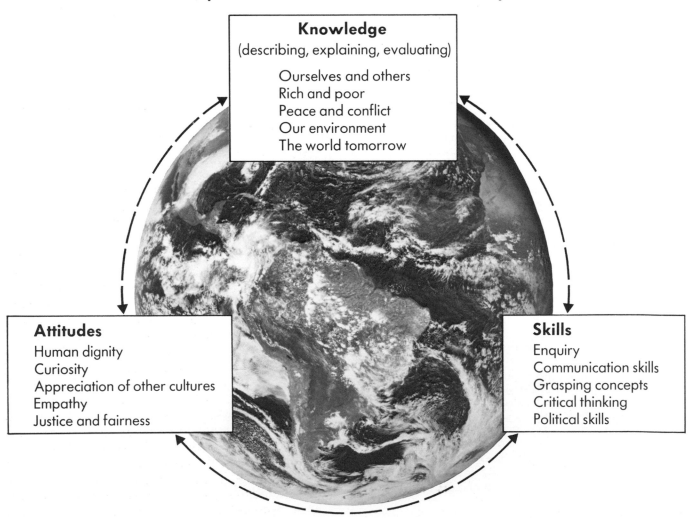

Knowledge
(describing, explaining, evaluating)

Ourselves and others
Rich and poor
Peace and conflict
Our environment
The world tomorrow

Attitudes
Human dignity
Curiosity
Appreciation of other cultures
Empathy
Justice and fairness

Skills
Enquiry
Communication skills
Grasping concepts
Critical thinking
Political skills

Figure 3.3

26

It is important to draw a distinction, under knowledge, between the ability to describe, to explain and to evaluate. *Describing* involves knowledge of basic facts such as dates, names of places and people, descriptions of events and so on. *Explaining* involves being able to compare and contrast, to analyse and to make generalisations. *Evaluating* involves selecting and justifying a particular explanation for an event or course of action, and making judgements about the importance of one idea or event rather than another.

These three abilities are in ascending order of difficulty and are consistent with the fact that competence increases with age. They cannot, however, be related and confined to one age level rather than another. Thus we would argue, as Bruner has done, that all the objectives are achievable in some intellectually honest form with, say, eight year olds, and also that they will be achievable in more complex ways as children grow older.

Attitudes and Skills

Fostering Attitudes

Many of the attitudinal objectives listed in Figure 3.2 are not unique to world studies; they are, rather, an essential part of good education. Taken together, however, they indicate the main features of a world studies approach.

One of the most fundamental of human needs is *human dignity*, to know that we personally – together with our family, group and background – have value and worth. If, whether consciously or unconsciously, we feel we are being undervalued then relationships, behaviour and work may all suffer.

It is essential, therefore, that we do not, by default, devalue children's backgrounds. To 'treat all children as the same' is, unintentionally, to do just that. We need to take due note of: gender differences, so that blatant and subtle sex-role stereotyping is not perpetuated (we need to question our assumptions about what girls should be like and what they are capable of, and what boys should be like and are therefore capable of); class differences, so that working class norms are not taken to be deviant, for example, and therefore in need of correction; cultural differences, so that ethnocentric and racist attitudes can be avoided. Good world studies teaching takes account of these differ-ences, and of the fact that the attitudes of others (both teachers and peers) play an important part in developing, or failing to develop, a sense of self-respect in every pupil.

Curiosity is essential to enquiry-based learning. It involves a need to keep asking questions, to go beyond the evidence, to speculate. Curiosity is an integral part of critical thinking. If teaching emphasises telling learners what they need to know then thinking may become a chore. If on the other hand teaching encourages a questioning attitude, a continuous challenging of assumptions, then it will certainly foster curiosity. In the context of world studies such curiosity will be channelled towards those issues related to living in a multi-cultural society and an interdependent world.

Empathy involves a willingness to put oneself in someone else's shoes. It is an attitude which arises out of concern for others and leads to imagining the feelings and viewpoints of others, particularly those in situations and cultures different from one's own. Since in the middle years of schooling children do seem to be more tolerant than in adolescence, it is very important that empathy is developed when they are young. Empathy may relate to curiosity. 'I wonder how *she* feels about that?' It may also, less directly, relate to the development of dignity and self-respect in that showing one appreciates someone else's feelings can enhance the other person's sense of worth.

Empathy is probably best developed through role-play and simulation games where one may have to act as if in someone else's shoes and then reflect on the meaning of that experience. Many of the experiential activities described later can be used in this way.

One important aspect of empathy is *appreciation of other cultures* whether within one's own country or in other parts of the world. Tolerance in a plural society, it can be argued, involves not only accepting the presence of other cultures but appreciating aspects of them as being of value to oneself.

Any study of the wider world and the events occurring in it must involve facing up to the existence of injustice. This will involve consideration of the nature of *justice and fairness* on a variety of scales from the local and national to the global. Any real valuing of democratic principles should begin with the pupils' own sense of fairness in relation to everyday life and classroom experience. We should not shrink from the fact that a commitment to justice and fairness may involve a fundamental questioning of the status quo, especially if enquiry reveals gross inequalities or injustice.

Developing Skills

There are several facets to the skill of *enquiry*, the ability to find out and record information being perhaps the most fundamental. If a teacher always presents pupils with ready-made answers, that is if the teacher takes the role of knower rather than facilitator, enquiry skills will not be encouraged, if indeed they are developed at all. Enquiry is not a matter of simply looking things up in a reference book. Rather, it is knowing *how* to investigate an issue using a variety of sources: printed, audio-visual, in the field, and talking to people. Only when a wide range of sources are being consulted regularly in a coherent fashion can enquiry skills be really developed.

Communication skills involve the ability to express one's views and feelings clearly and considerately in relation to others. This applies not only to one's own peer group but to others within the school and local community. Communication is also relevant to developing relationships with people of differing cultures and social groups.

The need for pupils to understand and grasp certain *key concepts* relating to world society is considered below. One longer-term aim of handling such concepts is to help pupils acquire the ability to make and test generalisations: for example, 'Conflicts often happen because people have different beliefs about things' or 'Conflicts can often be resolved non-violently if we analyse them carefully'.

Critical thinking needs to be founded on curiosity and an ability to ask questions. It should be (though it is not always) one of the main outcomes of developing enquiry skills and is a process which is well suited to the important middle years of schooling.

All the above skills are of little value unless they involve at the same time, or later, action to influence decisions in the real world. Such action involves *political skills*. Political decision making, centring as it does on the distribution of scarce resources and power, goes on all the time in schools, at home, and in the community. Political skills are needed by all citizens in a democratic society; they are certainly not the sole prerogative of politicians. Pupils need to begin to understand the social, economic and political processes that are at work in world society and how they themselves are, and will be able, to influence them. Learning these skills can begin with pupils participating in decision making at classroom and school level.

Figure 3.4

Planning with Concepts

Many teachers find it helpful when planning to use one or two key concepts or ideas, in conjunction perhaps with certain selected objectives. The value of using such concepts lies in their capacity to provide overall coherence and direction for a topic or course, and also in establishing the main focussing ideas. They also help solve the problem of potential information overload. The choice of concept(s) can lead to very different lines of thought and investigation between topics with the same title.

For example, one teacher might base a world studies topic, 'food', on the concepts of fairness and distribution of power, while another, using the same title, might choose interdependence and co-operation.

The first approach might well emphasise the disparities in food consumption in the rich and poor worlds, how international agribusiness companies work, what the basic human requirement for food is, and the working conditions of 'third world' food growers.

The second approach would quite likely highlight the many different international sources of our daily food, the intricate co-operation needed to bring, say, tropical fruit to the consumer's table, an aid project concerned with food production and the interdependence between a city and the surrounding countryside for food production and marketing.

The concepts listed in Figure 3.5 have much in common with other projects, such as the Schools Council *History, Geography and Social Science* and the Inner London Education Authority's *Social Studies in the Primary School*. They include ideas which are important to all areas of the curriculum and, like the objectives, can be used in separate subjects, in project work, or as a guide for a broader school policy. They were selected in the light of three main criteria:

(*a*) they are relevant to the lives of children now;
(*b*) they help to explain human behaviour and the nature of world society;
(*c*) they are relevant to many different areas of the curriculum.

Of course concepts can be understood at different levels, and for practical purposes we can distinguish four stages of understanding:[3]

recognising: being able to recognise a word in context as one that has been mentioned or seen before, one that has been talked about;
explaining: being able to give an explanation of that word and examples of the way it is used;
using: being able to use the word as part of one's own active vocabulary, whether in writing or in speech;
applying: being able to apply the word to one's own everyday life and situation, and to understand the implications of this for one's lifestyle.

The first three categories should certainly be possible for children within the 8–13 age range. The fourth, applying, is clearly the most difficult and, for many teachers and pupils, will be an ultimate rather than immediate goal.

The concept matrix on page 36 enables the teaching activities listed in Part 2 to be built into such a conceptual approach.[4]

With each of the ten key concepts listed in Figure 3.5 there is a brief indication of the sorts of understanding that one might be working towards.

It is important to note that, for any of the objectives or concepts referred to in this chapter to be grasped, children need to make use of and reflect on, first, their own experiences and then those of other people. Part 2 of this book shows how class work can often be initially focussed on children's immediate experience – real or simulated – as a basis for studying more distant events and issues in the wider world.

Reflection and Action

The Whole School

World studies cannot be confined to one area of learning. Its objectives and concepts, we have argued, need to become an integral part of the whole curriculum (if they are not so already), part indeed of the very ethos of a school. World days, One World weeks, United Nations days and the like are certainly important and useful as they stand, but they are likely to be much more so if they are firmly built into the regular study and life of a school.

The ultimate aim for many will be a 'world-centred' school, one, that is, in which a world dimension pervades the whole climate and atmosphere. This should of course come about in a way that suits each set of unique school circumstances best. There is no one blueprint, but there are pointers.

In such a school, one might expect teachers and pupils to be beginning to think and talk in a world context, as well as a local and personal context. They are keen to try out new and creative approaches to learning, to explore their own attitudes to important and controversial issues. In their planning, teachers are trying to maintain a balance between the essentially individual and personalised approach to learning appropriate for each pupil, the fostering of co-operative group attitudes and skills, and the pressing need to help all pupils understand and cope with, as they are able, the forces which are bringing about rapid change in the wider world. The school as a whole welcomes pupils, teachers and parents, and visitors with a wide variety of experience and backgrounds. It has links with relevant organisations and agencies; it may have a formal link with another school in this or another country; the relationships within it are as open as possible to encourage frank discussion; it remains emphatically part of, and open to, the local community it serves.

Concepts for use in world studies

Causes and consequences

Our actions and also events in the wider world have different sorts of causes. Similarly, actions and decisions, whether ours, other people's or those of governments or big business, have different sorts of consequences, often unintended or unforeseen. Understanding causes and consequences can give us more control over our own lives and also make events in the wider world more comprehensible.

Communication

People exchange information, views and feelings in a variety of different ways and languages, both with and without words. Clear communcation is essential if we are to understand the motives and actions of others and if we are to be understood by others. The mass media are primary communicators of information about the wider world and, inevitably, of bias and distortion also.

Conflict

We live in a world of conflict. Human beings continually disagree with each other, and often fight with each other. This happens in our own society, in other societies and between our society and others. Conflicts can be analysed and resolved in a variety of ways. Understanding how conflicts occur can make it easier to resolve them constructively.

Co-operation

Individuals, groups and countries often work together, or at least wish to appear to be doing so, in order to tackle common problems. Co-operation enables tasks to be performed which would not otherwise be possible. It is essential if conflicts are to be resolved peacefully. Co-operation can be as stimulating and rewarding as many forms of competition, requiring as it does a high level of communication and sensitivity to others.

Distribution of power

People and groups are able to influence what happens in the world. In most groups, countries, and in the world as a whole, power and wealth are distributed unequally. This affects people's life chances, their freedom and welfare. An awareness of this inequality raises important questions about fairness and justice.

Fairness

Fairness involves respecting the rights of other people and seeking solutions to conflict which take into account the interests of all parties. Some laws are an attempt to institutionalise fairness at national and international levels. For the world to be a fairer place, priority needs to be placed on the fulfilment of essential human needs through patterns of living which are equitable and in harmony with the planet.

Interdependence

People depend on each other in a variety of ways, ranging from caring and emotional support to the exchange of goods and services. This interdependence pervades every aspect of life, at individual, group and international level. It can have both positive and negative effects. The most urgent problems facing humankind need to be tackled at the global level and across national boundaries, as well as at the local level.

Similarities and differences

There are many different ways of doing things and not all human beings do the same as we do. But everyone has a similar nature deep down, the same physical needs and similar wishes and hopes, for example for friendship, love, happiness, enjoyment. It is important to find out about and understand both the differences between people, and those things which we all have in common.

Social change

Change is a constant feature of world society. It is brought about by people, whether deliberately or by accident. The best place to begin changing things for the better is where each individual happens to be, each with their own background, needs and aspirations. In order to do this people need to be free to take maximum control over their own lives.

Values and beliefs

People have different views about what is important. Ways of life, behaviour and traditions vary. Our values and beliefs, our sex, social and cultural background, affect the way we perceive people and events, and the way other people see us. Finding out about the values and beliefs of other people can help us to understand them, and ourselves, better.

Figure 3.5

Involvement in the World

In Chapter 1 it was suggested that world issues and events inevitably have an effect for better or worse on us as individual people and that, for the well-being of individuals and societies, people need, as far as possible, to have control over their own lives and to be able to participate in the debates and decisions which affect them. But this kind of involvement is demanding. It requires at least two essential elements: reflection and the opportunity for personal involvement. Reflection, that is looking back on what one has learnt and considering the wider implications of this, can occur in a variety of ways. Reflection may be verbal through reporting back, it can also be through pictures, charts, drama and story telling. It includes asking questions such as: What does this mean to me? What significance does it have for my life/my school/my community/the future? What sort of world do we want to move towards?

How would we like things to be in the world as a whole, in our country, locally, for me?

Personal involvement, either real or simulated, is equally essential. Action to tackle world society's problems and their causes is often taken from the top, by governments and international organisations, but it can also happen from the bottom, at local level, through individuals and groups.

The global and the local are inextricably intertwined, and concern for the global village needs to be realised by living responsibly in some small part of it. The major issues facing humankind in this latter part of the twentieth century can all be tackled at the local level. Such involvement can occur in many ways, for example:

- a survey of shopping facilities which also maps the origins of products and the living conditions of the producers;
- taking part in conservation work locally, either through school or with a local environmental group;
- taking part in an exchange visit between schools in different parts of the country;
- fund raising for local community projects;
- cultural evenings arising out of discussion with local ethnic minority groups;
- a study of the closure of a local factory, including an investigation of why it happened, and who gains and loses as a result;
- an investigation to show how far one or more of the major multinational companies influences the lives of pupils, and with what results;
- working with voluntary agencies such as Oxfam, Friends of the Earth or a local peace group;
- caring for the disadvantaged, for example the elderly or disabled, as part of the school's long term commitment to the community;
- being involved in local celebrations, festivals, meetings and rallies;
- writing to councillors, MPs, interesting people, pen friends, etc.;
- surveys and interviews of local opinions about national and global events.

Figure 3.6

It is sometimes argued that young people should not become involved in such matters. However, if they cannot begin to do so while at school, they will surely be ill equipped as adults to affect the course of events around them. We are, one way or the other, all involved. Each of us is, so the argument runs, either part of the solution or part of the problem.

The crucial question is not, 'Should I get involved?' but, 'Whose side [am I] on?' If a multinational company wants to build an oil terminal on the Scottish coast there are three options. One can give warm support, claim to be neutral, or come out in opposition. Whatever the rights and wrongs may be, the first two courses have the same effect – they support the company's efforts, whether by encouragement or default ... Conflict cannot be avoided, and neutrality is impossible. In an attempt to establish justice, taking sides is often the price of effective action.[5]

Conclusion

When teachers, students, parents and employers have been asked to say what the main goals of education are, most have agreed that they are to develop our most human capacities: the ability to learn without instruction, the ability to make one's own observations, the ability to live and work with others and the ability to care for one's community.[6]

Teaching and learning world studies in the ways described in this book will, it can be argued, go a long way to achieving such goals.

It is only as we become more conscious of the world that we become fully human. Helping children to become more conscious of the world involves making use of genuine experiences and showing their relationship to wider issues. This is best achieved through enquiry-based learning wherein the teacher acts more as a facilitator, manager or consultant than as a director or supervisor.

The capacity of children to think critically, to reason and reflect about unresolved issues is generally underestimated. Critical thinking should not be seen merely as a long-term aim but rather as something which can be systematically developed here and now.

One can hardly overstress the importance of discussion, between pupils as well as between pupil and teacher, in developing thinking and reasoning. Learning based solely on factual recall can only deal with outdated information.

Teachers involved in world studies have found experiential exercises such as those described in Part 2 especially helpful, and adaptable to many themes and situations. These nearly all encourage communication skills, especially speaking and listening, and lead to opportunities for reflecting on and discussing both the immediate and the wider world. They also encourage co-operation and involve working together on common tasks. Motivation is provided by the task itself, not by the need to compete or win. Such self-discovered self-appropriated learning is likely to influence pupils' overall behaviour, particularly when it includes considered constructive social involvement.

Further Reading

Blyth, A. *et al.*, *Curriculum Planning in History, Geography and Social Science*, Collins/ESL, Bristol, 1976.

Davies, H., Whitburn, R. and Jackman, M., *Social Studies in the Primary School*, ILEA Curriculum Guidelines, ILEA Learning Materials Service, 1980.

Wren, B., *Education for Justice*, SCM Press, 1977.

PART TWO

Classroom Activities

Introduction

Explanation

This part of the book is for the immediate use of teachers. It contains over a hundred separate activities intended to stimulate and develop children's interest in the wider world. Each activity is, at the same time, an opportunity for children to learn about themselves, their friends and their immediate situations.

The first part of the book set out the context for these activities outlining the main underlying assumptions and some important concepts and objectives to which they can contribute. They can and are being used in a wide variety of subject approaches, and also within integrated approaches.

While many of the activities can be readily adapted for young people of any age, and indeed for adults, they are primarily intended here for children between the ages of eight and thirteen. We do not specify precisely their suitability for any particular age group because chronological age is often a poor guide to competence and learning ability, and teachers themselves must be the judges of what is appropriate for their own pupils.

We do, however, sometimes suggest simpler and more complex versions of an activity. These correspond broadly to 'younger' and 'older' categories within the eight to thirteen span and should guide teachers in selecting the most suitable version for their particular class.

The activities are organised in four chapters: Here is the World; Getting on with Others; Other Worlds; and The World Tomorrow. This is one practical way of dividing up the concerns of world studies which teachers have found helpful in their thinking, and useful for the classroom.

It is important to note that each activity is focussed round some of the key concepts which have been discussed on pages 28–30. The activities can thus be systematically used to develop children's conceptual understanding, a process which is central to all education. The checklist on page 36 indicates which concepts are likely to be most valuable for each activity.

Each chapter has a similar structure:

- an introduction to the thinking behind the activities;
- the activities themselves, described in detail and grouped under related sub-headings;
- further brief suggestions which teachers may want to develop for themselves;
- a selective annotated guide to relevant resource materials.

Each activity includes all or some of the following headings:

Purpose	what the activity sets out to achieve;
Preparation	what the teacher needs to do beforehand;
Procedure	how the activity proceeds, step by step;
Discussion	some of the main points which should be raised and discussed by the class;
Follow-up	suggestions for ways in which the activity might lead to worthwhile investigation and further learning;
Variations	simpler and more complex versions of the activity.

Evaluation

How can we tell whether these approaches achieve what we intend? Do they 'work'? It is certainly possible to evaluate the factual aspects of world studies learning. Straightforward tests, for example, can be devised to check whether certain information has been learned and understood.

Tests and questionnaires can also be used to

assess the extent to which key concepts have been grasped, bearing in mind the four main levels of conceptual understanding suggested on page 29, i.e. recognising, explaining, using, applying. Another frequently used technique to gauge pupils' understanding is small group discussion, in which the teacher plays only a prompting role, listening, while pupils speak freely.

Other skills relevant to world studies can also be evaluated through discussion and observation. It should be reasonably evident, for example, whether children are improving their ability to find out and record information about world issues or not, and whether they are becoming more able to articulate and explain ideas.

It is much more difficult to evaluate changes in attitudes and behaviour. And harder still to know whether these are real changes or presentational ones, and to discover what factors, in or outside the classroom, have brought them about.

Nevertheless some such evaluation is possible, and a number of approaches can be used.

For example, one can ask pupils directly what they think and feel about a particular country or issue, and whether they think they have changed their opinions. What do they think they have learned? Perhaps even what do they think the teacher wanted them to learn, and to think?

Alternatively a set of questions can be devised and put to each pupil. These might be based on the world studies objectives on pages 25–6 and be related to a particular piece of work. The class can be presented with the results and asked for their reactions.

Another approach is to use a word association exercise or brainstorming (see page 79), in which pupils are asked, individually or as a group, to list all the words that come to mind on a particular country or issue. A simple analysis can be made of such lists indicating the most frequently occurring words and giving a breakdown of the positive and negative terms used. The same exercise can be done before and after a topic or course, and changes noted and explored. Another useful device here is the adjective test before and after learning about an issue. From a list provided, the pupils are asked to draw a circle round the four adjectives which they feel most accurately describe, say, Native Americans

(*a*) before the work starts;
(*b*) after the work is completed;
(*c*) six months later.

The techniques described on page 103 can also be used to gauge pupils' attitudes before and after a topic without them knowing, at least initially, this particular purpose of the activity.

A further possibility is to review pupils' written and creative work over a period, looking for signs of change: for example, an increasing interest in an issue or event, or a greater readiness to respect other peoples' viewpoints.

It is useful to keep a class diary in which incidents and remarks in and out of class are noted. After a time one can answer questions such as: Are conflicts resolved less violently now? What response do the children make to racist remarks? Do these remarks occur less frequently now? Do pupils have spontaneous discussions about events in the news?

A more general source of indirect evaluation is through parents, who may mention changes in a child's outlook.

In all these approaches, evaluation should be for the pupils' benefit as well as for the teacher's, helping them to identify changes in their own knowledge, feelings and assumptions, and inviting them to ask themselves and their friends why these changes have occurred and what the consequences might be, both in and out of school.

Selected Resources

The resource list that follows each chapter has two functions: (i) to provide information about appropriate *resources for children* to support their work, resources in the form of both hard facts and literature, which offer much in the way of insights and empathic vicarious experience; (ii) to provide further information and *resources for teachers* so that they can equip themselves with background knowledge, or develop any of the curriculum areas indicated in each chapter.

Each chapter bibliography is arranged under headings that relate to, but are not indentical with, the section headings within the chapters. Since many of the resources that appear in one section would be appropriate in several, teachers may need to refer to other sections and chapters; the notes on each publication provide guidance on its content.

Concepts and activities: a checklist

	Activities	Causes and consequences	Communication	Conflict	Co-operation	Distribution of power	Fairness	Interdependence	Similarities and differences	Social change	Values and beliefs
Chapter 4	Our Class in the World		•					•			
	What is our Classroom Made of?				•		•	•			
	Things We Use								•		•
	Our Word House	•	•		•			•			
	Interviewing People	•	•					•	•	•	•
	The World in our Newspapers	•	•					•			
	Making a Documentary		•		•						•
	Food from Overseas	•	•		•	•	•	•			
Chapter 5	Working Together (various)		•	•	•						
	Observing Conflicts in School	•		•			•				
	Role-playing Everyday Conflicts	•		•			•				
	Five Questions to Ask	•		•		•				•	•
	Which Way to World Peace?	•	•	•	•	•				•	•
	Doing Things Differently					•	•		•	•	•
	Who Does What at Home?					•	•		•	•	•
	Women in the World	•				•	•				
Chapter 6	What Do We Know Already?								•		•
	Using Photographs	•	•					•	•		•
	Detecting Bias	•	•			•	•				•
	World Population and Wealth			•		•	•	•	•		
	The Problem of Tourism	•	•	•	•		•	•	•	•	•
	Why Poor Countries are Poor	•		•		•	•	•			•
	Native American Issues	•		•	•	•	•	•		•	•
	Myths and Facts		•			•					•
Chapter 7	My Future	•								•	•
	Making Forecasts 1	•								•	•
	Making Forecasts 2	•								•	•
	Mental Maps		•	•	•				•		•
	Arming the World	•		•		•		•			•
	Projects for a Better World		•		•		•			•	•
	A New Society		•		•		•			•	•
	Using and Re-using	•			•			•		•	•
	In the Making	•	•		•	•		•		•	•
	Action for Change	•	•		•	•		•		•	•

4. Here is the World

Introduction

The activities in this chapter aim to help children discover evidence of the wider world around them. They point to the variety of cultural and economic links which affect everyday life, to the ways in which people, ideas and objects from elsewhere are constantly influencing the way we live.

In the modern world everything that people think, feel and do is permeated by the influence of others. In turn a great deal of our normal behaviour and lifestyles has an impact, for good and ill, on people many miles away. If we are to live responsibly therefore, we need to see our own lives and those of others in a world context.

We cannot, however, merely observe. It is important to go further and to question the ways in which this interlocking system works, and to look at the consequences. It would be easy, but wrong, for children to gain the impression that people elsewhere exist to grow our food and to provide raw materials and exciting holidays. We need continually to encourage and help them to look behind the obvious global interconnections to the inequalities on which they are based.

For example, most children in the middle years can formulate and sensibly investigate questions such as the following about a particular situation:

What is the historical background?
How and why have things changed?
Who gains and who loses?
What conflicts of interest are there?
How fair is the situation today?
How are things *likely* to change in the future?
How, *ideally*, should they change?

The activities in this chapter fall into three main sections.

Looking at Ourselves (pages 38–47) is concerned to draw out the immediate and tangible links that people have with the wider world through their families and friends, through language, through the materials which we make use of and consume, and to raise questions about the nature of these relationships.

Exploring the Neighbourhood (pages 48–53) widens the area of investigation to the surrounding locality. What people live nearby who could share pupils' experience of world events and major issues, or of the way local life has been affected by happenings in the wider world? How does the local press demonstrate, explicitly or implicitly, the existence of a world society? If people who have different backgrounds and interests see the same things differently, then the reasons for these differences need to be understood.

Unequal Trade (pages 54–65) contains a play which follows the progress of a single product, bananas, from the plantation to the consumer, and broaches the issue of who controls and benefits from world trade.

All the activities are self-contained. Each of them is also intended as a means of stimulating children's curiosity to investigate further the nature of human interdependence and communication and to explore the implications of these ideas for their own lives.

Looking at Ourselves
Our Class in the World

PURSOSE ▶

To indicate some of the ways in which pupils have direct personal contact with the wider world.

PREPARATION ▶

A supply of coloured stickers is needed and large chart similar to the one shown in Figure 4.1. should be displayed. Obviously the questions need to be handled sensitively.

PROCEDURE ▶

The chart can be filled in in a variety of ways. Most simply the teacher asks for a show of hands on each point and the correct number of coloured stickers is placed on each line. This provides a rapid survey of the class and enables the teacher to explore the results in more detail then or later.

More elaborately the class can be asked, after the chart has been explained, to jot down individually what they *expect* the results will be for each category, or, alternatively, to discuss them in small groups and produce a group forecast. Pupils then go up to the chart in turn and put up, as appropriate, coloured stickers with their initials or name written on.

DISCUSSION ▶

The results can be examined in the light of what the pupils had expected. How well do they in fact know each other? Are there other ways in which the pupils have links with the wider world? What does the existence of all these connections mean?

Our class in the world

Born in this area _____

Born elsewhere in Britain _____

Born outside Britain _____

Travelled outside this area _____

Travelled outside Britain _____

Recently received letters from abroad _____

Recently sent letters abroad _____

Spoken recently to someone from another country _____

Relatives or friends elsewhere in Britain _____

Relatives or friends outside Britain _____

Figure 4.1

Pupils can research the points on the chart further and mark the information on an outline map of Britain or the world. For example, they can find out details of where their classmates were born, mark the places on a map and draw arrows from there to the place where they now live and go to school. Similar maps can be made for parents and relatives. A good example of this can be found in Chapter 2 of the BBC publication *Multicultural Education* (see page 13).

Looking at Ourselves
What is a Classroom Made of?

PURPOSE

To show that every classroom is part of a worldwide network of producers and consumers. The global village is not distant, but right here.

PREPARATION

Examples of some or all of the following materials are needed: sugar, timber, oil, wool, cotton, copper, cocoa, lead. For younger pupils it will help to have ready a good supply of A4 sheets of paper, each with the name of one of the materials written on the top half.

PROCEDURE

The teacher introduces each of the materials listed above to the class, asking what they are, and what kinds of things they are used to make (Figure 4.2 shows a few examples). The teacher writes the names of the materials on the board.

The pupils are then asked to form small groups and each group is allocated one of the materials and some A4 sheets as labels. Their task is to find every object in the classroom which contains or consists of this material and to stick an appropriately worded label on it. Some groups may need assistance, and it helps if uses of the materials have been thoroughly discussed previously. Where a material is found in large numbers of similar objects one item can simply be displayed, for example a pullover, with a label on it and the number of similar items written on it: 'There are twelve pullovers made of wool'.

The next stage is for pupils to find out what part of the world the materials might come from. Most simply they can be told the principal sources, or referred to the figure. Preferably they will use reference books to find out.

Each group then returns to their labels and writes on them clearly the names of the two or three countries or regions which are the main sources of that material. Absolute accuracy is not essential. The main thing is for pupils to get a lively sense that the classroom contains within it commodities from many parts of the globe.

Finally, after the class has walked round and inspected the various labels, the activity can be completed by putting the information gathered onto a large world map.

Commodities in the classroom

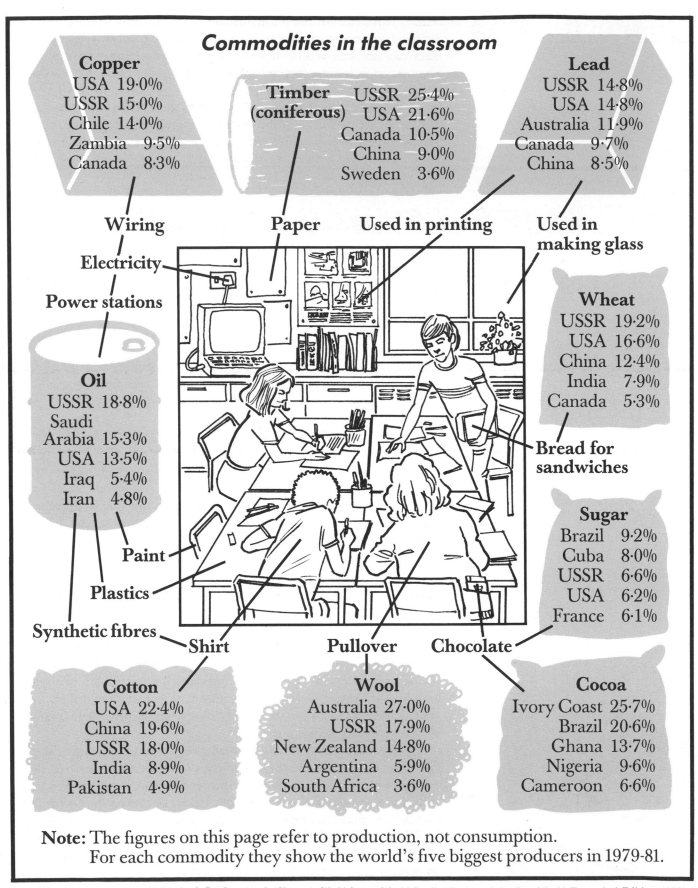

Copper
USA 19·0%
USSR 15·0%
Chile 14·0%
Zambia 9·5%
Canada 8·3%

Timber (coniferous)
USSR 25·4%
USA 21·6%
Canada 10·5%
China 9·0%
Sweden 3·6%

Lead
USSR 14·8%
USA 14·8%
Australia 11·9%
Canada 9·7%
China 8·5%

Wiring

Electricity

Power stations

Paper

Used in printing

Used in making glass

Oil
USSR 18·8%
Saudi Arabia 15·3%
USA 13·5%
Iraq 5·4%
Iran 4·8%

Wheat
USSR 19·2%
USA 16·6%
China 12·4%
India 7·9%
Canada 5·3%

Bread for sandwiches

Paint

Plastics

Sugar
Brazil 9·2%
Cuba 8·0%
USSR 6·6%
USA 6·2%
France 6·1%

Synthetic fibres

Shirt

Pullover

Chocolate

Cotton
USA 22·4%
China 19·6%
USSR 18·0%
India 8·9%
Pakistan 4·9%

Wool
Australia 27·0%
USSR 17·9%
New Zealand 14·8%
Argentina 5·9%
South Africa 3·6%

Cocoa
Ivory Coast 25·7%
Brazil 20·6%
Ghana 13·7%
Nigeria 9·6%
Cameroon 6·6%

Note: The figures on this page refer to production, not consumption. For each commodity they show the world's five biggest producers in 1979-81.

Figure 4.2 (source: based on Richardson, R., *Learning for Change in World Society*, World Studies Project of the One World Trust, 2nd Edition, 1979)

40

Initially this can focus on the number of countries which are represented in the classroom. It is important, however, that questions are raised – ideally by the pupils themselves – about justice and fairness in trade of this sort. For example: What sort of work is involved in producing this commodity? Which countries are heavily dependent on exports of one or two commodities? What are the historical reasons for this? What damage to the environment, if any, is caused by the production and use of the commodity? What are the conflicts of interest involved, and how are these resolved, if at all? What is likely to happen in the future?

VARIATION

Pupils can each be given the name of a country and asked to investigate how that country could be present, through its raw materials, in the classroom.

Looking at Ourselves
Things we Use

PURPOSE

For children to reflect on their own immediate environment and their style of living, and to see these in a world context. This activity also invites children to express and explore their feelings about their own lives and, more generally, about human priorities and values.

PREPARATION

Several boxes or plastic bags are needed, one for each small group. A tape recorder for each group would be useful.

PROCEDURE

Figure 4.3

The class is divided into groups, each of which is given a box (or plastic bag). They are asked to imagine that they will shortly be visited by a star traveller who will pick up their boxes and take them to a distant planet. There, children of their own age will unpack the contents and, from them, try to get a true picture of life on planet Earth.

The pupils put into their boxes whatever objects they feel will be helpful. They can do this *either* using the classroom only, or – with any necessary restrictions – they can use the school and its grounds.

The contents of the boxes are then presented by each group in turn to the class, and reasons are given for their choices. Would they have liked to include other items, or some more general information?

The teacher can make a list on the board of the main points that emerge.

An obvious starting point is how and why the contents of the boxes differ. Questions to consider would be: Do these objects actually reflect life on Earth? And whose life? Is there anything illustrating modern technology, wealth and poverty, different social and ethnic groups? What *are* the most important things to know about life on Earth? To what extent is the life and experience of these pupils typical? What do the objects indicate about how the pupils feel about their own lives and situations? If pupils put their most treasured possessions in a box what would they be?

VARIATIONS

If some time is allowed to elapse after the boxes have been packed, they can be presented to the class again for each group to unpack another group's box. As they do so they are asked to imagine that they have received them from the star traveller on a distant planet. What can realistically be deduced about the lifestyle of the earth's inhabitants? Group discussions can be taped and played back to the class. Alternatively groups can be asked to list their main conclusions on a large sheet of paper, display this and talk about it to the rest of the class.

Pupils can be given a week to collect items from the neighbourhood which indicate important aspects of daily life. These should be things that are freely available, such as packaging or newspaper cuttings or things brought temporarily from home.

A more specific task can be set. For example, pupils can be asked to illustrate a particular aspect of life, such as work, travel, food or sport.

Looking at Ourselves

Our Word House

This is a game for 16 to 32 people, lasting an hour to an hour and a quarter. It has been adapted, with permission, from *The People GRID*, published by Oxfam and Cockpit Arts Workshop.
The original game was based on the work of Alec Davison, then working for the Cockpit Theatre, and Margot Brown, working for Oxfam.

PURPOSE

To show how our everyday language is made up of words and phrases from all over the world. Many cultures have made valuable and lasting contributions to our everyday speech.

Note: While the selection of words from each cultural group has been made in good faith they may not all stand up to detailed etymological study. This is not important in the context of a game which is primarily to do with appreciating the rich international flavour of English language. It might, however, give rise to some investigation by pupils at the follow-up stage.

PREPARATION

The following materials are needed:

- A Word House sheet and family sheet for every two pupils (see Figures 4.4 and 4.5 on pages 45–7).
- A different coloured pencil for each of the eight families.
- A good number of strips of paper, approximately 3–5 cm wide (A4 length) for writing sentences on.
- A sheet of white A4 paper per family pair to make a family sign.

The classroom needs to be arranged so that the chairs and desks are in pairs in the shape of a circle.

PROCEDURE

The game is played in pairs which can be randomly chosen, though it is probably helpful to pair those who are linguistically confident with those who may be less so.

The class is asked to imagine that it is made of eight families, all from different countries which have influenced the English language. The classroom is Our Street. The families live next to each other in a row of terraced houses. The eight different families are Celts, Romans, Greeks, Scandinavians, French, Dutch, Italian and Indian. Pupils can choose their family or be allocated one. In a class of up to thirty-two, each family will consist of two pairs. Family pairs should not, however, sit next to each other.

Stage 1

Each pair is given their family sheet which has on it twenty of the many words their culture has contributed to the English language. They are to do two things: first, find out something about the cultural background of their family; secondly, write their family name and country of origin on the sheet of A4 paper.

Stage 2

When the preliminary research has been done and the signs are displayed, each family pair is given a copy of the Word House and a coloured pencil. On their Word House front door they should write their family name and cultural group and then, with the coloured pencil, colour in the twenty bricks which contain words from their own family sheet. Any words which they cannot understand should be investigated and discussed. *The teacher will need to check as far as possible that the families do understand their own words.* As these initial preparations take some time, the teacher may wish to cover the next stage (the game proper) in a separate lesson.

Stage 3 (allow a least half an hour)

In order to survive, people generally have to interact: to share what they have and give to others. In doing so they learn from the languages of other groups and countries.

In this game the aim is for each family to interact with the others and, in doing so, to get as many bricks coloured in as possible. The procedure is as follows.

1. Family pairs are given a handful of 3–5 cm wide strips of paper.

2. Each pair takes a word which they have not coloured and, on a strip of paper, writes a sentence to show what it means (for example: I need an *umbrella* when it's raining).

3. One of the pair takes the sentence and the family Word House round the other families to find out what country the word comes from. When the right family is found, the visiting pupil shows the family member the sentence. If they feel the word is correctly used, they colour in the word brick on the visitor's Word House, and the visitor then takes it home.

4. Meanwhile the second member of the family pair remains at home with their family sheet of words. When members of other families come visiting, asking about different words, they must be told whether their word comes from the family sheet or not. If it does, the whole sentence is read and if it seems correct the word is coloured in with the home family's coloured pencil on the other family's Word House.

5. When the visiting member of the family returns, the pair make up another sentence and then the one who had stayed at home sets off with it on a strip of paper.

DISCUSSION

The children will want to talk at first about what happened in the game. After that it will be useful to talk about what they think they have learned. There is no need for them to remember the exact origins of every word. Rather they should realise the international nature of our language and appreciate the richness and variety which it has as a result. Purity of language, like purity of race, is a myth.

A number of contributions to the English language (from the Caribbean, for example) do not feature in this game. Which other sources can the pupils think of? They can then research them.

FOLLOW-UP

One possibility is for pupils to make up a story set in their family's country using all the words in their word box. All the Word Houses can be pinned up close together like a row of terraced houses and the class can illustrate the surroundings of the street with a suitable international flavour, as they see fit. A display such as this can be a good way of interesting other pupils and staff in world studies. It can also be a useful stimulus to creative and imaginative writing.

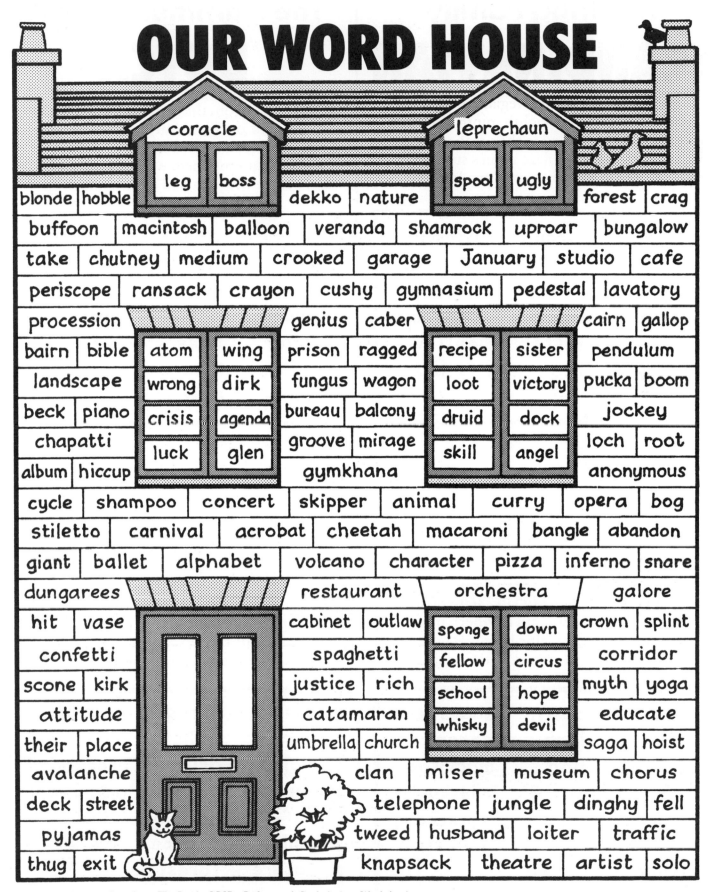

OUR WORD HOUSE

coracle

leg | boss

leprechaun

spool | ugly

blonde	hobble		dekko	nature			forest	crag
buffoon	macintosh	balloon	veranda	shamrock	uproar	bungalow
take	chutney	medium	crooked	garage	January	studio	cafe
periscope	ransack	crayon	cushy	gymnasium	pedestal	lavatory
procession			genius	caber		cairn	gallop
bairn	bible	atom	wing	prison	ragged	recipe	sister	pendulum
landscape	wrong	dirk	fungus	wagon	loot	victory	pucka	boom
beck	piano	crisis	agenda	bureau	balcony	druid	dock	jockey
chapatti	luck	glen	groove	mirage	skill	angel	loch	root
album	hiccup		gymkhana		anonymous
cycle	shampoo	concert	skipper	animal	curry	opera	bog
stiletto	carnival	acrobat	cheetah	macaroni	bangle	abandon
giant	ballet	alphabet	volcano	character	pizza	inferno	snare
dungarees		restaurant	orchestra		galore
hit	vase	cabinet	outlaw	sponge	down	crown	splint
confetti	spaghetti	fellow	circus	corridor
scone	kirk	justice	rich	school	hope	myth	yoga
attitude	catamaran	whisky	devil	educate
their	place	umbrella	church	saga	hoist
avalanche	clan	miser	museum	chorus
deck	street	telephone	jungle	dinghy	fell
pyjamas	tweed	husband	loiter	traffic
thug	exit	knapsack	theatre	artist	solo

Figure 4.4 (source: based on *The People GRID*, Oxfam and Cockpit Arts Workshop)

The Trigg Family
SCANDINAVIAN

The Scandinavians (Norwegian and Danish) came to Britain in the eighth, ninth and tenth centuries. They settled in the north and east. Many Scandinavian place names survive today: for example, those ending -by, -fell, -beck.

snare	wrong	ransack
hit	fell	crooked
take	their	husband
wing	beck	ragged
ugly	sister	outlaw
saga	leg	fellow
skill	root	

The Dammers Family
DUTCH

The Dutch (from the Netherlands) have long traded with Britain. Many people from the Netherlands came to live and work in England. Among them were weavers, artists and people who drained the fenlands.

scone	dock	landscape
deck	waggon	knapsack
hoist	rich	spool
boom	hope	groove
loiter	boss	hobble
luck	hiccup	skipper
splint	uproar	

The Ifans Family
CELTIC

The Celts were among the earliest inhabitants of Britain but later settlers drove them into the western and northern margins of the country. The Celtic languages are Gaelic, Welsh, Erse, Manx and Cornish.

crag	cairn	shamrock
clan	loch	coracle
down	bog	macintosh
glen	bairn	whisky
galore	dirk	leprechaun
caber	kirk	jockey
druid	tweed	

The Jacques Family
FRENCH

The French, or Normans, came to Britain in 1066 and Norman French as well as Latin became the language of the court, the law and the church for the next 300 years, English remaining the language of the country only.

vase	mirage	restaurant
artist	ballet	avalanche
blonde	prison	procession
bureau	garage	abandon
cafe	crayon	balloon
gallop	justice	cabinet
nature	forest	

Figure 4.5 (source: based on *The People GRID*, Oxfam and Cockpit Arts Workshop)

The Theodore Family
GREEK

Greek civilisation was at its height in the fifth century B.C. and made major contributions to European art, science and philosophy. The Greeks were conquered by the Romans, and many Greek words came to Britain via Latin.

crisis	museum	gymnasium
angel	acrobat	telephone
atom	theatre	character
devil	bible	orchestra
myth	alphabet	periscope
cycle	church	anonymous
place	chorus	

The Benedictus Family
LATIN

The Romans came from Italy via Gaul, conquering and occupying Britain from A.D. 43 to A.D. 418. Roman missionaries brought Christianity to Britain in the sixth century. Latin became the language of education for over a thousand years.

crown	recipe	January
exit	fungus	educate
giant	animal	pendulum
album	street	lavatory
circus	school	sponge
miser	genius	agenda
	medium	victory

The Giovanni Family
ITALIAN

The Italian influence on Britain was strongest during the Renaissance in the sixteenth century. Many rich Britons visited Italy to enjoy the music, painting and architecture.

opera	concert	spaghetti
piano	confetti	umbrella
studio	stiletto	carnival
solo	volcano	pedestal
traffic	inferno	macaroni
pizza	balcony	attitude
	buffoon	corridor

The Kallie Family
INDIAN

The Indian contributions (e.g. Hindi, Gujarati, Bengali, Punjabi and Tamil) to the English language were mainly made in the nineteenth century when Britain controlled the Indian subcontinent as part of its colonial empire.

curry	chutney	dungarees
loot	bangle	bungalow
thug	dinghy	veranda
yoga	cheetah	pyjamas
cushy	jungle	shampoo
pucka	chapati	gymkhana
	dekko	catamaran

Interviewing People

PURPOSE

To show that one connecting link between a neighbourhood or town and the wider world is the people who live there. Through carefully conducted interviews pupils can see recent events and trends in the wider world through the eyes of local people who have personal experience of them. Similarly the global aspects of local events and issues can be investigated and made explicit.

PREPARATION

Younger children may need to practise interviewing. Role-play is an effective way of doing this, with pupils taking it in turns to be questioned.

Appropriate contacts need to be made, if these are not already to hand. A register of suitable people can be built up over a period of time as a result of personal meetings and local press articles.

Such people might include:

- those who have been directly involved in major world events and initiatives such as armed conflicts, conferences, trade agreements, disaster relief;
- those who have lived and worked for some time in other countries;
- those who can remember and illustrate the effects of major world events on daily life and the local neighbourhood;
- members of minority groups who have experienced prejudice and discrimination and who are working to change attitudes and perhaps the law;
- those who grew up in a culture or setting different from that of the pupils and can describe aspects of their schooling, family life, games, songs and stories;
- those who are directly involved in developing alternative ways of living and working in, for example, city farms, work-sharing, education at home, small-scale technology and recycling;
- those who have experience of important world organisations such as the Commonwealth, the United Nations and the EEC;
- those involved in trying to change government attitudes towards important issues via groups such as Friends of the Earth, Shelter, the World Disarmament Campaign and the World Development Movement.

PROCEDURE

This approach – an alternative to the more usual format of pupils simply putting pre-arranged questions to a visitor – is that of a tribunal of enquiry interviewing an expert witness. It has five stages:
1. The visitor has five or ten minutes to talk about their experience, as previously arranged with the teacher;

2. Pupils make a list of questions which they would like to put to the visitor. They can do this as a whole group with the visitor listening, or in small groups, each of which is to produce, say, three questions.
3. The questions are written up on the board, beginning with the more concrete and then going on to the more speculative.
4. The questions are put to the visitor by the teacher or by one or two pupils. The class can put additional relevant questions to the visitor during this period if time permits.
5. The interview can conclude with the visitor having time to make any comments he or she feels are appropriate.

Afterwards pupils can be asked, individually or in pairs, to jot down four important things which they have learned. These can be the stimuli for further work and discussion. They can also be made into a single list by the teacher and displayed in the classroom or school foyer under a heading such as 'Some important things we learned when X came'.

VARIATIONS

A small group of pupils can record an interview 'on location', for example in the street or on a farm.

One or more recorded interviews can be turned into a short radio style programme for the rest of the school to hear.

Exploring the Neighbourhood
The World in our Newspapers

PURPOSE

To use local newspapers to show some of the many connections between the local neighbourhood and the wider world.

PREPARATION

The class will need either identical sets of nine or ten cuttings from local newspapers cut up separately, or complete issues of local newspapers (one for every two pupils).

PROCEDURE

Pupils are given one set of local newspaper cuttings between two. Each cutting is read out and discussed with the class to ensure that it is fully understood. With younger classes it may be best to concentrate only on the headlines. Pupils then work in pairs to sort the cuttings into two piles: those which have something to do with other countries or areas and those which are solely to do with the immediate neighbourhood or town. After, say, ten minutes the pairs form groups of six to share their findings and to try and reach agreement on the two piles of cuttings.

It is important to note that cuttings can relate either explicitly or implicitly to the wider world. Explicit references involve the names of places or people, or mention of particular world issues and problems. Implicit references are likely to be more numerous, and also more difficult to spot. For example, a new film coming to the area may have been at least partly made outside Britain. A company undertaking a local development may well have overseas branches and personnel. An advertisement for a car is implicitly related to world society via the components and metals from other countries.

It is not necessary or possible for pupils to have absolute knowledge of all the implicit connections. It *is* important for them to make sensible hypotheses and guesses, some of which could be followed up later.

Class discussion can now take place and reasons for the allocation of cuttings to a particular pile can be explained. The exercise can end by relating each 'international' cutting to its correct place on a world map or globe.

VARIATIONS

Another, more demanding, activity is for pupils to be given one or two issues of local newspapers. In pairs they cut out all those articles or headlines which are clearly and directly to do with the wider world and those which they think may be indirectly to do with it. They then sort them into three categories: people, ideas, goods. If the pupils all have the same issues of the paper then discussion can proceed in groups as above and the exercise follow the same pattern.

An alternative to sorting the cuttings into piles would be to make them into a poster or wall chart, or paste them into a scrapbook.

Instead of taking just one or two issues of a newspaper it can be very valuable to monitor several issues over a period of weeks. Pupils can cut out items relating to other countries and compile their own 'world' version of the local paper.

A different focus is created if pupils are asked to rank (see page 90) a set of nine newspaper cuttings in response to the instruction: 'You are writing a letter to a penfriend in a distant country. Which of these will you enclose to show the world as seen in your own country?'

50

Goodwill trip to twin town

NORCHESTER'S CIVIC LEADERS left by chartered Trident jet this afternoon to spend the weekend in Norchester's twin town Mittelstadt, West Germany.

They were invited as part of the local British Week which is held to encourage West Germans to buy British goods.

Before boarding the 'plane, Labour Group Leader

BIRTHDAY CLUB

Congratulations to Delroy Bennett who is 10 today. He lives in Waterloo Street, Norchester, and attends St Barnabas Junior School. His hobbies are stamp-collecting and swimming, and he never misses his favourite TV programme, Doctor Who. He hopes to be an airline pilot when he grows up.

Because today is a school day, the party will be on Saturday

Battle to save jobs

Trade Union Leader *John Davidson* appealed today to the management of Sellall Ltd not to go ahead with plans to cut 500 people from the workforce.

He said: "If this goes ahead we will soon have the highest rate of unemployment here since before the Second World War".

No choice

But Sellall's managing director said last night: "We have no choice. The competition from overseas is so strong that if we don't cut costs we shall go out of business".

At a recent board meeting it was agreed that immediate cuts

CAMPAIGN LAUNCHED

"IT'S AMAZING!" was all Annette Kirkpatrick could say after Tuesday's meeting of the World Disarmament Campaign which was attended by over 200 people.

As local organiser she said she had never dreamed that so many people would come with so many new ideas for campaigning.

Ms Kirkpatrick said the Campaign would now be appealing for funds to mail information to every household in Norchester.

Membership of W.D.C. has risen sharply since

Food Prices UP

"SHOCKING". This was the verdict last night of local Euro MP Janet Newby on the rising cost of food.

"The Government *must* act to prevent the price of basic foods such as bread, butter, cheese, coffee and tea from going up further before there is real hardship in the region."

Addressing a meeting of constituents in the Victoria

Teenager Wins Prize

Mark Johnson, 18, of Australia Road, East Norchester, is off on a tour of Europe after winning a £5000 Premium Bond prize. He expects to spend several months travelling and will return in time to start a course at Norchester Polytechnic in October.

Mark's winning bond number, which previously

POLICE TRY OUT BRITISH BIKES

NORCHESTER POLICE are revving up for a battle against West German and Japanese motorcycle manufacturers.

The force are trying out new British-built cycles which they hope will be good enough to replace their fleet of German BMWs.

The prototype machines, which have frames of a completely new design,

High Flyer

More than £10,000 made by the air display held at the Downley USAF base on Thursday is to be handed over to Oxfam.

Sheila Manzini, the charity's area director, said: "Every penny of this will go to help the poor help themselves.

"The continuing drought in countries bordering the Sahara

BLAZE DESTROYS CAFE

Police are investigating a fire which last night gutted the popular Canton Restaurant in Silver Street.

Firemen arrived too late to save the fine Gothic building but they were able to save the shop next door from serious damage.

The alarm was given at 11.30 pm by local resident Mrs Mary

Figure 4.6

Understanding the news: an example of work with twelve year olds

The initial reaction from the children was not favourable. For example: 'Oh we don't watch BBC, Dad won't have it on;' 'Mum is always watching the other side;' 'It's too posh for me.'

After watching the first selected edition no one could remember any of the items and they were quite pleased with themselves. It proved their point: boring! A few allowed a little enthusiasm to show when asked to point out various countries on an outline world map. Even more joined in stopping the spinning globe and seeing to which country their finger was pointing. The news programme was considered again, taking the countries mentioned, and looking at where they could be found on the globe and on the world map.

From this shaky start the children's interest and commitment grew. To begin with only some of the items were remembered and discussion of them developed rather slowly. Drawings and notes were also produced which were displayed beside the world map and linked to the country concerned.

As time went by more items were remembered until the time came when all items from a programme were being remembered. Discussions became more lively, with a little encouragement these involved everyone. The importance of this discussion work should not be underestimated; each individual gained confidence to speak to the group. To maintain the right to finish relating a news story, they had to learn to organise their thoughts and to express them clearly and accurately or have the subject taken from them by someone else.

This lack of tolerance by the group as a whole for individuals who stumble can be turned to good use.

One child starts to tell the first news item and may only be interrupted when they hesitate or make a mistake. Points may be awarded for completing a story and for taking over after a hesitation or mistake.

Once the basic approach had been mastered, variations could be tried out. One alternative was to follow through with discussion of all topics, but then for the children to prepare a report on just one story. This worked quite well, but it was pointed out by the children that extra information was often needed. Although the school had no such resources, we obtained a selection of booklets and newsheets from a variety of charities.

Newspapers were also brought in regularly: both 'popular' and 'quality' papers. These were used as a source of topical cuttings and as a source of background information.

Another idea was for each individual to watch the programme and try to spot some detail that they hope no one else has seen. This involved each individual writing down what they had seen and then each being asked in turn to recount their chosen item. This proved a very useful introduction as some children had no idea what to look for and now they devise questions for each other.

Feed-back from the children is a vital aspect of this work and is essential if interest and involvement are not just to be maintained but increased. Casual chats with individuals are useful but group discussions can be even more productive provided that all of the children are encouraged to speak freely about what they thought of the lessons and to make any suggestions they could for changes.

John Burns, a teacher in Somerset

Figure 4.7

Exploring the Neighbourhood
Making a Documentary

PURPOSE

For pupils to explore different ways of viewing their own local neighbourhood. It can be a first step towards introducing different perspectives on other countries and on world issues as well as a consideration of bias.

PREPARATION

A collection of about twenty photographs of the local neighbourhood is needed. These should illustrate a variety of features and characteristics of the area. Enough copies are needed to provide a set for every two or three pupils involved at any one time in the activity.

PROCEDURE

Pupils work in small groups, each with a set of photographs. Their task is to select a manageable number, say twelve of them, and to

Figure 4.8

write a commentary with the title 'This is our neighbourhood'. Each group will thus produce a simple documentary on the area, but they have to do this from different standpoints: for example, someone who has just arrived in the area from another country; an old age pensioner who has always lived there; an out-of-work teenager; someone of the same age and outlook as the pupils themselves; a reformer who wants to change the area for the better; a conserver who wishes to keep things as they are; an artist; a police officer; someone who was brought up in the area, left, and recently returned.

There will need to be discussion with the pupils as to what each viewpoint entails in order to avoid stereotyped viewpoints being presented. If there is time, pupils should do some research before writing their commentary, looking, for example, at the recent history of the area, at any issues that have arisen, at new developments. They could very usefully interview one or more people who actually hold the viewpoint which they are trying to portray.

They will also need guidance on how to construct a coherent commentary. This should as a minimum have an introduction to the standpoint or person being represented, an overview of the area, a description of the qualities of the neighbourhood (What is good about it? What is bad? What is beautiful or ugly?) and a conclusion.

The next step is for the 'documentaries' to be presented to the class. This can be done by asking the remainder of the class to rearrange their copies of the photographs as instructed before each small group gives the commentary. Alternatively a set of slides can be made from the photographs and shown.

DISCUSSION

The initial discussion might well centre on whose documentary was most convincing, and how each group managed their task. Further important questions include: Whose version was nearest the truth? Is there in fact one single right view of the area and its possibilities?

VARIATIONS

A simpler approach is for pupils to write a brief caption for each photograph from their chosen standpoint, and for these to be displayed rather than presented to the class.

It is equally possible for pupils to use photographs to portray a particular event or issue in the school or locality.

Instead of taking different viewpoints, pupils can be asked to illustrate particular themes such as the world in our town, transport, recreation, work, or, more ambitiously, to illustrate a key concept such as communication, interdependence, distribution of power or fairness.

Instead of producing a documentary, pupils can produce booklets on the neighbourhood incorporating both photographs and commentary.

53

Food from Overseas: A Case Study of Bananas

To illustrate some important aspects of world trade by looking at the example of bananas. To raise some questions about the fairness of the world trading system.

By way of an introduction to world trade generally, and to the food trade in particular, there is the familiar activity in which pupils are asked to collect food wrappers and packaging with overseas origins marked on them. These are displayed around the classroom or on a large world map and linked to the country of origin to illustrate our dependence on the wider world for food. While this may suggest a satisfactory mutual arrangement, a close look at one example, the banana trade, raises some provocative and far-reaching questions.

Copies of the play on pages 56–9 need to be available (at least one between two). It was written by Steve Pratchett and published by Christian Aid in 1983. The minimum props for the play are some bananas, a box to put them in, and 100 counters or tokens to represent 100 pence. A number of other possible props are mentioned in the text.

The play provides an introduction to the banana trade. It can be used in many ways: for example, as a small group activity, as a presentation to the class, or at a school assembly. It is very important to take up the points it raises with the children and to encourage them to see this trade from the differing standpoints of the participants. What is convenient for some is unjust for others.

After the play has been acted out and understood, children need to extract the information about the banana trade and put it in an easily understandable form such as a flow chart or diagram. This would begin with the plantation in Jamaica and end with the British shopper. Then, using the information in the play, they can write or draw on the flow chart the amount of money accruing to each person in the chain. Alternatively they can produce a chart similar to the one in Figure 4.9 entitled 'Where does the money go?' These charts can be presented to the class and the system they describe discussed in some detail. World trade is made up of myriad systems such as this, which together contribute a major factor in the perpetuation of underdevelopment.

DISCUSSION

A natural and crucial question which arises is to do with the fairness, or otherwise of such a trading system. An important point to be made is that over the years the price paid to the grower – which is set by the firms involved, not the producing countries – has steadily declined, while the cost of goods needed to produce crops and promote development has increased enormously. In 1950 the tractor which Mr Honore wanted to buy cost the equivalent of 3 tons of bananas. In 1970 it took 11 tons. By 1982, 25 tons were needed, and the amount was still increasing. The situation is the same with other commodities such as coffee, tea, sugar, cotton and copper.

Other questions which can usefully be raised include: What would be a *fair* breakdown of one hundred pence spent on bananas among the people involved in the trade? In what circumstances would the pupils and their families be willing to pay a higher price for a product such as bananas?

FOLLOW-UP

Pupils can investigate the trade in other commodities such as coffee and tea, both of which have been well documented, by Campaign Co-op and the World Development Movement respectively. An additional advantage of choosing these is that they offer examples of successful initiatives aimed at increasing the amount of money staying in the country of origin – Tanzania in the case of coffee, and Sri Lanka in the case of tea – by marketing an alternative product to those offered by multinational companies. Pupils could become involved in promoting Campaign Coffee and World Development Movement Tea.

The Gingerbread People Project: an example of work with younger children

I wanted my class to understand that they were dependent for their food on the labours of many people throughout the world and to build on their concepts of interdependence.

Early discussions with them showed that many felt that food came off the supermarket shelf and confirmed the need to develop this theme.

It seemed appropriate to start on a small scale and to use the practical context of a cookery session to stimulate interest. I organised for the children to bake some gingerbread people and these were very soon eaten. They made some more in small groups on their own and were asked to write down the names and addresses of all the companies whose products were used in the recipe – including currant buttons and facial features. We found all this information on the labels. Individual children were then asked to write to one company each, requesting information about the source of their product. I enclosed a covering letter to explain the general purpose of the enquiry. While we waited for the replies, the children wrote stories about gingerbread people and did paintings of them, carefully matching the colours.

Eventually all but one of the companies replied and we were able to trace the origin of these ingredients and in some cases the routes by which they arrived in Britain. We recorded our findings on a world map. This was displayed with their paintings and stories. We had achieved our objectives of discovering where our gingerbread people had come from, and very global characters they were!

Nick Clough, a teacher in Bristol

55

The Journey of the Bananas and the Return of the Pennies

Narrator	(*Holds up a 'hand' of bananas*) Have you ever wondered where our bananas come from? Do you know who grows them? Do you know how they get to us?.
	Today we are going on a journey – a long journey – the journey of a banana. Our journey begins on the island of Jamaica, one of the many islands of the Caribbean where bananas grow. The journey ends here in Britain where the banana disappears into my stomach. (*Narrator peels banana and takes a bite.*) Now let's go to the start of the journey and meet Mr Honore and his family who live in Jamaica.
Mr Honore	Hello, my name is Lennox Honore and this is my wife Lystra.
Lystra	Hello.
Mr Honore	These are my children – Jasmin, she is the youngest, she is nine – Tyron, my son, he is eleven – and Luella my elder daughter, she is thirteen. We have a small farm of ten acres on which I grow mixed crops. Children, would you like to show everyone what we grow?
Children	(*Each child holds up a fruit or vegetable in each hand.*)
	Oranges . . . coconuts
	Yams . . . sweet potatoes
	Dasheen . . . bananas
Mr Honore	The bananas are our most important crop for earning a living. We call bananas a cash crop. I sell the bananas to the exporters who send them to other countries. The money I earn from bananas keeps my family. Come on Tyron we must make an early start.
	(*Mr Honore and his son walk off to the plantation. They arrive next to a banana tree.*)
Mr Honore	This is a special knife. I use it to cut down the stems of bananas. On a good tree I can get as many as twelve or fourteen hands on each stem. You can see the bananas are covered with a polythene bag. This protects them against the banana spider. It has taken ten months for this tree to produce bananas. The bananas, as you can see, grow upwards from a purple flower and I cut them when they are green.
	(*Tyron stands underneath with a board on his head.*)
Tyron	I'm ready dad.
	(*Mr Honore chops down the bananas.*)

Mr Honore	Now I have to cut down the whole tree because it only produces one crop of bananas. (*He cuts down the tree*).
Tyron	I often take days off school at this time of year to help my father with the banana harvest. I have to be very careful not to drop or bruise the bananas or they will go bad and we cannot sell them. (*Tyron walks along with bananas on his head. He arrives at the dipping tanks.*)
Luella	My sister and I help after school. I dip the bananas in this special liquid. This stops the sap oozing out of the ends of the bananas.
Jasmin	I dip the bananas in this tank to preserve the bananas and stop them going bad.
Luella	Now we must pack them carefully into boxes. We mustn't bruise them. (*The girls pack the bananas into boxes.*)
Lystra	I'm busy preparing the dinner. (*She holds out a saucepan.*) I have wrapped some breadfruit in cabbage leaves and I am roasting it over an open fire in the kitchen. I will also cut up some mangoes. (*Holds one up.*) It has been a hot day and my family will find the juice refreshing.
Mr Honore	Come on children let's get the boxes down the road to the banana depot. We'll use the donkey. (*They all load up the donkey and carry some boxes themselves. When they are walking along the road a landrover speeds past blaring out a message over a loudhailer.*)
Loudhailer	Men are needed on the banana plantation. The rate is £6 a week. The hours are 5 a.m. to 6 p.m. We need hole diggers – we pay 1p a hole – and planters . . . Men are needed, etc., etc.
Mr Honore	They don't mention the housing for the men on the plantation. They live in shacks, ten feet square with no electricity, no running water, and no toilet. The company charge £2 a week to pay for a bed. (*The family arrive with their bananas at the docks.*)
Docker 1	I am a docker. I load the bananas onto the boats. My job depends on the banana. You see there is not much other work around.
Docker 2	We have to get the bananas onto this ship within twenty-four hours of being picked, or they will go bad. (*They load boxes onto the boat.*)
Exporter	I work for a British banana company. I get the orders from customers all over Britain. I am called an exporter. (*The exporter gets on the boat.*)
Exporter	Let me introduce you to the Shipper.

Shipper	My banana boat has a crew of forty-eight men. The boat belongs to the banana company. I have room in the ship's hold for 48 000 stems of bananas, that is 160 railway truck loads. In the hold the bananas are kept at a cool temperature so that they don't ripen too fast. (*The boat sets sail for Britain.*)
Narrator	While the ship is sailing, here is something for you to think about. Did you know that roughly one out of every two bananas that you eat comes from the West Indies? (*Peels another banana.*) These really are delicious. (*The boat arrives in Britain.*)
Insurer	I work for Lloyds Insurance Company. We insure this banana boat in case of accident. If it sinks we will buy the shipper a new one. I've come to inspect the safety and conditions of the ship. (*He climbs on board and looks it over.*)
Dockers	Our jobs depend on the banana trade. We unload the bananas here in Bristol. (*They pass the boxes of bananas to the Ripeners.*)
Ripener	We unpack the bananas and take out the ripe ones. Then we scientifically ripen the rest in a special room where we can control the temperature. Sometimes we find spiders in the boxes so we wear gloves.
Packer	We re-pack the boxes of bananas ready for the shops and load them onto the lorries. (*They load the boxes onto a lorry.*)
Transporter	I run a fleet of lorries to get the bananas to the shops and big supermarkets. My drivers (*points to one*) drive big container lorries up and down the motorways of Britain.
Retailer	I am a retailer, that means I sell the bananas to members of the public. I have my own shop and I also run a stall at Romford Market . . . Come on ladies, a lovely bunch of bananas, thirty pence a pound! You can't beat the quality luv!
Housewife	I'd like a £'s worth of bananas please. (*She takes out a piggy bank.*) I hope you don't mind me paying in pennies but you see I've just emptied my piggy bank at home. (*She turns to her little boy.*) Come on Willie give the man his money.
Retailer	That's all right luv. (*He checks the money.*) Yes that's correct luv, a hundred pence, I could do with the change. Here's your bananas. (*Use the hundred counters to represent the money.*)
Narrator	We have followed the journey of the bananas all the way from the island of Jamaica in the West Indies to a market stall in Romford. Now let's do a return trip and follow the hundred pence to see where they all go.
Retailer	Thirty-two pence of this is mine. I've got a shop and market stall to run and I want to take the family to Majorca this year for a holiday.

Ripener	Nineteen pence of this is mine for ripening the bananas in my special store rooms. I have a wife and three children to support and I've just bought a new car.
Insurer Shipper }	Eleven and a half pence is ours.
Insurer	For insuring the banana boats in case they sink or catch fire . . . My wife and I both run a car.
Shipper	For the cost of sailing the banana boat between Britain and the West Indies . . . I've just bought a new colour television and video recorder.
Transporter Exporter Packer Docker	Twenty-six pence is ours.
Exporter	For exporting the bananas from Jamaica.
Packer	For packing the bananas into boxes.
Docker	For loading and unloading the bananas off the boats.
Transporter	For carrying the bananas to the shops in my lorries. (*The Retailer, Ripener, Insurer, Shipper, Exporter, Packer, Docker, Transporter, all group together and build their money into a stack of eighty-eight and a half pence. They unfurl the Union Jack.*)
All	This eighty-eight and a half pence stays in Britain with us – the rest can go back to Jamaica. (*The boat sets sail with the money left over.*)
Narrator	The banana boat is returning to Jamaica to fetch a fresh cargo of bananas. Eleven and a half pence goes back to Jamaica with the boat.
Grower	This eleven and a half pence is ours for producing the bananas in our country. This eleven and a half pence stays in Jamaica. (*They hold up the Jamaican flag*).
Mr Honore	Out of this I must pay the rent for my land and support my family. I also need to buy fertilisers, weedkillers, insecticides and fungicides from Britain if my bananas are to grow well. I need the crop spraying aeroplane to come and spray my banana trees to kill the banana spiders and stop leaf spot or I could lose many bananas. But I can't afford to pay for the plane to come. I would like to save up for a tractor which I could share with other farmers around me but we cannot afford one. My wife too would like a washing machine but the price I get for my bananas is not enough to buy one. I wish I could get a fairer price for my bananas.
Narrator	Next time you eat a banana think of all the people who help to bring it to you and spare a special thought for Mr Honore and others like him who need a better price for growing your banana in the first place.

The Journey of the Bananas and the Return of the Pennies written by Steve Pratchett from *Show You Care*: ideas for worship with younger children produced annually by Christian Aid.

Figure 4.9 (source: *Show You Care*, Christian Aid)

Tractors and bananas

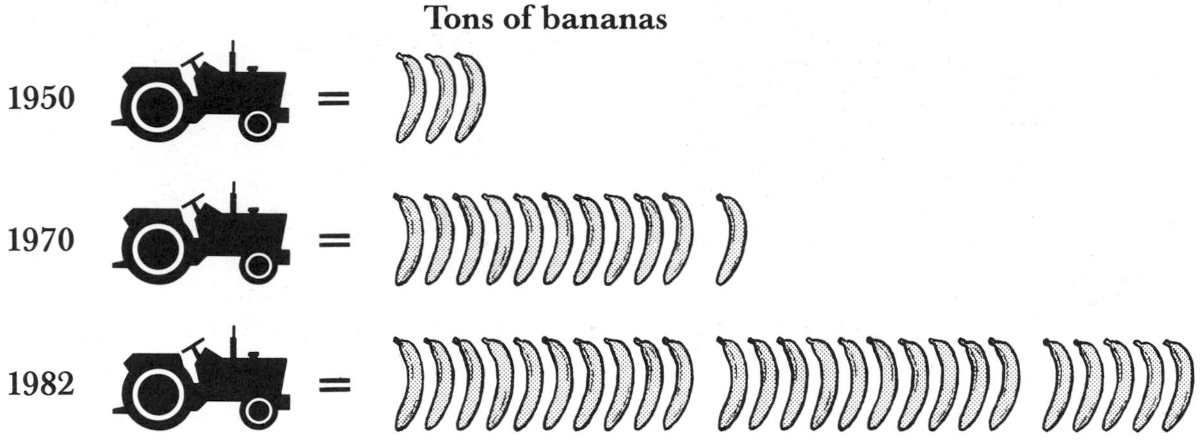

Tons of bananas

1950 =))))

1970 =))))))))))))

1982 =))))))))))))))))))))))))))))))))

Some background information on bananas

The continent which grows the most bananas is Africa where people eat them cooked as the main food. In one area of Uganda, daily consumption of bananas is 4–4.5 kilograms per family.

Banana trees grow about 2.5 metres high. Each tree bears only one stem of bananas with many hands. Male and female flowers produce a lot of sticky pollen and nectar which attracts bats, birds, bees, ants, wasps and any other large insects. At night the scent is particularly strong to attract the nocturnal bats who pollinate the plants. The time between planting the small trees and harvesting the bananas varies according to the soil and climate. It can be anything between nine and eighteen months.

Bananas can be damaged very easily. Leaves or branches rubbing on the fruit produce bruises; grasshoppers and snails leave black marks on the skin. There are numerous diseases and pests which banana farmers have to watch out for. In Surinam between 1906 and 1911 the whole banana crop was wiped out by banana wilt. The most worrying moment for the banana grower is during the hurricane season. High winds can flatten the plantation and no harvest will be celebrated that year.

The banana industry developed at the end of the nineteenth century and beginning of the twentieth. Jamaica developed first, sending the fruit in schooners to North America. A world total of 20 million tons of bananas is now grown, though only 4–5 million are traded internationally. The two main fruit companies are United Fruit Co. and Standard Fruit Co. Geest is one of the smaller British companies. Bananas first arrived in Britain in 1882 from the Canary Islands. It is not necessary to use refrigerators to transport bananas. As long as they are picked at the correct green stage they can be eaten on arrival. Companies aim to allow two weeks between harvest and destination.

Figure 4.10

This jar of coffee costs 100p in the shops. Where do the pennies go?

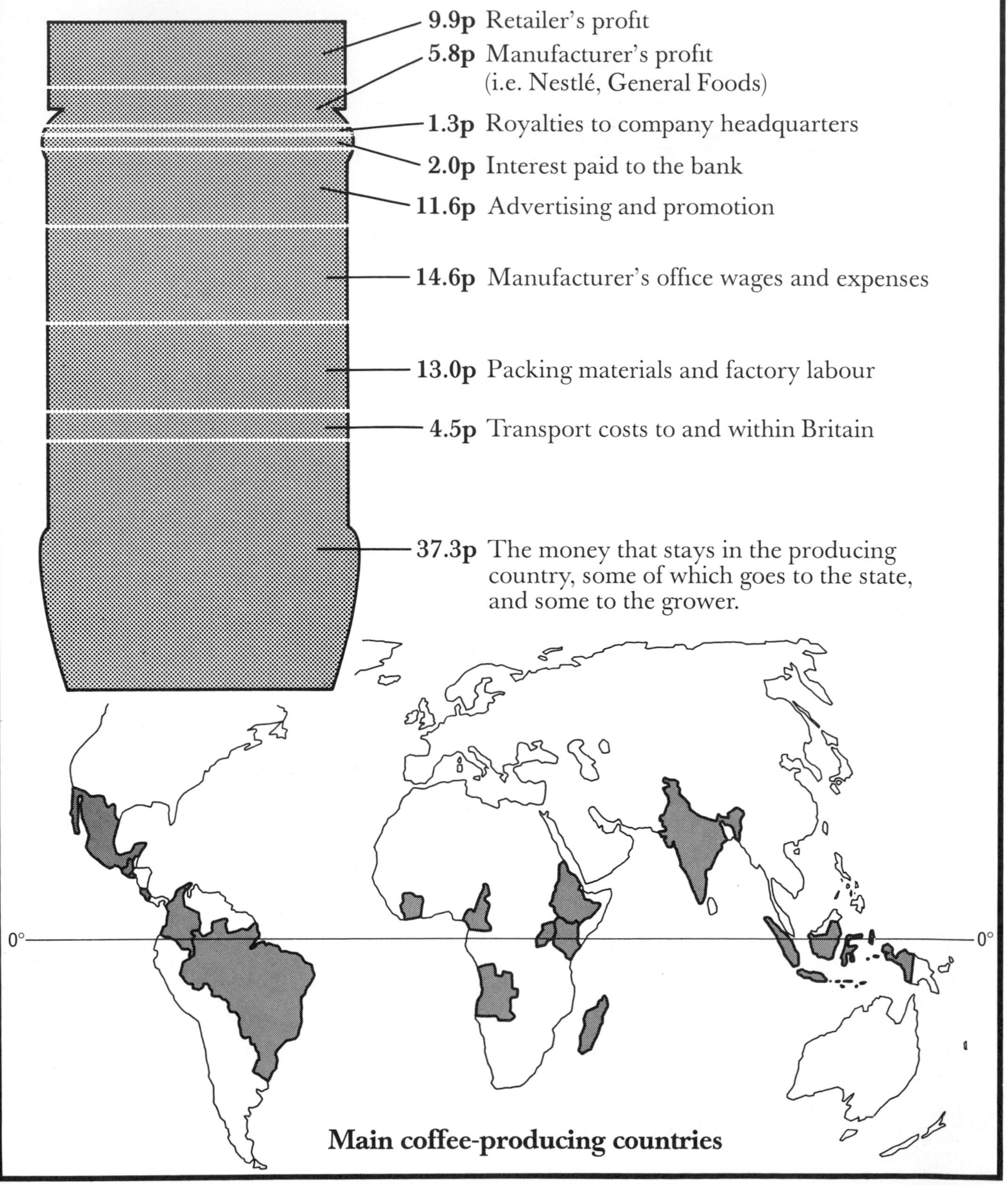

9.9p Retailer's profit

5.8p Manufacturer's profit
(i.e. Nestlé, General Foods)

1.3p Royalties to company headquarters

2.0p Interest paid to the bank

11.6p Advertising and promotion

14.6p Manufacturer's office wages and expenses

13.0p Packing materials and factory labour

4.5p Transport costs to and within Britain

37.3p The money that stays in the producing country, some of which goes to the state, and some to the grower.

0°   0°

Main coffee-producing countries

Figure 4.11

Starting Points

The World in our Town

Pupils study their local area, including shops, firms and current issues and events. They look at some of the raw materials processed by local industry and at how things have changed. They then make a set of detailed instructions and notes for a walk through the area which other pupils can follow. This town trail draws out the links with other countries. It shows evidence of (*a*) the wider world in our town, and (*b*) our town in the wider world.

An Imaginary Community

One way to introduce children to the idea that their own class group is in some important ways a miniature version of world society is for them to imagine starting a new community from scratch. As a result of a plane crash the class are marooned on a small island. How do they organise themselves to meet their basic needs, and to respond to particular events? How do they make decisions and make sure they are kept to? A version of this for older pupils can be found in *Fighting for Freedom*, by Robin Richardson (Nelson), pages 26–7.

A Local Issue

The teacher chooses an issue reported in the local paper: a new site for travelling people, or a disagreement over plans for a new road, or cuts in education provision, or the location of a new rubbish tip. Children role-play the different groups of people affected. They look at alternatives and likely effects. They examine different points of view and try to assess whether media reports have been fair and what the final outcome should, ideally, be.

Questions

Pupils brainstorm a list of questions about the local neighbourhood. With the teacher's help they select those which offer the most scope for exploring the links between it and the wider world. The pupils then discuss and research possible answers.

Making a Programme

A group of pupils tape record the views of some pupils and staff about a particular world issue or event. They edit the interviews and play them to the pupils and staff of the school.

Reviewing the Curriculum

The class and teacher look back over the past term or year's work. How much time was spent on countries other than Britain, and on cultures other than the dominant ones in the school? How often did ideas such as conflict, prejudice, tolerance, fairness, come up? How often were potentially violent conflicts resolved peacefully? Was time spent thinking about the future as well as the past?

A Local Event

Pupils take a locally reported event and investigate its international background. For example, pupils could look at the reasons for the closure of a textile factory. They can invite someone involved to be interviewed. What is the effect on employment here? How does the resulting unemployment compare with that in the 'third world' countries. Who needs jobs most?

Food

Pupils collect labels, packaging and actual items of food to present a display on 'Things We Eat'. They experiment with cooking different sorts of meals and relate them to their countries of origin.

A Visit

Pupils listen to or watch the local news. They prepare questions to find out how the news was collected and the items chosen. They visit the local radio or television newsdesk and question how the news was collected, selected and presented.

Involvement

Pupils take part regularly in various forms of local activity which contribute to the welfare of the global village: for example, community relations, recycling, city farms, helping old or disabled people. They also develop active links with organisations such as Shelter, Help the Aged, Friends of the Earth or their local peace group.

Selected Resources

T: for the use of teachers
P: for the use of pupils

Images and Assumptions

This section applies also to how we look at people in other countries. Refer again to this list in the context of Chapter 6.

Bethell, Andrew, *Eyeopener*, Cambridge University Press, 1981, Books 1 and 2. (P) Two small books that go some way to teaching children how the media select images to give the message they want. Distortion and stereotyping of even a subtle kind are brilliantly exposed.

Birmingham Development Education Centre, *Values, Cultures and Kids: Approaches and Resources for Teaching Child Development and About the Family*, 1983. (T) Valuable classroom resource for teaching against stereotyped views and towards a global and multicultural perspective. Provides information, photographs and suggests activities.

Dickinson, Peter, *The Devil's Children*, Penguin, 1972. (P) Medieval conditions arouse superstitious fear in a future Britain, of which a group of Sikhs becomes an inevitable target.

Guy, Rosa, *The Friends*, Penguin, 1977. (P) Phyllisia comes to the USA from Trinidad, is mocked at school for her accent and her prissiness and treats Edith, the one girl who befriends her, with alternate dependence and contempt. Raises issues most sensitively and is finely written. Age eleven and over.

Hicks, David, W., Bias in schoolbooks: messages from the ethnocentric curriculum, in James, A. and Jeffcoate, R. (eds.), *The School in the Multicultural Society*, Harper & Row, 1981. (T) Looks at images of the 'third world', textbook analysis, classroom implications and guidelines.

Klein, Gillian, 'Children's books – what to look for' in *Resources for Multicultural Education – An Introduction*, Longman/Schools Council, 1982. (T) Guidelines on selecting materials that positively reflect other cultures and ethnic minorities in the UK, based on a concern that the messages in currently used books are often racist, or otherwise damagingly biased.

Large, Martin, *Who's Bringing Them Up? Television and Child Development*, available from TV Action Group, 25 Reservoir Road, Gloucester. (T) Aimed mostly at parents, this is a convincing argument that indiscriminate television viewing is detrimental to children's development.

Macdonald Insiders Series: *Newspaper* by Penny Junor, 1979, *Television Studio* by Judy Lever, 1978. (P) Typical MacDonald picture-book format: a rather glossy version of both, but very informative.

Maclean, Eleanor, *Between the Lines: How to Detect Bias and Propaganda in the News and Everyday Life*, Housmans Distribution Service, 1982. (T) Written by a Canadian, the book focusses on the mass media. Its main concerns are misreporting of 'third world' issues. Lavishly illustrated, stimulating and relevant.

Philo, Greg, Hewitt, J., Beharrell, P. and Davis, H., *Really Bad News*, Writers & Readers, 1982. (T) The Glasgow University Media Group has followed *Bad News* and further reports with this analysis of later news broadcasts, showing how (and *why*) television distorts the content of the news and also determines what *is* newsworthy.

Looking at Ourselves

Barratt, Sylvia, *The Tinder-box Assembly Book: Starting Points, Stories, Poems and Classroom Activities*, Black, 1982. (P) Rhymes, stories, songs, etc., built round the themes of self, others, surroundings, times of difficulty, celebrations. For juniors.

Berger, Terry, *Big Sister, Little Brother*, MacDonald Educational, 1979. (P) Colour photographs and a brief text exploring the feelings of both children, feelings which would be shared by the readers even though they are not black Americans.

Harper, Anita, *How we Live; How We Work; How We Feel* and *How We Play*, Penguin, 1979. (P) Picture-book format explores a range of lifestyles, homes, families, occupations, amusements, emotions in a fresh, non-stereotyped way. Though for a young age group, they could provoke thought.

ILEA English Centre, *City Lines: Poems by London School Students*, 1982, available from English Centre, Ebury Bridge, Sutherland Street, London SW1. (P) The feelings of young people in London, expressed in verse. Many deal with issues of racism, family difficulties, as well as aspirations and dreams.

ILEA English Centre, *Our Lives: Young People's Autobiographies*, 1979, available from English Centre, Ebury Bridge, Sutherland Street, London SW1. (P) School students have written their own stories, many to do with their experience of settling in London from another country.

ILEA Learning Materials Service, *Caribbean Anthology*, 1981. (P) Pack of poetry books plus two cassettes, on which the poems are read by Caribbean voices, often those of the poets themselves. Gives insights into feelings and issues of dialect. Designed for classroom use and suitable for age eleven and over.

Mendoza, George, *House by Mouse*, Deutsch, 1982. (P) Henrietta Mouse is the ultimate architect: each house she designs takes account of the special requirements of her clients: Squirrel, Mole, Fox, etc. (Cat needs beds everywhere, for that sudden snooze). Beautifully realised and illustrated and affording great scope for discussion. Age eight to twelve.

Miller, Jane, *Many Voices: Bilingualism, Culture and Education*, Routledge & Kegan Paul, 1983. (T) Wise and readable book for teachers reassessing bilingualism as an asset; demonstrating that language is our way of making sense of experience and of representing it to ourselves and others.

Raleigh, Mike, *The Languages Book*, 1981, available from ILEA English Centre, Ebury Bridge, Sutherland Street, London. (P) Lively and entertaining classroom book that places standard English firmly in its place as just one effective form of communication, and provides teachers and students with models for exploring language diversity.

Sutcliffe, Rosemary, *The Eagle of the Ninth*, Penguin, 1975. (P) How it feels to be the outsider: the Roman boy Marcus becomes a spy in hostile Scottish territory. Age eleven and over.

Exploring the Neighbourhood

Bethell, Andrew, *Roots, Rules and Tribulation*, Cambridge University Press, 1983. (P) Here's a play, commissioned for the Cockpit Theatre, which could be acted – or done as a rehearsed play-reading – by a class (nearly thirty characters). It explores one 'soft option' for six young offenders: working in a park.

Birmingham Development Education Centre, *The World in Birmingham – Development as a Local Case Study*, 1982, available from Selly Oak Colleges, Bristol Road, Birmingham B29 6LE. (P) Wallet of photographs plus booklet, aimed to raise social issues with pupils in a local context.

Centre for World Development Education, *Change and Choice: Britain in an Interdependent World*, 1980. (P) Resource pack primarily for courses in geography, social studies, religious education. Mainly for older pupils, but case studies of the world in a British school and in a British town can be used at junior level. Items available separately.

Community Service Volunteers, *Learning in the Community – A Teacher's Handbook*, available from 237 Pentonville Road, London N1 9NJ. (T) Community involvement for students and teachers: case studies and examples include projects with the aged, the disabled, environmental projects, etc.

Coussins, J., *Taking Liberties: A Teaching Pack for Boys and Girls on Equal Rights*, National Council for Civil Liberties, 1979. (P) Workcards for classroom use, lively and imaginative, with excellent resources section.

Smith, Barbara and Rhymes, Helen, 'Letters from strangers: talking to friends' in *Multicultural Teaching*, Vol. 1, No. 3, 1983. (P) Pen-pal scheme between two fourth-year classes, not ten miles apart, but in sharply different schools, illustrates one way that children can learn about others very different from themselves.

5. Getting on with Others

Introduction

Competition and Co-operation

If we are to solve, or at least cope with, many of the world problems facing us today, people need to be able to work together in their local communities and on a global scale, across national boundaries. To resolve conflicts of interest justly, however, may require not only co-operation but the dismantling of systems which help to perpetuate global inequality.

Many of our interrelationships and institutions are characterised not by co-operation but by the competitive ethic. While this may bring out the best in some people, it does tend at the same time to militate against co-operative initiatives, whether local or international, causing human problems and conflicts to be seen primarily as contests to be won – violently if necessary – or at least not lost, rather than, for example, as common problems which can be solved by the interested parties acting together.

Another harmful effect of the competitive ethic is that, while it may mean winning for a few, it means losing and failure for most. With children, competition can reinforce a poor self-image and set up barriers to learning.

The fact that it is desirable to help pupils work together does not deny that competition has some value. Competing against an objective standard, such as one's own previous achievement or a stopwatch, can be extremely helpful, for instance. It does, however, mean that we need to become more aware of the ways in which classrooms and schools hinder co-operation and encourage negative competition, so that we can consider making relevant changes. Further, we can make our schools places where co-operation is systematically encouraged. Only in such a context can we work effectively with pupils to develop constructive and creative ways of learning and behaving.

This chapter is therefore about fostering more just and co-operative human relationships. It begins, in the first section, Working Together, with face-to-face personal relationships in school and at home, and includes games and exercises to develop pupils' ability to communicate and co-operate with each other.

The second section, Resolving Conflicts, recognises the fact that conflict is an everpresent feature at all levels of human society. It suggests several ways in which pupils can begin to learn about resolving conflicts in their own lives and in the wider world.

The third section is concerned with sex differences. It draws attention to the gender stereotypes which children develop from an early age and puts forward some ways of beginning to challenge these. It also suggests that the issue of equal opportunity in schools and classrooms is an extremely important one.

Working Together

All the classrom activities suggested in this book can help increase the level of co-operation in a classroom and school. Those in this section, however, are specifically designed to encourage a co-operative and purposeful classroom atmosphere, open to communication at all levels.[1] They are also concerned with fostering three closely associated qualities:

  self-respect: through an approach known as affirmation, in which pupils learn how to express positive feelings and judgements about each other face to face;
  communication: listening to and conveying ideas clearly, with and without words;
  empathy: imagining the feelings and viewpoints of others, including others' views of oneself.

These activities have two further uses. First, they can help children to understand what is needed to create non-violent and peaceful situations. Children experience problems to do with trust, co-operation, communication and confrontation naturally in their everyday lives. In these activities they learn to recognise such problems for themselves, a necessary precondition for managing and solving the conflicts which they are involved in.

Secondly, looking beyond the classroom, the activities can be used to illustrate and explain problems and issues in the wider world. All of them demonstrate aspects of human behaviour which can be seen equally on the small and large scale. Problems to do with poor communication, lack of trust and mutual respect, an inability to co-operate, are evident at the level of world society and in our national life, as well as in the local community and classroom. The classroom is, in this sense, the world in miniature. Parallels can be drawn as appropriate. Through comparisons of this sort, interest aroused by personal experience can be channelled towards issues which may at first have seemed beyond the scope of younger children. As one teacher commented: 'I have been amazed at the children's understanding of fairly complex issues. I do not think we as teachers realise the *levels* of understanding that even younger children can aspire to.'

Resolving Conflicts

We live in a world in which conflict seems to be inevitable. This is most obvious from the television and newspapers which continually inform us of fighting between countries and between groups within countries. But most conflicts are not obviously violent, nor very far away. They occur whenever the powerful and the powerless meet, where resources are limited and human interests, needs and wishes diverge. Thus the word 'conflict' describes the rivalry between children for their parents' attention; the relationship between teachers and their classes, and between teachers themselves; a dispute over a new urban development; an industrial strike; discrimination based on race, sex or class; the division between rich North and poor South, and between capitalist West and communist East. In all such conflicts, violence may occur, for they all contain two or more opposed elements which need in some way to become reconciled. These conflicts will of course resolve themselves in some manner or other but often the outcomes have much more to do with the relative *power* that each side possesses than with any concern for fairness or justice.

Conflict resolution is about resolving such situations fairly and, as far as possible, so that all parties concerned may benefit.

Children in the middle years are beginning to be capable of a rational and quite sophisticated approach to conflict resolution. It is important,

therefore, that they begin to consider seriously the idea of conflict: to recognise it in their own lives and in the wider world and to think about how particular conflicts can be resolved imaginatively and peacefully.

Figure 5.1

Sex-role Stereotyping

One of the advantages of a world perspective is that it sheds fresh light on the customs and social behaviour of one's own society. Situations and relationships which had before seemed natural, inborn, self-explanatory, are suddenly seen as being the result of particular political, cultural, social and economic factors. It becomes clear that in other places and at other times things may happen quite differently.

Such is the case with the relative position of men and women in our own society, where roles and opportunities are sharply differentiated on the grounds of sex, particularly in employment and in the home, and where women are frequently at a disadvantage.

That these differences are not due to biological factors is confirmed by the variations in status and role taken by men and women in different societies. Sometimes, in fact, a division of labour on grounds of sex simply does not exist, either in the home or at work. (See pages 90–3.) Certainly the evidence from other societies quite clearly demonstrates that the inequality of opportunity between the sexes in our own country is not inevitable.

Sex differentiation and discrimination are matters of concern to teachers because they profoundly affect the life chances of their pupils. Attitudes to gender are formed during the early and middle years of childhood. From the age of about seven onwards, girls learn to play with girls and boys with boys, and the normal domestic pattern is for mothers to do things more with daughters than with sons. By the age of eleven, if not before, girls tend to prefer activities such as shopping, sewing, baking and cleaning, while boys prefer 'typically masculine' ones such as sport, gardening, home-maintenance and car cleaning. The early emphasis on outside jobs for boys, and inside ones for girls is one that continues into adult life.[2]

Although some schools are beginning to challenge this state of affairs, many often reinforce it.

From the age of seven, when boys and girls are frequently separated for games and sometimes for crafts, the division becomes ever more clear. It is re-emphasised in procedures such as lining up boys and girls separately, getting boys to shift furniture, asking girls to look after visitors, and so on.

Evidence has accumulated in recent years to show that, while girls achieve at a higher level than boys in primary school, teachers have lower expectations of them in class. In the words of one report, girls at primary school 'learn to be losers'.[3]

The whole process is a largely unconscious one which begins, in school as in society generally, with the unquestioning acceptance of traditional sex stereotypes. If schools are to begin to challenge this state of affairs and open up more possibilities to both girls and boys, teachers need to reappraise carefully their whole approach to pupils and to learning.

A checklist such as the one shown in Figure 5.2 can be a useful starting point.[4] The process is one which needs to continue and expand until it permeates the whole curriculum and the school itself.

The activities in this section are designed to make pupils more aware of the basic assumptions about gender which they have and which wider society reinforces, and to help them challenge these assumptions in the light of the experience of societies other than their own.

A checklist for sex stereotyping

1. In topics and projects, do you emphasise the achievements of women as, for example, astronauts, sailors, politicians, explorers, scientists?

2. Do you wherever possible include reference to roles which are non-traditional, particularly at work and in the home?

3. Do you use stories in which women and girls have adventures, are active, brave, enterprising, inventive, independent, and men and boys are sensitive, co-operative, obliging, conscientious, calm?

4. Do you make sure that girls take an interest in space travel, engines, sport, armaments, and boys in clothes, food, home life?

5. Do you use mathematics work-cards which have men going shopping and women using bank accounts, driving cars, and so on?

6. Do you ensure that all classroom chores (carrying things, collecting, tidying, putting things out) are done equally by both boys and girls?

7. Are you wherever possible using books and materials which assert the equal importance and value of men and women, or which give particular emphasis to the viewpoints of women?

8. Are you helping pupils to look critically at materials of all kinds so that they can discover sexist references and omissions for themselves?

9. Do you ensure that all crafts are learnt equally by boys and girls?

10. Do you teach explicitly about the history of sex discrimination, the role of women in various societies, and women's struggle over the years to secure equality of opportunity?

Figure 5.2 (source: slightly adapted from a checklist published by the Equal Opportunities Commission)

Working Together
Listening Time

PURPOSE ▶ To help children listen attentively.

PROCEDURE ▶ Pupils are asked to listen for one minute to any sounds coming from outside the room. They then say what they heard. This is an effective way to begin a session as it helps focus pupils' attention on the here and now. It also illustrates different interpretations of sounds and leads to questions about the importance of evidence.

Working Together
"Whispers"

PURPOSE ▶ To encourage careful listening and articulation.

PROCEDURE ▶ Pupils sit in a circle. A sentence is whispered to one person to see if it can be passed round correctly to the last person. If the message gets distorted a list can be made of things which help people hear words correctly. Different sentences of varying difficulty can be tried.

VARIATIONS ▶ Pupils can be asked to close their eyes and hold hands. They then pass a non-verbal message by specific squeezes of the hand round the circle.

Pupils can send the same message, or different ones, both ways round the circle simultaneously.

Working Together
Magic Microphone

PURPOSE

To help pupils regulate their discussion in groups.

PROCEDURE

This activity can help develop discussion on any topic. An object is chosen to use as a 'magic microphone' (for example, a shell, box, hat or book). Only the person holding the object is allowed to talk. To obtain it, others must raise their hands and wait for it to be passed to them. Co-operation occurs when the 'microphone' travels between people carefully and respectfully.

VARIATIONS

The object can be tossed quickly from one pupil to another. Pupils must speak when they have it.

The object can be passed round in a circle. Pupils may speak or stay silent when it reaches them.

Working Together
Pictures and Words

PURPOSE

To encourage the learning of basic vocabulary in an affirming and co-operative way.

PREPARATION

A supply of reasonably straightforward pictures is needed. They can be related to a theme the class is studying, illustrating words such as busy, friendly, sad, angry, lonely.

PROCEDURE

Pupils individually or in groups choose a picture they think illustrates one word clearly. They paste the picture on to a piece of paper and alongside it write clearly their name and four words. One of these is illustrated by the picture, the other three are not. When this is done, pupils can hold up their sheets in turn, and read out their words so that others can guess the answer.

If the pictures contain people, pupils can then be asked to empathise with them: to say how the characters might be thinking and feeling. This can be a first step in helping them become more aware of others and their problems.

VARIATIONS

Pictures which show an action can be used, and pupils can think of verbs.

Pupils can make up four different sentences about a picture, only one of which describes accurately what is going on.

Working Together
What's in a Picture

PURPOSE

To encourage precise observation and communication.

PREPARATION

A set of photographs or cartoons is needed. These should be relevant to an issue or topic which the class is studying.

PROCEDURE

THERE'S SOME THINGS YOU JUST CAN'T DO BY YOURSELF !!

Figure 5.3 (source: Houseman's 1984 Peace Diary, 1 January)

Pupils are in pairs, with pen and paper ready. One member of the pair puts their picture face down on the table. The other member of the pair describes their own picture in detail for their friend to draw, making sure that the picture can't be seen. After a few minutes they compare the picture and the drawing. The process and the roles are then reversed.

At this point, if they have not already done so, pupils can consider the content of the pictures. They can list as many questions about one picture as possible and then speculate on the answers. Or they can list three points about each picture which they would like to share with another pair.

The exercise can be rounded off by giving everyone a slip of paper and asking them to write a sentence beginning 'I learned . . .', 'I felt . . .', or 'I noticed . . .' These can then simply be read out to the whole class or they can be collected in and redistributed so that everyone reads out someone else's sentence.

Rumour Clinic

PURPOSE

To let children experience problems to do with communication and memory.

PREPARATION

A large picture or wallchart is needed.

PROCEDURE

A volunteer leaves the room and a large and fairly intricate picture is shown to the rest of the class. They examine it carefully so that they can describe it. The picture is put away and the volunteer returns. The class then describes as accurately and fully as they can what they saw in the picture. The volunteer gives his or her own description before the picture is brought out again.

DISCUSSION

Questions which can usefully be discussed include: What was remembered and what was left out? Were there disagreements about some aspects of the picture? Do these differences in memory and understanding cast light on everyday life? How can we know what is really going on here or elsewhere? How do we know the true picture? Are some conflicts caused by different understandings of the same basic evidence?

VARIATIONS

The volunteer can draw the picture by receiving instructions from the class instead of summarising their suggestions.

Three or more people can go out of the room. The first one comes back and is told about the picture by the group. They then, in front of the class, describe what they have been told to the second person, who repeats it, again in front of the class, to the third person.

Fables can be used instead of pictures. The fable about the Star Traveller on page 2 is a possibility.

Self - Portraits

PURPOSE

To encourage children to make appreciative comments to each other, thus building up self-confidence and mutual esteem.

Long sheets of paper are needed (1–2 metres long), felt pens, paint or crayons, and a good supply of pieces of blank paper or cards.

PROCEDURE ▶

Pupils work in pairs. Each pupil is given a strip of paper as long as they are tall. One child in each pair lies down on the paper, and the other draws carefully round their friend with a felt pen or crayon. They then change round.

Each pupil now fills in their own features and clothing using crayons, paints and pieces of cloth stuck on with glue. They write their names prominently and the pictures are displayed around the room. Pupils can be asked to talk about their feelings while making their self-portrait and to make positive comments about the portraits of others.

Pupils then form groups of six and sit in a circle. Each pupil is given a piece of paper (or card) and asked to write his or her name on it. The six cards are then passed round the circle and each member of the group writes on them, in turn, one thing that he or she *likes* about the others. Group members will therefore write, on five different cards, something complimentary about all members of the group except themselves.

The cards are then returned to the 'owners' and pupils can read out in turn what has been written about themselves. Finally the cards are put next to the self-portraits.

DISCUSSION ▶

It is valuable to draw out pupils' feelings with questions such as: What did they feel like when the other children spoke about their portrait? What did they feel like when they were reading out the comments about themselves?

I took care to keep a light-hearted banter going on. I felt some of the children were nervous and determined to spare embarrassment for anyone. However, the response was amazing. The youngest children were the most vociferous and said the kindest things. An overweight ten year old boy was told he was 'a good referee'. All the comments affirmed everyone. There was little repetition of complimentary epithets. The children for whom I felt considerable worry received real accolades – 'David is good at Maths', 'Pamela is kind to the infants', 'Jacob says nice things about people', 'Briony has nice thoughts about everyone', 'Nicola's handwriting is beautiful'.
The lesson fired everyone's thoughts.

Mike Fearon, a teacher in Cumbria

Pupils can draw round faces instead of the whole body. With hand mirrors they can do self-portraits of their own faces.

Working Together
Co-operative Shapes

PURPOSE

To encourage co-operation and empathy.

PREPARATION

This activity is for groups of five pupils. Enough copies of the maps in Figure 5.4 are needed for each group in the class to have a complete set. The maps should be cut up by the teacher along the lines indicated, and the pices of the maps labelled A to E as shown. The appropriate pieces from each set of maps should then be sorted into five envelopes labelled A to E. Each group in the class will receive a complete set of envelopes, with five map pieces in each envelope.

PROCEDURE

Each group of five sits round a table, and each member of the group is given an envelope with a different letter on it. The envelopes must not be opened yet. The following instructions are given:

Each of you has an envelope with some pieces of world maps in it. Your group is going to make five maps which are exactly the same. You will not have finished until everyone has a map which looks the same as everyone else's.

There are two simple rules. First, there is to be no talking during this game or any other kind of communication: no signs, winks or nods of the head. Second, you may not *take* a piece from someone else. You are only allowed to *give* pieces to other members of your group who you think need them.

DISCUSSION

Pupils will probably want to talk initially about what happened. They can then go on to talk about their feelings: frustration, irritation perhaps; anxiety at being unable to make a complete map; envy of those who can; *dismay* at having to dismantle their own map for the good of the group as a whole.

The class can further be asked how easy or difficult it was to put themselves in the position of other members of the group when at the same time they were probably anxious about their own map. And what of the difficulty of empathising with the group as a whole, of

74

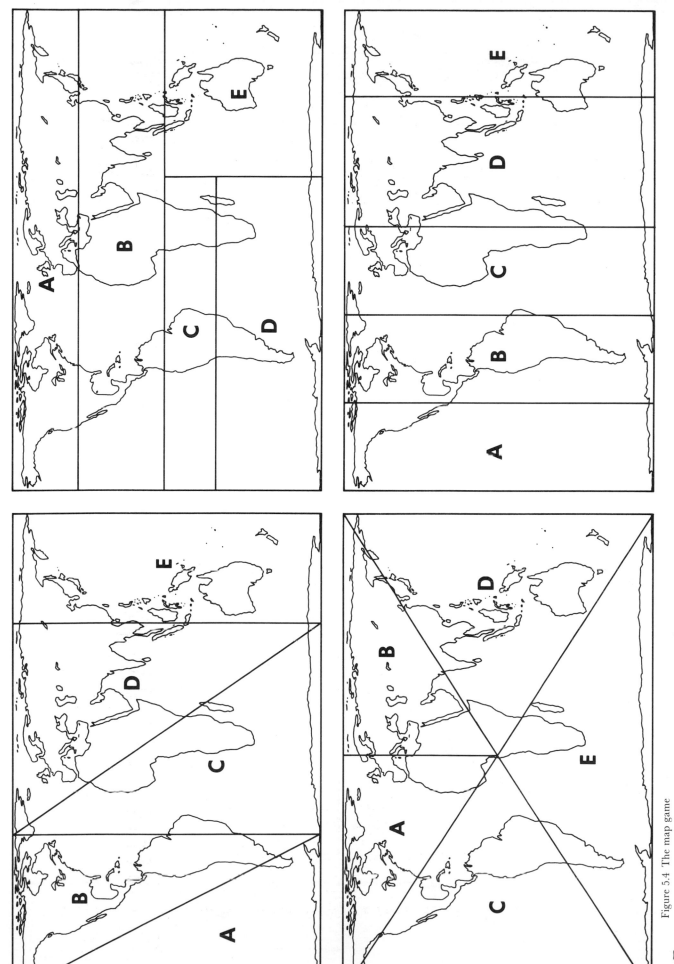

Figure 5.4 The map game

75

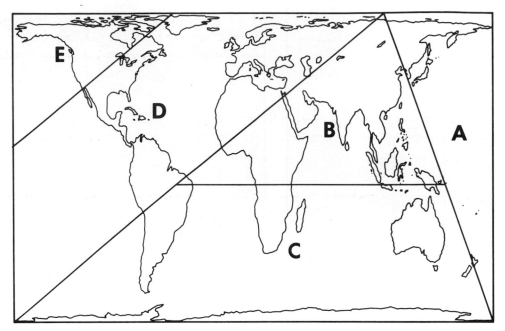

Figure 5.4 *continued*

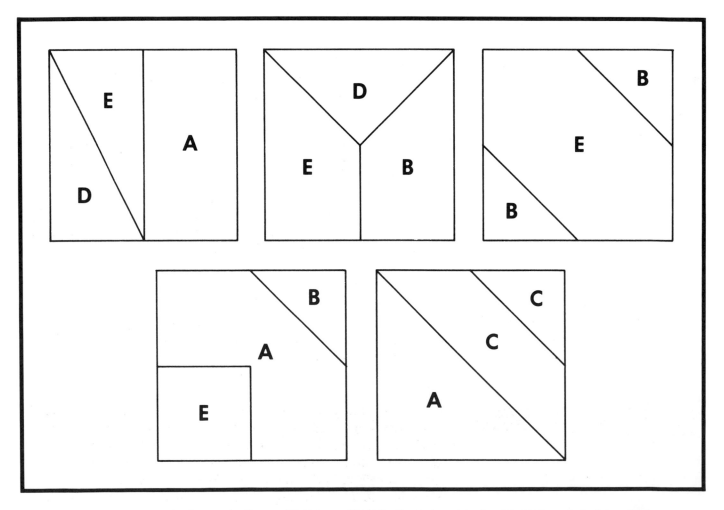

Figure 5.5 (source: Richardson, R., *Learning for Change in World Society*, World Studies Project of the One World Trust, 2nd edition, 1979)

seeing the exercise as a task for all the members of the group to solve together rather than as a contest to be won or lost by individuals? How did pupils feel when others saw what pieces they needed and supplied them?

VARIATION

A more difficult version of the same activity uses squares[5] instead of maps, cut along the lines indicated in Figure 5.5.

Working Together
If I were You

PURPOSE

To encourage empathy.

PREPARATION

A list of about ten questions is drawn up, either from the list in Figure 5.6 or as a result of a class brainstorming session (see page 79). Enough copies are needed for one between two.

PROCEDURE

Pupils works in pairs. One of them puts the questions to their partner. They can add one or two supplementary questions if they wish and make notes as necessary. When the question have been answered the roles are reversed.

Then, in small groups, each pupil introduces their partner to the others using the first person 'I' and the information given during the interview. ('My name is . . ., I live at . . .')

DISCUSSION

After this has been done, it is important to explore what pupils felt as they took their partner's identity, and also how they reacted to someone else 'impersonating' them. How convincing did members of the group feel they were in their different roles?

VARIATION

With older pupils this exercise can be used with reference to their counterparts in other parts of Britain or another country. In this case pupils work out individually what they think that person's answers would be. Then in small groups they take it in turns to speak, as before, in the first person. When all have finished, differences and similarities can be taken up, and viewpoints or facts questioned as seems appropriate.

What kind of a person am I?

Name	Are there special names by which you are known to parents, family or friends? Are there reasons for this?
Clothes	What kind of clothes do you like to wear?
Food	Have you any particular dislikes or likes? What did you have for breakfast?
Games	Which are your favourite games, hobbies?
Jobs at home	What do you always do? What do you sometimes do?
People	Who do you like and why? Which famous people do you admire most? What kind of people do you dislike most?
School	What subject do you like most? Which do you dislike most? Which are you best at? If you could change one thing in this school, what would it be?
Special reactions	Does anything make you squirm or shiver?
Feelings	What makes you afraid? What makes you angry? What makes you laugh? What makes you sad?
Values	What would you like to become? What would you most like to own? If your house was on fire and you could only save one thing, what would it be? If you had to choose, would you rather live in the past or the future? If you had one wish that would come true, what would it be? Which country would you most like to visit?

Figure 5.6

Working Together
Brainstorming

PURPOSE

To enable a group to build up a list of useful ideas on any topic in a short time. Brainstorming is a widely applicable activity which enables pupils to consider a problem together.

PREPARATION

The only materials needed are a blackboard, overhead projector or a large sheet of paper.

PROCEDURE

The problem or topic (for example: questions about the future; images of Africa; ways of resolving a particular conflict) is written up and pupils call out as many ideas as they can on this. They are *all* written down, without comment, on the blackboard or sheet of paper.

The rules are that:

- ideas should be stated in very few words so that they can be written down quickly and easily;
- combinations and improvements of others' ideas are encouraged;
- no comment or criticism is allowed by anyone while this is going on;
- innovative ideas are fine;
- quantity is more important than quality.

When the ideas have been listed, each one is considered in turn to see how useful it may be. Those which get no support are crossed out. The remaining ideas can then be discussed in more detail and a list of key questions, solutions or whatever arrived at.

It is a good idea to practise brainstorming once or twice before using it for a serious purpose. The subject of a practice brainstorm can be almost anything. For example, 'How many things can you do with a rubber band, a shoe, or a paper clip?'

The success of brainstorming lies in the cross-fertilisation of ideas that it can produce and the many more ideas that come up than would be the case in ordinary discussion.

VARIATION

The range and number of suggestions can be increased by asking the pupils first to write down their ideas individually before calling them out in a class brainstorm.

Resolving Conflicts
Observing Conflicts at School

PURPOSE

To enable pupils to investigate conflicts at first hand.

PREPARATION

Pupils each need a clipboard with two or three copies of a question sheet like the one shown in Figure 5.7.

PROCEDURE

To begin with, fights and arguments are discussed in the class, and pupils are invited to contribute from their own experiences. Then they are asked to make suggestions about the main reasons for such conflicts and the ways in which they are usually resolved. These should be noted down.

It can now be explained that, over a period of time, the class will be studying conflicts in the school to see if some of the suggestions made previously are true. To do this, pupils will need to observe closely the behaviour of other pupils in school so that later they can pool their experiences and draw some conclusions.

In a junior class small groups of children can watch a group of infants at play without creating a distraction. Playtime or break is an obvious opportunity for such unobtrusive observation. Over a week it is possible for all members of a class to spend some time observing and recording incidents ranging from fairly mild disagreements and arguments to perhaps more violent confrontations. It is best for pupils to work in pairs.

Pupils then describe their experiences to the class using their notes, while the teacher compiles a summary chart or table. This should include a list of the *causes* of the conflicts, with different categories such as insults, hitting someone, arguments over possessions, and the ways they were *resolved*. These will tend to fall into four categories: fighting and aggression; retreat; discussion and negotiation; arbitration by someone else.

DISCUSSION

Findings can be graphed and tentative conclusions drawn. To what extent have the initial hypotheses about conflict been proved correct? Could fights and disputes be avoided more often? Would that be a good thing? Are 'non-violent' ways of ending conflicts better than violent ones?

Looking at a conflict

Name: ....

Date: ....

1. What was the very first thing that happened?

2. What happened after that?

3. What was the very last thing that was said or done?

4. How many people were involved?

5. Were they boys or girls?

6. Why did this conflict happen?

7. How did it end?

8. What happened to the people after it was all over?

9. What did you feel about it?

Figure 5.7

Resolving Conflicts
Role-playing Everyday Conflicts

PURPOSE

To explore through drama the causes and consequences of conflicts which are within children's everyday experience.

PROCEDURE

The teacher chooses a situation, perhaps one of those in Figure 5.8, and explains it in detail, stating clearly who the characters are and what each person's point of view might be. It may also be helpful to stimulate the children's imaginations by getting them to brainstorm (page 79) different ways in which the situation might develop. Pupils should be encouraged to feel their way into their parts as thoroughly as possible.

In small groups pupils talk through the situation, focussing initially on questions such as: How are the different people feeling? What will probably happen next? What would be the best solution?

They then act this out, either simultaneously, or, in turn, to the class as a whole. It is quite possible that the solutions they act out will differ from the ones they planned earlier. This offers interesting possibilities for discussion. A further stage can be for pupils to change roles and re-enact the scene.

Conflicts in everyday life

School

Broken chair

A teacher comes into the classroom and finds a chair broken. She asks who did it, but no-one answers. She says 'If you don't tell me who did it you'll all have to stay behind after school.' One of the class says, 'But, Miss, I'm playing in the school football team. I can't stay.' Another says 'Then it's not fair.' The teacher . . .

Pencil case

A nine year old girl has lost her pencil case. Suddenly, in the middle of a lesson, she sees one that looks exactly the same on the desk of a boy. She goes over and takes it. The boy stands up. 'That's mine! Give it back or I'll hit you!' The teacher . . .

Home

Bedtime

A father tells his ten year old son that it is time for him to go to bed. He replies that he isn't tired and that he needs to read a book for school. The father stands up, furious. 'Why don't you ever do what I say? Come here!' The boy's mother . . .

Television

A brother and sister, aged nine and seven, are happily watching a television programme. The door bursts open and their older sister, aged twelve, comes in. 'Oh no!' she says, 'You're not watching that. It's time for my serial and I've been watching it for weeks.' She goes to switch channels. The brother . . .

Neighbourhood

Football fans

Four football fans are leaving the ground very merrily after their team has won. They meet three fans of the losing side who say loudly that the winning side only won because, as usual, they fouled and cheated. The four . . .

Apple tree

Two friends are looking out of a window. They see three young people of the same age climbing over a neighbour's fence to take some apples from a tree. The friends go outside and one says 'Don't do that. They're not yours.' One of the other group answers 'It's none of your business. Keep away or . . .'

Figure 5.8

82

It is important to draw ideas together with the whole class. Leading questions include: What happened in each group? What did it feel like to act these parts? What were the underlying causes of the conflict? How do the different solutions compare? Who gains and who loses by each? Which is fairest? Can the class agree on one preferred outcome? What advice would the pupils offer to each of the people involved in the conflict?

Figure 5.9   **"Old Wilkins never forgave Henderson for pinching his best conker."**

Each character in the drama can have a person standing nearby who says what he or she thinks the character is thinking and feeling, as opposed to what the character is in fact saying.

The class as a whole can act out the situation, perhaps as a more formalised role-play with written descriptions of each role.

Situations can be taken from real conflicts and dilemmas found in the newspapers and on radio and television.

These scenes can also be dramatised with simple puppets, perhaps made by the children. Groups of pupils can prepare and present a brief show to the whole class. Puppets are a very effective stimulus for discussion and the show itself provides an affirming, confidence-building, activity for those involved, particularly shy children.

Five Questions to Ask

PURPOSE

To consider current unresolved conflicts with children in a systematic way. The suggestions here are relevant on any scale, from the personal to the global.

PREPARATION

Copies of the questions shown in Figure 5.10 need to be available for each pupil.

PROCEDURE

Pupils are each given a copy of the five questions (and the flow diagram) and, working in groups, are asked to consider each question in turn in relation to a particular conflict selected by the teacher. The simple model outlined in Figure 5.10 can be used to analyse conflicts as diverse as the arms race, the rich world/poor world divides, Northern Ireland, industrial disputes, neighbourhood issues, even school disputes. It lends itself to a variety of activities and approaches which are described elsewhere in this book. Some illustrative examples are given here.

In question 1, the aim is for pupils to try to see and describe the conflict as a whole, and for their own subjective ideas about it to be acknowledged as valid and important. One effective way of tackling this is through the device of a mental map (see page 141). Pupils draw a picture of a particular conflict for the benefit, say, of a star traveller visiting Earth for the first time. They then show and describe these to each other. In doing this they will become aware that their own view of an issue is only one of a number of possible perceptions of it.

This process leads into question 2, an investigation into the causes of the conflict, into the current situation, and the demands, aims and interests of the various parties involved. Pupils could spend some time making their own investigations from classroom and resource materials produced by the teacher. They can role-play the arguments between parties using the information gained, perhaps exchanging roles and repeating the exercise to encourage them to appreciate more than one perspective.

Question 3 involves listing every possible way of resolving the conflict. What are all the imaginable solutions, probable or improbable? Brainstorming (see page 79) the question 'What next?' is one way of quickly making such a list.

Five questions to ask

1. **Images**
   What do you, and others, think this conflict is really about?

2. **Background**
   What has actually happened so far, and why?

3. **Solutions**
   What are all the possible solutions that we can think of?

4. **Choices**
   What are the best possible solutions?

5. **Action**
   What, if anything, can we do about the issue?

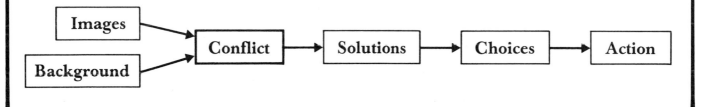

Figure 5.10

The task in question 4 is for pupils to consider which solutions they think are both *possible* and *desirable*, and to try to establish an order of priority, using a ranking exercise. In small groups pupils begin by choosing, individually, three or four 'best' solutions from the list and writing each one clearly on a slip of paper. They put them all face up on the table and eliminate by agreement all except nine. They then rank these in a diamond shape (see page 90), before sharing their conclusions and thoughts – including any differences of opinion – with the class as a whole. Why did pupils prefer one solution to another? Have any of the preferred solutions been tried yet?

Finally question 5 involves considering what steps are necessary for any of the solutions discussed to become a reality. Are these questions solely of use as an exercise in thinking or is there something that can usefully and responsibly be done? Are we already involved in some way: for example, by paying taxes to fund overseas aid or arms manufacture?

VARIATION

A model such as this can be used for investigations into particular conflicts where the main sources of information are the media. Pupils monitor a particular conflict over a period of time and build up a dossier of evidence under each heading and then present their reports to the class.

Studying peace and conflict

After some time observing and discussing conflicts amongst pupils in the infants class the children began to think and write about themselves, about times when they themselves had been angry. They wrote about their own fights. Who had been involved? What had caused the fight? What had happened next? How did the fight end? They also wrote about a time when they had felt like fighting but had managed to control themselves. What had they done to avoid conflict?

Some of these ideas were developed further using drama. The children were given the task of setting up an 'everyday' conflict situation. Most children chose an incident set either at home, in the local park, in the playground or in school. They then had to work out how they could solve their problem. Most scenes were in fact sorted out by the introduction of an authority figure such as Mum, Dad or teacher. However, one group did manage to solve it between themselves through co-operation. This provided a real lesson on how to restore peace without calling on outside help.

So far, the approach taken in studying peace and conflict had been from the personal point of view. The next step was to look at conflict in our local area. The school is situated in St Pauls, Bristol. Many of the children had witnessed the 'riot' that had taken place on April 2nd, 1980, and which, at the time of our study, was again in the news because the people arrested were now up for trial. I gave those children who wanted to, an opportunity to write an account of what they had seen on that day, what they thought about the whole incident and how they thought the riot might have been avoided in the first place.

After this piece of work we looked at conflict in the world. In a discussion we briefly touched on a variety of situations that the children had been made aware of, mainly through watching the news on television. The aspects of global conflict mentioned by the children included El Salvador, South Africa, Afghanistan and the Iran/Iraq situation. With more time available it would have been interesting to take one of these situations and explore it more thoroughly, but we had spent about five weeks on the work so far, and it was unfortunately time to round everything off.

We decided to present all the experience and information gathered to the rest of the school in the form of an assembly. Some children acted out their drama sequences, other read out their accounts of the 'riot', while others said their own made-up prayers asking for peace, not only amongst themselves, but in the local community and throughout the world too. In this way we were able to share our findings on peace and conflict with the whole school.

Elaine Hicks, a teacher in Bristol

Which way to World Peace

PURPOSE

To help pupils develop and clarify their images of peace and justice.

PREPARATION

A list of characters and viewpoints such as the one in Figure 5.11 needs to be provided for each pupil.

PROCEDURE

Pupils are asked to imagine that the world's people have had enough of war. There is to be a worldwide election to choose the people best able to ensure that peace and justice come about. But what kind of peace is it to be? That is what the class have to decide. They have to choose the three candidates from the list that they would most like to bring about peace.

At its simplest, this 'values clarification' exercise involves five stages:

1. The teacher goes through the election candidates with the class, explaining, simplifying, developing the position of each, as appropriate.

2. Pupils as individuals choose the three people they would like to see elected. Then in small groups they explain their choices and reasons to each other and alter their selection as they wish.

3. In the class as a whole, pupils argue for their preferred candidates, putting forward and discussing some of the arguments and issues which they feel are important.

4. The pupils vote, as individuals.

5. The three highest-scoring candidates are named.

DISCUSSION

What do these choices tell us about the things we feel are important in the world? What things seems to be less important? What other candidates and approaches should there have been? What choices would other people have made: our families, teachers, politicians, world leaders?

FOLLOW-UP

Pupils can research further the ideas advocated in the 'election', their history, and the people advocating them today.

VARIATION

The election could involve pupils individually or in small groups preparing and making short speeches to the class in favour of their preferred candidates.

Workers for peace

Pax Green
He can organise demonstrations all over the world so that more and more people will come to believe that we must fight for peace with love and truth only, not with weapons.

Revell Lenning
He can organise armies in many countries to force governments to make their countries more fair and peaceful.

Karla Julius
She can make the world's people share out their wealth and resources so that everyone has enough to eat, a house to live in, and a job.

John Bull
He can spread the British ideal of democracy so that all other countries will have the same kind of government and the same values as in Britain.

Una Globe
She can set up a world government chosen by the people of the world, with world laws and a world army to make people do what it says.

Mehdi Teshun
He can train people to think and pray so that they begin to stop quarrelling and fighting in their everyday lives.

Simvid Fishix
She can make teachers teach about war and peace, power and fairness, so that pupils all over the world learn to make up their own minds about how to make the world more peaceful.

Joseph Franco
As a strong dictator who will share his power with no-one he can force people to choose: either they stop fighting and making weapons or he will drop bombs on them.

Vespa Ranto
She can teach everyone to speak the same language so that all people will be able to understand each other.

Dag Thant
He can make sure that the weapons owned by the United States of America and the Soviet Union are exactly equal, so that one side will not think of attacking the other.

Figure 5.11

A ranking exercise such as that described on page 90 can replace the idea of an election.

Figure 5.12

A ranking exercise such as that described on page 90 can replace

---

Sex-role Stereotyping
Doing Things Differently

PURPOSE

To help children become aware of some of their assumptions about male and female occupations. To prompt them to consider alternatives both for people in general and for themselves in particular.

PREPARATION

Copies of the photographs in Figure 5.13, or similar ones, will need to be made and cut up, enough for one set between two pupils.

PROCEDURE

There are many ways in which these pictures can be used,[6] It is best to let children discover for *themselves* that the central theme of the pictures is sex roles. Pupils work in small groups. One member of each group has a picture which he/she describes to the others who cannot see it. They have to draw it according to the description. When they have finished they compare their efforts with each other and with the original, before another picture is described by a different member of the group.

VARIATIONS

Pupils in pairs can lay out a set of the photographs face up on a table. After one minute they turn them over; they then make a list of the photographs which they can remember.

Each pupil can receive the same set of six pictures and be asked to choose the one they find most interesting, or most surprising. They then in turn describe and explain their choice to their small group.

Pupils in pairs can receive a set of nine pictures and be asked to rank them as above. They can do this in a straight line, from very interesting to uninteresting, or from like to dislike. Alternatively they can arrange the pictures in a diamond formation like this.

$$
\begin{array}{ccccc}
 & & 1 & & \\
 & 2 & & 2 & \\
4 & & 4 & & 4 \\
 & 7 & & 7 & \\
 & & 9 & & \\
\end{array}
$$

The picture at the top is the first choice, the next two are equal second, the three across the centre are fourth equal, and so on.

Pupils in pairs can receive a set of the pictures, a sheet of sugar paper, blu-tack and felt pens. They are asked to stick the pictures down in any way they like on the paper, and to write or draw on it as clearly and colourfully as possible in order to make the arrangement clear and interesting. They then explain the outcome to another pair. Finally all the pieces of work are displayed and discussed by the class as a whole.

Pupils can divide the pictures into three or four categories with an equal number in each category and then make their arrangement on sugar paper as above. Whatever the categories may be, the reasons for them should be made clear on the paper.

Sex-role Stereotyping
Who does what at Home

PURPOSE

For children to think about the way essential tasks are allocated at home and to compare this with another contrasting society.

PREPARATION

Each pupil needs a chart like the one in Figure 5.14. In addition a much larger chart is needed which can be seen by the whole class, and a supply of small sticky labels in two colours.

Activities such as this which look at patterns of organisation and behaviour in the home need to be sensitively handled to take account of one-parent families, for example, and those who might feel the school is being unduly inquisitive.

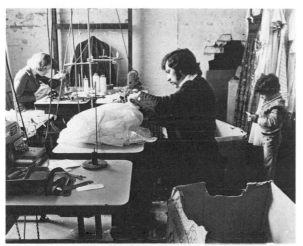
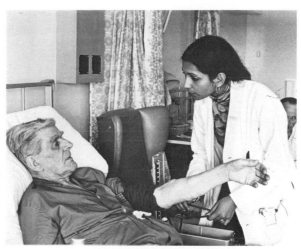

Figure 5.13

91

1. Pupils fill in the first column of the chart for their own homes. They should put the symbol ○ for a girl or woman, △ for a boy or man, and both if the task is shared.

2. In pairs, they review their charts and note any differences. This gives each of them confidence in their own results and a chance to air views with one other person which they may later feel able to share with the whole class.

3. The teacher then plots individual results on the wall chart with a different coloured spot for each of the two symbols. At this point pupils may well want to discuss what the differences in their results are, and why they exist.

4. The teacher then points out that among some of the peoples of South East Asia *all* the jobs listed on the chart are shared between men and women. This should be indicated on the summary chart, using stickers as before, and on the pupils' own charts. Pupils then consider this short passage:

> From the time they are born the children learn that what they do and the jobs they will later have do not depend on whether they are boys or girls. Most jobs in the house and outside are done by either men or women, and often they do the work together. Men and women decide together how money is spent in a family and all other important matters. When there is a new baby everyone is happy whether it is a boy or a girl, though girls are specially welcome as they are more likely to stay in the village when they are grown up. Both parents help bring up the children, who begin when still very young to work in the house and in the family's vegetable plot. These people have a saying 'A girl is also a boy, and a boy is also a girl'.[7]

5. Finally, in pairs or small groups, pupils fill in the column on their charts marked 'My ideal', if possible reaching agreement on each task. They can include other jobs which are not mentioned on the chart: for example, cleaning/repairing the car, mowing the lawn, putting up cupboards and shelves.

DISCUSSION ▶

Questions that may arise during this or in a final class discussion include: What are the disadvantages for women and girls if they are only allowed to do certain things? What are the disadvantages for men and boys if they also are confined to certain roles and activities? What changes would need to take place at home if both boys and girls are to have more choice in what they do? What changes would need to take place in school, and in this classroom?

Who does what at home?

	My home	South East Asia	My ideal
Cooking 			
Washing up 			
Cleaning floors 			
Washing clothes 			
Sewing and mending 			
Going shopping 			
Looking after a sick child 			
Taking a child to the doctor 			

Fill in this grid using ○ for a girl or woman, △ for a boy or man, and both together if the job is shared.

Figure 5.14

93

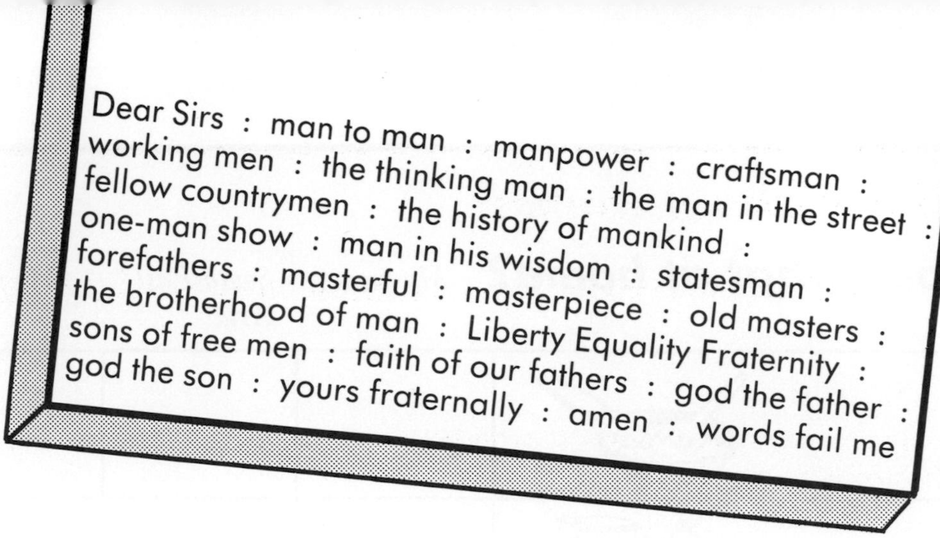

> Dear Sirs : man to man : manpower : craftsman :
> working men : the thinking man : the man in the street :
> fellow countrymen : the history of mankind :
> one-man show : man in his wisdom : statesman :
> forefathers : masterful : masterpiece : old masters :
> the brotherhood of man : Liberty Equality Fraternity :
> sons of free men : faith of our fathers : god the father :
> god the son : yours fraternally : amen : words fail me

Figure 5.15 (source: Dowrick, Stephanie, 'Words fail me', The Women's Press)

Sex-role Stereotyping
Women in the World

PURPOSE

For pupils to learn some basic information about the position of women in the world, and to explore the meaning and implications of this.

> Women make up half the world's population, do nearly two-thirds of the world's working hours, receive one tenth of the world's income and own less than one hundredth of the world's property.
>
> UN Report of 1980

PREPARATION

Sets of statements or facts such as those in Figure 5.16 need to be cut up into individual slips of paper, with one fact on each slip. There should be enough for one set between every two pupils.

PROCEDURE

1. Pupils, in pairs, are asked to choose the two or three statements which they find the most important, or the most surprising, or the most contradictory.

Some facts about women

Born equal
Girls are born with the same ability as boys to learn, think, feel, work and play.

Reading and Writing
Two out of every three of the people who have not been taught to read or write in the world are women.

Jobs
In many countries women have some of the toughest jobs. For example, half of those working as builders in India are women.

War and peace
In both world wars none of the leaders or generals of the fighting countries were women. But women can become soldiers in many countries.

Life and health
Women live longer than men in all parts of the world. As mothers, wives and daughters, or as nurses, they look after nearly all the sick people in the world.

Housework
Women with young children in the West spend on average seventy-seven hours a week looking after home and family. If they were properly paid for this they would each receive quite a large salary.

Smaller families
In almost every country in the world women are having fewer children than their mothers. This is because they are marrying later, are better educated, can more easily find paid jobs outside the home and because of more effective methods of birth control.

Wages and wealth
£1 out of every £10 earned in the world goes to women. They own £1 out of every £11 of the world's property and wealth.

Work and rest
Women do two out of every three hours worked in the world. Married mothers with a paid job have less than two hours free time for every three enjoyed by their husbands.

Food
Women produce over half the food grown in the 'third world' and prepare nearly all the world's food for eating.

Figure 5.16

2. Using various materials they then translate each of these statements into visual terms. The format could be almost anything: collages, diagrams, posters, cartoons, statistical tables and so on. Pupils should be encouraged to make liberal use of illustrations from magazines and to put in arrows, boxes and other graphic means of explanation.

3. The work is then numbered and displayed round the room, and pupils circulate in pairs, listing each picture by number and writing down which statement or fact they think it portrays.

4. The answers are then provided by the class and each pair notes its successes and failures.

5. The statements most often selected can be identified and pupils asked to give their reasons for choosing them, and for rejecting others.

6. The activity can end with pupils learning the information for a 'test' in the traditional manner. The pictures, diagrams and collages will probably be found to be very helpful and the possibility of 'visualising' other pieces of information can be taken up.

DISCUSSION

It is important for pupils to express their feelings about the statements they have been working with. How do they react to them as girls or boys? Did they find them surprising, annoying, confusing?

VARIATIONS

A multiple choice quiz can be constructed, based on such a set of statements or facts, and used before the class sees the information. This can stimulate the pupils' interest and provide a guide to their existing knowledge. After the results have been given and discussed pupils can construct their own multiple choice quizzes based on these or other statements and test the knowledge of pupils in other classes.

Pupils can take part in a brainstorm on two or three of the facts, listing as many questions as they can think of which arise. The questions can then be categorised, perhaps into those which can be answered with a little research by the class itself, and those which are more far-reaching and speculative. Pupils could then each research a question and report to the class as a whole.

Pupils can rank the slips in the order in which they find them interesting or surprising. This might be done initially with boys and girls working separately.

Pupils can rewrite the statements from a different standpoint. For example, they could all be written from a male perspective. What effect does this have?

Figure 5.17

96

Starting Points

I'm Going to – No You're Not

Pupils are in groups of six. Each group then divides into two: one party of four pupils wants to do something, the other two will not allow it. The group has 15–20 minutes to make up a little play, then each performs in front of the whole class. The problems and solutions are then discussed in the class as a whole. Are peaceful solutions more effective than unpeaceful ones? Is compromise a good option or a sign of weakness?

Instant Solutions

Pupils are in pairs. They are given the names of two characters in a role-play and asked to choose which part they wish to take. Then the teacher describes an unresolved conflict to them and gives them one minute to role-play it. After this the whole class discusses how people felt and what solutions they found. This can usefully be done two or three times in succession. It is a way of helping children think quickly and positively.

Drawing Pictures

Pupils draw, individually or in small groups, two pictures of their school. One depicts the school working badly, the other shows it working well. They then list the differences between the two pictures and try to identify what are the conflicts which need to be resolved for the 'good school' to come about.

Strip Cartoons

Each pupil is given a sheet with six or eight squares drawn on it and two or three pictures depicting part of a story about conflict already filled in. Pupils are asked, individually or in pairs, to finish the story by drawing pictures in the remaining squares. They then describe and display the solutions to the whole group for discussion. It is important to emphasise that the exercise has nothing to do with drawing ability: stick people are perfectly adequate.

Designing a New Neighbourhood

This question is put to pupils: 'Imagine we are building this area again from scratch. Everything can change. What would you like to see in it?' In small groups they share their thoughts. What do we need to survive? What do different groups of people need: for example, old people, teenagers, families? Group members decide co-operatively on the outline shape of the new neighbourhood and draw it on a large sheet of paper. They then draw on smaller pieces of paper things they would like to see included. They glue these to the large sheet and thus assemble their new neighbourhood. Groups then explain their pictures to each other and affirm each other's work.

Job Questionnaire

Pupils answer a questionnaire on what jobs they would most like to have when they leave school, and what jobs they would least like to have. The answers are tabulated for boys and girls and used as a basis for exploring differences in choices between boys and girls and sex differences in society at large.

Advertisements

Pupils look through a selection of magazines and cut out the advertisements which portray and describe women and men. They display these as a collage and write about what the 'ideal' woman and the 'ideal' man are like, according to the advertisements. How does this compare with real men and women?

Rewriting Fairy Stories

Pupils rewrite fairy stories with the roles reversed. All male characters are female and vice versa. These are then read out and lead to a discussion about sex roles generally and, specifically, about how children's stories often reinforce a stereotyped view of men and women.

Equal Opportunities Group

Several staff form a working party to review the school curriculum and the life and rituals of the school. They look in particular for examples of unequal opportunities between boys and girls and make recommendations for change where appropriate.

Famous Women

Much of history is written as if it were a male affair. To redress the balance, pupils can investigate the lives of women who have made an impact in their field. Obvious examples are Joan of Arc, Florence Nightingale, Elizabeth Fry, Mary Seacole, Emily Pankhurst, Harriet Tubman, Golda Meir, Winnie Mandela. There are many other less well known but equally important women.

Survey on Sexism

Pupils monitor the local or national newspapers over a period, looking for material relating to sex roles and the position of women. They particularly look for articles and cuttings where there is an assumption of male superiority. They put their evidence in a scrapbook and present it to the newspaper concerned, personally or in writing.

Kitchen and Workshop

Without any introduction, the children do two quick drawings, one of a kitchen and the other of a workshop. Each picture should have at least three people in it. When they have finished, the drawings are analysed by the sex of the people in each room. Most of the pictures will probably show women or girls working in the kitchen and men in the workshop. The question then is 'Why did you draw the people you did?'

Selected Resources

T : for the use of teachers
P : for the use of pupils

Drama and Games

Adams, Susan, *Games Children Play Around the World*, John Adams Toys Ltd, Wargrave, Berkshire, 1979. (T) Games are a way of learning to share and communicate: these are simply the 'rules' of each, indicating the country of origin. They include group games, ball and board games.

Barratt, Sylvia and Hodge, Sheena, *Tinderbox: Sixty Six Songs for Children*, A. & C. Black, 1982. (T) Songs from all round the world, with the music, notes about origin and related movements or activities. For classroom use with juniors.

Byrne, D. and Dixon, S., *Communication Games*, NFER, 1979. (T) A collection of exercises and games designed for English Language teaching. Many practical ideas, easily adaptable for world studies.

Cockpit Theatre and Oxfam, *The People GRID* (growth, relationships, inter-action, development), Oxfam, 1980. (T/P) Three games and activities for ages eight to twelve. One on the international quality of language (Our Word House), one (The Growing Up Game) examining symbolically how each person grows up differently from another, and The Global Cake, which explores the world trading system.

Orlick, Terry, *Co-operative Sports and Games Book: Challenge Without Competition*, Writers & Readers, 1979. (T) Alternatives to all those games that have to be won to be fun: action, puzzles, etc. for ages three to seven and eight to twelve.

Prutzman, P., Burger, M. L., Bodenhamer, G. and Stern, L., *The Friendly Classroom for a Small Planet: A Handbook on Creative Approaches to Living and Problem Solving for Children*, Avery, New Jersey, 1978. Obtainable from Housmans' Bookshop, London. (T) Worth ordering specially. This manual sets out ways to examine feelings: feelings about oneself and others, about sharing and conflict, in the safe context of the classroom.

Rhue, Morton, *The Wave: The Classroom Experiment That Went Too Far*, Kestrel, 1981. (P) Cast as an American teenage novel and compelling reading, this story is based on a true incident in California in 1969, and could be effectively used in the classroom. A teacher sets out to answer the question 'How did the Germans stand back and allow the atrocities?' by creating a fascist movement in the school which gets out of control.

Scher, Anna and Verrall, Charles, *One Hundred + Ideas for Drama*, Heinemann, 1980. (T) A book of advice and suggestions for working with groups and whole classes, improvising situations and plays, simulations and role-play.

Searle, Chris, *The World in a Classroom*, Writers & Readers, 1977. (T) The outcome of a teacher's efforts to counteract the 'false knowledge' of stereotypes of new settlers and to extend all children's imagination and understanding of the feelings of settlers and black Britons. Most of the book is the writings of his twelve to fourteen year olds themselves.

Conflicts

Fair Play for Children, *All Children Play: Background Information on Play in Multiracial Britain*, wallet from 248 Kentish Town Road, London, NW5. (T/P) Some of the activities on the cards would translate well to junior classrooms.

Foreman, Michael, *Moose*, Picture Puffin, 1973. (P) Caught between the warfare of bear and eagle, Moose constructs a shelter with the help of the other animals. Age six and over.

Heater, Derek, *Peace and War Since 1945*, Harrap, 1979. (T) An attempt to explain, for older children, international conflicts in their historical context; begins with the Cold War, looks at Europe and at struggles in the Far East, West Asia and Africa.

Leaf, Munro, *The Story of Ferdinand*, Puffin, 1977. (P) Classic (1937) tale of the bull who wouldn't fight matadors, so was taken home. Age six and over.

Marches: Multiracial Britain: Images from This Century, ILEA Learning Materials Service, 1981. (T/P) Black and white photographs, to be used with the videocassette programmes *Marches from Jarrow to Cable Street* and the teachers' book *Marches: Unemployment and Racism*. Each photograph captures a specific event or moment (for example, a West Indian in the 1930s being refused accommodation, a Jewish tailor's workshop before 1914) with notes on how to use them.

Nicholas, Frances (ed.), *Conflict, Change and Our Future*, available from Ely Resource and Technology Centre, Back Hill, Cambs. (T/P) Looseleaf ring binder pack designed for nine to thirteen year olds. Takes children from an exploration of themselves and their immediate experience, out into the wider world. Four co-operative games are also available to go with the pack.

Oakley, Graham, *The Church Mice at Bay*, MacMillan, 1978. (P) Sampson, the Vicarage cat, has vowed never to harm a mouse, least of all the church mice here threatened by the trendy visiting curate. Their non-violent campaign escalates in the way of all good picture books and reads hilariously. The prose is dry and adult, as is the theme, but it will appeal to children of eight and over.

Richardson, Robin, *Fighting for Freedom*, Nelson, 1979. (P) Oppression – of individuals, women, minority groups and nations – and ways of resisting. Also *World in Conflict*, Nelson, 1977. (P) Prejudice, wars and conflict, considered at personal and global levels.

Sex Roles

Adams, Carol, *Ordinary Lives: A Hundred Years Ago*, Virago, 1982. (T/P) The daily lives of working-class women, from childhood to parenthood; their households and their place in the world presented from contemporary reports and documents.

Doing Things in and About the Home, Photographs and Activities About Work, Play and Equality, Serawood House, 1983. (T/P) A group of teachers working from Maidenhead Teachers' Centre has prepared this wallet of photographs with accompanying teachers' notes, designed to set children thinking – and talking – about role stereotyping and fixed views and attitudes.

Jansz, Natania and Jansz, Litza, *Prudie Finds Out*, Routledge & Kegan Paul Pandora Press, 1983. (P) Sophisticated verse and concept, delightful pictures that challenge role stereotyping. Could be used for classroom discussion or just read for fun.

Kemp, Gene, *The Turbulent Term of Tyke Tiler*, Penguin, 1977. (P) Lively and amusing school story that confronts children with role stereotyping. Age nine and over.

Oakley, Ann, *Subject Women*, Fontana, 1982. (T) Draws on examples from many different countries in investigating how women's role has changed this century, and the reasons for today's pattern of sex roles in industrialised societies.

Spender, Dale, *Invisible Women: The Schooling Scandal*, Writers & Readers, 1982. (T) 'Schools cannot teach what society does not know' asserts Spender, and then gives the hard information on the defined areas of 'appropriate' knowledge, the power in schools, the position of girl students.

Stones, Rosemary, *Pour Out the Cocoa, Janet: Sexism in Children's Books*, Schools Council, 1983 available from Longmans Resource Unit, Tanner Row, York. (T) Manifestations of sexism discussed and examples given, but useful too in considering what, given the existing books, we do about this.

Tompert, Ann, *The Clever Princess*, Lollipop Power, Chapel Hill, 1977, available from Sisterwrite. (P) The advisers to the kingdom are horrified when the ageing King wishes to abdicate in favour of his only daughter, Lorna, who refuses to marry, but passes all the tests they set her. Age seven and over.

Vestly, Anne-Cath, *Hallo Aurora*, Penguin, 1977. (P) Aurora learns that there are many ways of living and working, and that she should be guided by her parents and not by the norms of the new neighbourhood: this is a beguiling collection of stories. Age eight and over.

6. Other Worlds

Introduction

The Importance of Learning from Others

It is important that pupils learn about a variety of countries and cultures in school if they are to understand the affairs of the modern world, indeed if they are to grapple intelligently with many of the problems of their own locality, family and school. Our daily lives constantly affect, and are affected by, people from all over the world and members of minority groups within our own society. Learning about others also helps pupils learn about human nature, that is about themselves.

On the larger scale, countries and cultures are fundamental parts of the global village. Its inhabitants have different ways of doing things but people from different cultures, countries and hemispheres need to understand and respect each other if the world's problems are ever to be effectively tackled. Such understanding requires the ability to see things from other viewpoints.

We know also that children acquire attitudes towards other groups of people at a very early age, perhaps as early as four or five, and that they tend on the whole to be most open and tolerant between the ages of eight and twelve. After this, attitudes and prejudices often become more rigid. There are, therefore, good reasons for introducing issues relating to other cultures to this age range.[1]

The activities in this chapter relate to all the objectives for attitudes set out on page 25. Children need first to respect their own social group and culture. Being curious about and appreciating groups and cultures other than one's own can only begin to happen when one has a basic confidence in oneself. Curiosity and appreciation can lead to empathy, which in turn can give rise to a concern for justice and fairness, first in other peoples' situations, then in one's own. This applies as much, if not more so, in one's own immediate social situation as in the wider society and world.

Avoiding Bias

The choice of cultures or countries to be studied may be based on many criteria: for example, the wish to increase pupils' understanding of the East–West divide, the conflict in Northern Ireland, world poverty and North–South relationships, racial tension in Britain. Certainly many teachers would wish pupils, over a period of time, to consider a range of situations, from 'superpower' to 'third world', from capitalist to socialist and to look into both the benefits and disadvantages of interdependence. But, whatever the content, it is important to avoid ethnocentric bias, that is the tendency to judge other cultures by one's own values.

In as much as all human beings are born into a particular culture, all of us tend to be culture bound in our views. But the degree to which we are solely dependent on one culture for our world view is open to change. The need is, perhaps, to expand our own and our pupils' awareness of the many different perspectives and value frameworks that exist, often within one country, certainly in the world as a whole.

One danger of an ethnocentric worldview is that it can give rise to irrational and harmful behaviour. In the case of Britain, its historical colonial relationships with substantial areas of Africa, Asia and Latin America resulted in attitudes which were not only ethnocentric but also racist in the sense that they were based on an assumption of superiority over non-Europeans.[2]

Today, as surveys have shown, the British public, doubtless not untypically in the world, exhibit 'parochial and introverted attitudes, and are unsympathetic to a world perspective, clinging to the past and untutored to approach the future constructively'.[3] These attitudes underpin the discrimination against black people which pervades many aspects of British society, notably in education, housing and employment.

It is extremely important, therefore, to look carefully at what images we give when teaching about countries and cultures other than our own.[4] It can be a help in this process to use checklists such as those shown in Figures 6.1. and 6.2. Both highlight pitfalls which emphatically need to be avoided.

Approaches such as the ones mentioned in Figure 6.1 are both patronising and ultimately racist because they make people appear less than human beings, without dignity, dreams and a will of their own. They all ignore the fact that the gulf between rich North and poor South did not exist before European contact with the countries of the southern hemisphere. Europe's wealth in the nineteenth and early twentieth centuries came about largely as a result of using the 'third world' as a cheap source of raw materials. This process continues today, notably through world trade, as illustrated in the story about bananas (see pages 54–61).

Minority groups are also a popular topic with teachers of younger children. While this may sometimes be for the wrong reasons ('they're exotic'), there are important justifications for such choices. First, several of the major areas of conflict in the world have majority/minority relationships at their core, notably the Middle East, South Africa and Northern Ireland. Many other conflicts also relate to minority issues, including those involving the Basques, Tamils, Native Americans, and Aborigines to name but a few.

Secondly, learning about the problems facing a minority group, however apparently remote in space or time, helps to bring about an understanding of the minority predicament in general, and often leads naturally to a consideration of similar, and perhaps more controversial issues closer to home. Most obviously this provides an opportunity to introduce ideas about prejudice, discrimination and racism at a 'safe' distance before children begin to look at such matters in their own country and immediate community.

Again, however, there are dangers to guard against if one is not to run the risk of reinforcing negative attitudes. When studying a minority group, unnecessary dwelling on the 'exotic' or the past should be avoided. Groups should be given their own preferred names: Native Americans not Red Indians, Inuit not Eskimo. Studying the hopes and feelings of a particular minority group today is just as interesting as drawing untypical igloos or tipis. Why, for example, are many Native Americans involved in legal battles relating to nineteenth-century treaties? And why are Aborigines struggling against the big multinational mining companies?[5] It is much more appropriate to start with issues such as these in the present, and look back to the past to explain them, rather than teach about the past and perhaps never even reach the present.

The questions in Figure 6.2. may therefore be useful in planning a study of a minority group.

Teaching so as to avoid and, where necessary, counter racist images such as those indicated in the checklists is challenging. It is also extremely worthwhile and rewarding.

Teaching about 'developing' countries: a checklist

1. *The tourist-eye view*
Is everything portrayed as quaint and curious? Is there an emphasis on elephants and snake-charmers and the exotic? Are the local community or members of the class used merely as audio-visual aids for a project on the country they originate from?

2. *The packet-of-tea approach*
Are people overseas shown as existing to grow our tea/cotton/sugar, or to provide us with exciting holidays? Is it implied that this is a very convenient arrangement: they are happy natives singing in the sunshine and we are happy tea-drinkers snug around the fire at home?

3. *The pathological view*
Is everything shown as absolutely desperate: people everywhere are dying of starvation, floods, hurricanes, earthquakes? Are we shown as the only ones able to rescue them from such disaster?

4. *The pat on the head*
Is it implied that 'they' have been a bit behind with their mud huts and things but if they follow our example they'll come out all right in the end? Is it implied that high technology, fast cars, automated industry, are the things that make a country 'developed'?

5. *Poverty as an act of God*
Is poverty treated as something that is simply there although, of course, we deplore it? Are some of the fundamental *causes* of poverty given or only descriptions of its symptoms?

Figure 6.1 (source: adapted from Clark, B. (ed.), *The Changing World and the Primary Classroom*, published by CWDE, 128 Buckingham Palace Road, London SW1W 9SH)

Teaching about minorities: a checklist

1. *Motives*
What are your reasons for choosing to teach about a particular minority group? Is it merely because they appear colourful or quaint?

2. *The present*
Will the study look at the present situation of the particular minority as well as its past and at the issues which confront its members today?

3. *Status*
Will the study show the social and economic status of the minority group and its disadvantaged position in society as regards the majority?

4. *Prejudice*
Will the study acknowledge the presence of prejudice and discrimination in majority/minority situations?

5. *Origins*
Will the study consider the origins of the minority situation, e.g. colonisation, migration, separatism?

6. *Empathy*
Will the study attempt to foster sensitivity and empathy for the minority experience? Will it attempt to combat prejudice in any way?

7. *Culture*
Will the study look at the minority group's culture and history in a positive way, including views of minority group members themselves?

8. *Victims*
Will the study make it clear that the minority group itself is *not* the problem, or will it blame the victims for their own oppression?

9. *Response*
Will the study show the breadth of minority response to discrimination, ranging from despair to direct action?

10. *Self-esteem*
What would be the likely effect of this study on the self-image and self-esteem of children from that, or other, minority groups?

Figure 6.2

The Activities

The activities in this chapter fall into three main sections. The first section, Images and Assumptions (pages 103–8), suggests ways of finding out what children are already thinking about countries and cultures other than their own. This is an essential prerequisite for planning a topic or course, indeed for any teaching and learning on this theme.

The second section, Too Much or Too Little (pages 109–18), recalls that we cannot and should not look at the 'third world' in isolation. Rich and poor worlds are inextricably bound up and, as the activities illustrate, the wealth of some often results in the poverty of others.

While there are many different cultures that could be looked at, Minorities (pages 119–28) acknowledges the popularity of certain minority groups in primary teaching and raises questions about how we portray them. Consideration is also given to popular misconceptions about the multicultural nature of British society.

What do We Know Already?

PURPOSE

To establish what pupils think they know and how they feel about a country or topic before a course of study begins. This is important for at least two reasons: first it establishes for the pupils that what they already know is valuable and can be voiced in the classroom; and secondly it enables teachers to plan much more effectively, to decide which aspects of life need to be emphasised and which negative stereotypes need to be challenged.

PREPARATION

A relevant set of A4-size or larger photographs needs to be put round the classroom for step 3. Examples of useful photopacks would be *Living with Land* (about Ghana), *Choices in Development* (about Tanzania and Kenya), *Western India: City and Village Life*, all from the Centre for World Development Education (see page 182) or *The World in Birmingham: Development as a Local Case Study* (see page 65).

PROCEDURE

1. The teacher puts the name of the country, group or topic to be studied on the board and gives pupils two or three minutes to write on a sheet of paper every idea that comes into their heads which relates to the words on the board. Pupils will be interested to see what others have written and can discuss in pairs the differences and similarities between their individual lists. Then the teacher compiles an overall list of the words that have been written down and how often each idea was referred to. This can form the basis of discussion, then and there and also at the end of the course of study.

Such a list of ideas can be very revealing. The list will undoubtedly be a mixture of fact, fantasy and possibly prejudice. It should certainly not be attacked or pulled to pieces. Rather one should ask questions such as 'How can we find out if that is true or not?' 'Who agrees or disagrees with this?' 'Where did you get that information from?'

The last question will, in particular, illustrate the sources of children's attitudes and opinions, i.e. television, comics, books, parents, peer group. They will already have some definite ideas about, for example, the Russians, the Germans and the Irish. These ideas will probably not be very tolerant nor appreciative. If one list contains a substantial number of negative images it should not be left on display in case these are reinforced. It should, however, be referred to at the end of the topic to see how pupils' attitudes have changed.

2. Pupils are given a list of questions such as the following and asked to write down what they think the answers might be:

What sort of clothes do you think are worn and why?
What sort of schools do you think there are?
What sort of homes do you think people have?
What sorts of food do you think are eaten?
What sort of things do you think people like doing?
What sort of work do you think is important?
How do you think the lives of boys and men differ from those of girls and women?
What sorts of beliefs do you think people share?

This should be done individually and the teacher should refrain at this stage from commenting on what pupils have written. When completed, the answers can be collected and provide a series of reference points during the topic.

3. A set of photographs depicting the relevant group or society is put around the walls of the classroom (see Figure 6.3). Pupils are asked in pairs to look at each photograph and make a list of questions they would like answered. They can then compare their list with that of another pair and speculate on how they could find the answers. The questions are collated to form a manageable list for display. Answers to these questions can then be sought during the term.

The first two exercises can be repeated at the end of a topic or course; pupils are then asked to compare their earlier and present thoughts and feelings and to note the main differences. This can give rise to useful discussion about what has been learnt and also provides a means of assessment for both teacher and pupil. The teacher can gauge the extent to which certain objectives have been achieved. Pupils and perhaps parents can see and reflect on what has been learned.

Images and Assumptions
Using Photographs

PROCEDURE ▶ To help pupils learn from and evaluate pictorial information and, in doing this, to empathise with the people and situations shown. Also to promote discussion skills.

PREPARATION ▶ A set of A4-size or larger photographs are needed for display around the classroom. Examples of useful photopacks would be *Living with the Land* (about Ghana), *Choices in Development* (about Tanzania and Kenya), *Western India: City and Village Life*, all from the Centre for World Development Education (see page 182) or *The World in Birmingham: Development as a Local Case Study* (see page 65).

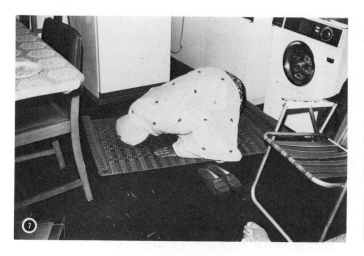

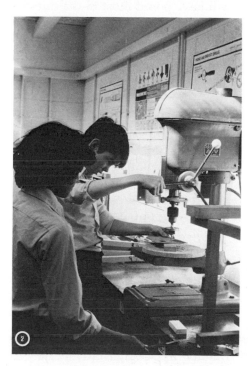

Figure 6.3

105

It is not necessary to display all the photographs in the pack. The teacher should make a selection based on the particular needs and abilities of the class. It is often useful to mount the photographs on large sheets of paper so that comments and questions can be written around them.

PROCEDURE

Pupils are asked to look at each photograph and to think of as many questions as they can about it. They then write these around the edge of the photograph (on the sheets mentioned above). These questions, it should be observed, will fall into two main categories: those which can be *answered* by the photograph if the details are examined really carefully, and those which are *raised* by the photograph, but not in fact answered by it. Having raised these questions, pupils next need the chance to answer them or discuss them. Since they will have posed most of the questions themselves this will add to their interest in solving them.

DISCUSSION

Photographs can, of course, be used to raise questions about particular issues to do with, say, the environment, or poverty and wealth. They can also stimulate questions relating to particular key concepts, i.e. similarities and differences, values and beliefs, distribution of power, co-operation and so on.

VARIATIONS

Pupils can look at a photograph for, say, a minute and then, when it has been removed, write down a brief description of the photograph, or draw it. Subsequently they can consider 'What did you notice most clearly?' 'What did you forget?'

Each pupil can look at all the photographs and select one which they are particularly interested in. Then, working in pairs, each describes their chosen photograph as precisely as possible to their partner who has to find that particular photograph in the pack from the given description.

Individually, or in pairs, pupils can write their own captions for some or all of the photographs. Alternatively they can choose what they consider to be the most appropriate caption for each photograph from a list drawn up by the teacher.

Pupils can be asked to consider the role of the photographer in relation to the pictures they are looking at. What was he or she trying to convey? What sort of things are highlighted in the composition of the picture? What might he or she have been thinking and feeling when taking it?

Pupils in pairs can discuss and agree on three things that particular people in the photographs might be thinking or feeling. These can be written on slips of paper and put next to the relevant photograph. They can be used as a basis for wide-ranging discussion. Later the class may select what they feel to be the most probable thoughts or feelings for each person discussed. These can then be written in speech balloons cut out on paper and fixed in the appropriate places.

Detecting Bias

Figure 6.4

" Yes, I'm on Social Security . . . No, I've never done a hand's turn in my life . . . Yes, I'm of Irish extraction . . ."

PURPOSE

To enable pupils to identify with the humanity of others and to challenge negative stereotypes.

PREPARATION

This activity needs to be planned in conjunction with work on a particular group or situation in which stereotyping and bias are common. Examples would be people from 'third world' or communist countries, minority groups, sex roles, events in the news.

It is vital that positive materials and information are available to pupils as well as materials that contain negative images. The latter are, of course, easier to come by. Materials produced by the group in question itself are particularly useful. A good example is *Unlearning Indian Stereotypes*, a slide–tape sequence in which young Native Americans talk about images of the Indian in American society.[6] Other materials are recommended in Selected Resources at the end of this chapter.

1. The teacher provides pupils with appropriate resources (posters, books, artefacts, music) for creating and highlighting all the positive attributes of the group in question. In discussion work, the skills, wisdom and values involved in, say, indigenous lifestyles should be stressed. Thus Inuit (Eskimo) life and traditions today should not be measured against technological 'progress' but seen as embodying sensitivities which we are perhaps little aware of. At this point, discussion should also stress our common humanity, similarities rather than differences.

2. Having identified in a positive sense with the people being studied pupils need to become aware of the injustice faced in the past, and today, by that group. Attention should be paid to how it feels from the recipient's perspective. A simple role-play can be useful here and an example is given later in the section on Native Americans.

3. Once alert to the nature of the injustices and indignities suffered, pupils can:

(*a*)   note comments, reports, pictures in the media;
(*b*)   recall examples in everyday speech and events;
(*c*)   study a selection of books.

This can lead to analysis of language (Red Indians, primitive people, savages, just like a woman, backward, thick, etc.), of visual illustrations (exotic and/or stereotyped images), of historical accounts (whose history?). The key questions are: How does it feel? Is this fair? Who benefits?

4. Once pupils are alerted to bias and stereotyping, particularly in teaching materials, they can:

(*a*)   prepare an explanatory display for the rest of the school;
(*b*)   write letters themselves to authors and educational publishers;
(*c*)   help choose new books and evaluate those already in the classroom or the library.

Racism: a definition

There are three basic components to racism:

1. the belief that people can be classified into clearly defined 'races';

2. the belief that some 'races' are superior to others;

3. the belief that superior 'races' should control the inferior, and attempts to put this into practice.

On the basis of the first two components, racism is only one example of *prejudice*. It is the third component which is most harmful since it leads to *discrimination*, either deliberate or by default.

Figure 6.5 (source: based on Hodge, J. L., Struckmann, D. K. and Trost, L. D., *Cultural Bases of Racism and Group Oppression*, Two Riders Press, Berkeley, California, 1975)

Those often taboo areas of religious, moral and political issues are now freely discussed. I, like most teachers, have no wish to be accused of bias and I was therefore somewhat wary of this aspect of world studies. I have since been surprised, however, at the level of maturity at which my pupils can operate when really interested. At an open evening one parent remarked 'You do a lot of current affairs in this class, don't you? My son is always wanting to discuss the news – its like living with Robin Day – mind you, I'm learning a lot!'

Steven Barnes, a teacher in Bristol

Figure 6.6

Too Much or Too Little
World Population and Wealth

PURPOSE

To provide an overview of where wealth and population are found in the world. This activity also helps pupils acquire very basic information about where countries and continents are.

PREPARATION

Pupils work in small groups. Each group needs two sets of coloured stick-on dots, each of a different colour; a copy of the tables in Figure 6.9; an outline map of the world on a large sheet of paper with the areas listed in the tables written in and the rough boundaries drawn.

PROCEDURE

First, each group of pupils is asked to place the correct number of dots of one colour closely together in the right places according to the information in the table relating to population. Thus they will put six dots on North America, ten on Europe and so on.

Then they do exactly the same for wealth, putting the dots of the other colour in the remaining spaces in each continent. If they have difficulty fitting the dots in, this can in itself be a matter for discussion.

DISCUSSION

The maps can be displayed and pupils asked to comment on what they show, perhaps in the form of a written statement beginning with the words, 'I learned that . . . ', or 'I notice that . . . ', or 'I wonder why . . . '

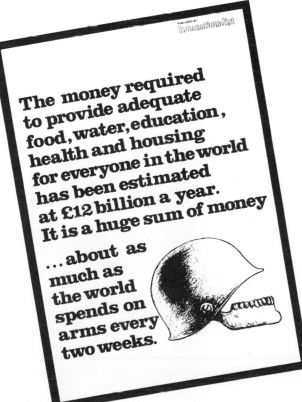

The money required to provide adequate food, water, education, health and housing for everyone in the world has been estimated at £12 billion a year. It is a huge sum of money ... about as much as the world spends on arms every two weeks.

Figure 6.7 (source: New Internationalist)

CONSUMPTION MAY BE HAZARDOUS TO YOUR HEALTH

Figure 6.8 (source: *CCPD Network Letter*, No. 5, January 1977)

If there were 100 people in the world this is where they would be		If there were 100 banknotes in the world this is where they would be	
Africa	9	Africa	3
Eastern Europe and USSR	9	Eastern Europe and USSR	18
East Asia	34	East Asia	14
Latin America	8	Latin America	5
North America	6	North America	28
Oceania	1	Oceania	1
South Asia	20	South Asia	2
West Asia	3	West Asia	2
Western Europe	10	Western Europe	27

Figure 6.9 (source: Richardson, R., *Learning for Change in World Society*, One World Project of the One World Trust, 2nd edition, 1979)

The optimists

'Think of all the foreign money it will bring in.'

'There will be plenty of jobs.'

'We'll learn a lot from the tourists.'

'Hey, it will be great with the discos and bars.'

'It will bring in other industries.'

'We'll have money to develop those poor areas in the north of the island.'

'The government can help start up new industries, and build new houses.'

The pessimists

'Those foreign hotel owners get all the profits – and by the time the government have paid back that loan we shan't get our new houses.'

'I suppose they'll give us all the rotten jobs – waiters, cleaners and that. Not much money there. That happened in Jamaica too, you know.'

'But the tourists only come in one season – what happens to our jobs for the rest of the year? What if fashion changes and they decide to go somewhere else?'

'Well, my family don't want to move, just because some Americans want to build a hotel on that beach.'

'Yeah, and who'll get the money anyway? Right, those with shops and cafés and they're rich already!'

Figure 6.10 (source: Prosser, R., *Tourism*, Nelson for the Schools Council, 1982)

Too Much or Too Little
The Problem of Tourism

PURPOSE >

To examine some of the dilemmas raised in developing countries by tourism, an industry which highlights some of the problems of 'too much and too little'.

PREPARATION >

It will be necessary to obtain brochures and photographs as the basis for a classroom display. These can be acquired from travel agencies and other national information services. They can be selected to illustrate one or several places in developing countries where tourism is important. Examples could be taken from Tunisia, the Caribbean, Egypt, Tanzania, Thailand, Sri Lanka, India and so on.

The information obtained from such agencies needs to cover the location of places, illustrations of hotels and local attractions, the cost of holidays including travel and travel arrangements. It is also important to have available information and illustrations relating to normal everyday life. *The Development Puzzle* gives examples of sources of such information (see page 13). Also needed, ideally, are quotations from local people about how tourism has affected their lives.

PROCEDURE >

1. Pupils work in pairs to list the things that make a place good for a holiday. It should be stressed that this should not be limited to Britain: 'You can go anywhere you like in the world'. Pairs can be asked to rank (see page 90) their criteria and, in discussion, to explain their choices.
2. Pupils study a series of photographs or holiday brochures which illustrate the tourist industry in a developing country. They list the particular attractions (climate, sandy beaches, hotels, convenient flights) as a basis for discussion on 'What has . . . to offer that makes it attractive to holiday makers?'
3. Pupils read the quotations in Figure 6.10. They are from people who observe at first hand the effects of tourism. Pupils list both the advantages and the disadvantages of tourism and then, in small groups, try to agree whether on balance tourism is helpful or harmful.
4. They write two paragraphs about tourism in the country being studied. One paragraph has the heading 'Advantages' and the other 'Disadvantages'.

VARIATIONS ▶

A debate can be arranged on the subject of 'Tourism in (name of country): for or against'.

Pupils can take on the roles of the five characters described in Figure 6.11 and argue their viewpoints.

Older children at school may find themselves faced with real moral dilemmas related to the tourist industry in a developing country, as the following example shows.

> Nigel has brought a letter home from school about a holiday planned for next spring. Four teachers are arranging a school package tour of Tunisia and they want the names of pupils who might be interested in going. Nigel would very much like to take this opportunity of seeing Africa. However, he has just finished studying the effects of tourism in such countries. He feels that the disadvantages often outweigh the benefits. Pupils have to decide in pairs or small groups what Nigel should do.

Figure 6.12 (reproduced by kind permission of *The Guardian* and Bryan McAllister)

Of course tourism gives rise to problems in all countries where it occurs, not solely in the poorer countries. It may be possible to raise the more general issue of whether tourism inevitably trivialises, even destroys, the culture of the host country. What evidence can we see of this happening in Britain, Spain, the United States?

Figure 6.13

112

People's views

Local elder

He represents many of the older people and is very proud of the village traditions. Although he knows how poor the people are, he opposes the plan for tourists. He believes the traditions belong only to the local people and does not want the dances and the crafts to be 'commercialised'. He is afraid that the money, and the desire for more, will destroy the way of life and that outsiders will control the trade.

Travel company representative

She is a young Englishwoman, ambitious for promotion with her travel company. She is very keen to bring in coach parties, but insists that there will not be too many, that the tourists will love the dances, the music and the crafts and will spend lots of money. She says that most of this money will stay with the local people. The tourist trade, she says, will help the traditions survive and flourish, will provide jobs and help young people to stay and make a living in the valley. She knows, however, that her company want to keep as much of the profits as possible.

Part-time basket maker

She is very undecided about the plan. She has five children and is very poor. She makes basketwork and knows that she could sell her goods to tourists. Her sister has worked in a hotel and they would like to open up a café or even a restaurant for the tourists. However, both sisters are afraid that their young daughters would be attracted by the 'outside world' and would leave the village. They are worried too, in case their husbands neglect the farmland to earn money from the tourists. Yet they are proud of their traditions and way of life and would like to show off this pride.

Farmers

These brothers live with their parents on a small farm and are opposed to each other. There is no room for the younger one on the farm and he needs a job. A sister has already left to work in a hotel. He supports the tourist plan because he is a fine dancer and hopes to earn his living and stay in the valley. The elder brother has lived away from the area while doing some agricultural training. He is politically active and is very proud of his people, strongly resents the tourists and opposes the plan. He sees the tourists as 'ripping off' his culture and believes these wealthy visitors will regard him as inferior.

Figure 6.11 (source of text: Prosser, R., *Tourism*, Nelson for the Schools Council, 1982)

Why Poor Countries are Poor

Figure 6.14 (source: *Development Forum*, Vol. 10, No. 8, 1981)

I sit on a man's back choking him and making him carry me and yet assure myself and others that I am sorry for him and wish to lighten his load by all possible means – except by getting off his back

Tolstoy

PURPOSE

To illustrate one important historical reason for the poverty found in many developing countries today.

PREPARATION

This falls into four main parts, the first three of which relate to maps, photographs and information.

- A series of illustrations (books, posters or slides) on pre-colonial civilisations is required to bring them effectively to life. It is probably best to take *one* such civilisation, for example, Zimbabwe, Songhay, Aztec or China as seems most appropriate. (See Figure 6.15.)
- Some familiarity with a world map is needed. If a large political map of the world is always present in the classroom, and regularly referred to, pupils soon develop an awareness of places. Outline maps of the world and Britain are needed for step 4 of the procedure.

- Pictures or actual examples of raw materials and manufactured goods should be available, for example a cocoa pod and a bar of chocolate, sugar cane and a packet of sugar, oil palm nuts and a bar of soap, and so on.
- It will also be a great help if pupils have already carried out the activity on world population and wealth (see page 109).

1. Pupils find the location of a chosen pre-colonial empire on the world map and in an atlas. Is there any evidence of its existence in the place names today? They mark its extent and main settlements on a prepared outline map and find out about some of the works of art that were produced then. Where can they be seen today? (See, for example, Figure 6.15.)

2. Pupils then locate on the world map some of the 'third world' countries which were European colonies (see Figure 6.16). They find out what life was like before the Europeans came and what the Europeans did when they arrived. How did the Europeans treat people at first, and later? How did they gain the co-operation of the ruling groups in these countries?

3. Pupils are given two lists: one of raw materials and one of manufactured goods. They have to match them in pairs. They can either rewrite the lists so they match up, or the exercise can be based on slips of paper which have to be sorted into pairs. (See also 'Unequal Trade' in Figure 6.17.)

4. Pupils mark on an outline world map the location of the ex-colonies which produce raw materials (see Figure 6.17) and indicate with different coloured dots the raw materials that each had to produce for Europeans. On a map of Britain they mark with coloured dots the towns where these raw materials were processed.

These points can usefully be raised with the class: What effect do pupils think the developments in colonial trade had on the lives of people in Britain at the time? What effects do pupils think colonial trade had on those who lived in countries that had been made colonies? (It would be important here to distinguish between the ruling groups, who often benefited greatly in wealth and status, and the rest of the population.) Most of the countries that became European colonies originally grew their own food and were able to feed themselves. Why do pupils think a lot of the land became used for other purposes? What might be grown there even today? Who do they think benefited most from colonialism? Most colonial countries regained their independence during the 1950s and 1960s. How might they have a felt about this?

The play about bananas (see pages 56–60) can be used to illustrate how the unequal pattern of world trade continues today. It is important to link current trade situations with the patterns that caused them in the past.

Christian Aid (see page 182) can supply a copy of *The Feast Game*. This is a very interesting role-play which explores issues to do with food.

Great Civilisations

Many developing countries which are poor at the moment were once the site of rich and powerful empires. In West Africa, for example, between A.D. 300 and 1500 three great empires – Ghana, Mali and Songhay – rose and fell. They grew rich as a result of trade in salt and gold and were famous for metalwork and fine pottery.

Further south the empire of Zimbabwe was based on wealth from iron and gold. The picture above shows some of the ruins still to be found today at Great Zimbabwe. When we talk about ancient civilisations we tend to think of Greece and Rome, but there have been important and influential civilisations elsewhere in Africa, Asia and America.

Figure 6.15

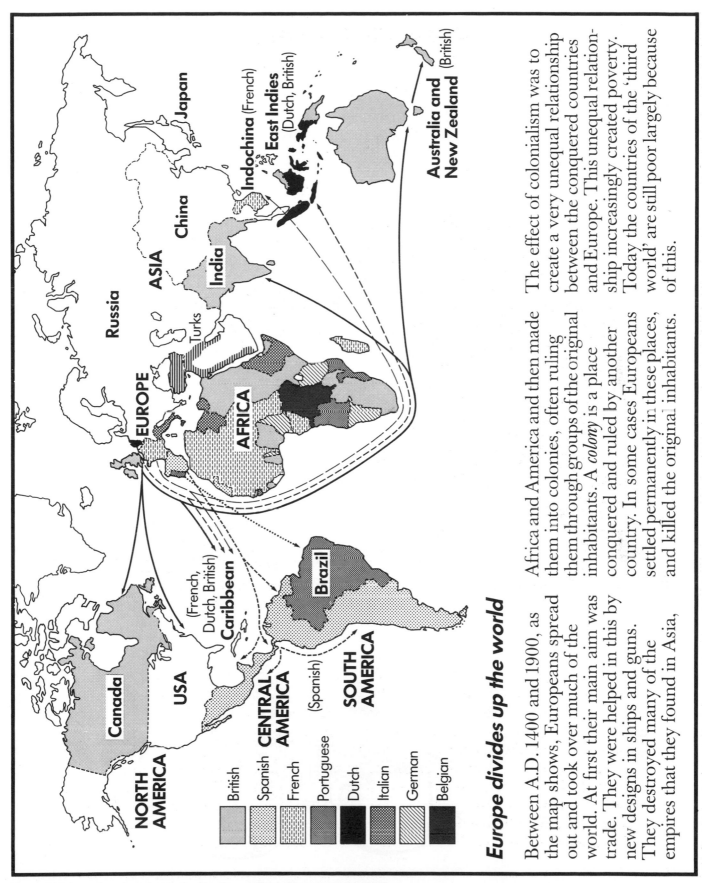

Europe divides up the world

Between A.D. 1400 and 1900, as the map shows, Europeans spread out and took over much of the world. At first their main aim was trade. They were helped in this by new designs in ships and guns. They destroyed many of the empires that they found in Asia,

Africa and America and then made them into colonies, often ruling them through groups of the original inhabitants. A *colony* is a place conquered and ruled by another country. In some cases Europeans settled permanently in these places, and killed the original inhabitants.

The effect of colonialism was to create a very unequal relationship between the conquered countries and Europe. This unequal relationship increasingly created poverty. Today the countries of the 'third world' are still poor largely because of this.

Figure 6.16 (maps based on Stuart, S., *The Unequal Third*, Edward Arnold, 1977)

Unequal trade

During the nineteenth century, European governments and business people wanted two things:

1. to obtain *raw materials* for their factories;
2. to sell lots of *manufactured goods* to make profits and to build more factories.

Raw materials are things which are grown or dug out of the earth, or which come from animals. The main ones are:
Foodstuffs: grain, meat, fruit, cocoa, sugar, tea, coffee
Soft commodities: cotton, wool, sisal, hides, wood, rubber, palm oil
Minerals: coal, iron, oil, diamonds, gold, and all other metals.

Manufactured goods are things made by people. Usually these mean things made in a factory; from razors to rockets, from clothes to chemicals.

The colonies which were able to produce raw materials were made to send their produce to Europe (which had factories) to be manufactured into useful goods. Some of these goods were then sold back to the colonies.

In the British Empire this meant that:

The West Indies grew sugar and cotton, but the sugar was refined in London, not Jamaica. India had supplies of tea, cotton and jute but textile workshops in India closed. Jute mills were opened in Dundee, and cotton mills in Lancashire.

Farmers in West Africa produced cocoa beans but there were no chocolate factories on the Gold Coast. They were in York and Birmingham.

Rubber produced in Malaya was made into tyres, not there, but in the Midlands.

Palm oil came from West Africa but the soap factories were built in Liverpool, not Nigeria.

Figure 6.17 (source: based on Stuart, S., *The Unequal Third*, Edward Arnold, 1977)

Native American Issues

> ## The Third World: a definition
>
> The set of exploited peoples everywhere (the Lapps in northern Norway, the Catholics in Ulster, the American Indians, women, peoples in Latin America, Africa, and Asia) is the Third World. Thus, the Third World is a structural concept, not a geographical one. It is not what was left after the Old World had conquered the New World in North America, nor what is left when one subtracts developed capitalist and socialist countries, nor what is left when one subtracts superpowers and the other industrialized countries. The Third World has its pockets in the Old World and in the New . . .
>
> Johan Galtung, *The True Worlds: A Transnational Perspective,* New York: The Free Press, a Division of Macmillan, Inc., 1980

PURPOSE

To explore the nature of the Native American experience and to counter traditional stereotypes.

PREPARATION

Use the checklist 'Teaching About Minorities' on page 102, as a guide to planning. It is also important to have read 'Detecting Bias' on pages 107–8.

Copies of the passages in Figures 6.18 and 6.19 are needed for each pupil in step 2 of the procedure, and copies of the questions listed there. For step 3, copies of the fact cards in Figure 6.21 are needed, enough for each group of five pupils to have a complete set. Each group will also need a copy of the instructions listed in step 3 of the procedure. Books and other materials on Native Americans are easy to come by, although many are more useful for the stereotypes they contain than for authentic images and up to date information. Some suggestions for books are made at the end of this chapter. In particular it is essential to have pictures of Native Americans in the 1980s.

PROCEDURE

1. Before preparing any visual displays, or even discussing the proposed work with the class, the teacher asks pupils to write down all the words that come immediately into their heads on hearing the words 'Red Indian'. A composite list is made indicating how many times different words such as tipi, buffalo, tomahawk, savage, scalping, etc. come up.

Native American voices

Here are some of the things said by or to Native Americans when they were fighting to protect their lands in the nineteenth century.

No white person or persons shall be permitted to settle upon or occupy any portion of the territory, or without consent of the Indians to pass through the same.

Treaty of 1868

The whites were always trying to make the Indians give up their life and live like white men – go farming, work hard and do as they did – and the Indians did not know how to do that, and did not want to anyway . . . If the Indians had tried to make the whites live like them, the whites would have resisted, and it was the same way with many Indians.

Wamditanka (Big Eagle) of the Santee Sioux

I have heard that you intend to settle us on a reservation near the mountains. I don't want to settle. I love to roam over the prairies. There I feel free and happy, but when we settle down we grow pale and die. I have laid aside my lance, bow, and shield, and yet I feel safe in your presence. I have told you the truth. I have no little lies hid about me, but I don't know how it is with the commissioners. Are they as clear as I am? A long time ago this land belonged to our fathers; but when I go to the river I see camps of soldiers on the banks. These soldiers cut down my timber; they kill my buffalo; and when I see that, my heart feels like bursting; I feel sorry . . . Has the white man become a child that he should recklessly kill and not eat? When the red men slay game, they do so that they may live and not starve.

Santana, Chief of the Kiowas

We have been south and suffered a great deal there. Many have died of disease which we have no name for. Our hearts looked and longed for this country where we were born. There are only a few of us left, and we only wanted a little ground where we could live. We left our lodges standing and ran away in the night. The troops followed us. I rode out and told the troops that we did not want to fight; we only wanted to go north, and if they would let us alone we would kill no one. The only reply we got was a volley. After that we had to fight our way, but we killed no one who did not fire at us first. My brother, Dull Knife, took one-half of the band and surrendered near Fort Robinson . . . They gave up their guns and then the whites killed them all.

Ohcumgache (Little Wolf) of the Northern Cheyennes

Figure 6.18

The trail of tears

In 1838 and 1839 laws were passed by the white American government taking away all the Cherokee lands. The army was then sent to round up all the Cherokee men, women and children at gunpoint. Those who resisted were killed.

In the autumn of 1838 12,000 Cherokee were forced to march west away from their land to Oklahoma. 4,000 of them died on the march. Eyewitness accounts of this still exist. Here is a description by Private John Burnett who was one of the soldiers taking part. He called it his 'Birthday Story', and addressed it to his sons and grandsons.

Children:

This is my birthday December the 11th 1890, I am eighty years old today . . . The removal of the Cherokee Indians from their life long homes in the year of 1838 found me a young man in the prime of life and a private soldier in the American Army . . . I saw the helpless Cherokees arrested and dragged from their homes, and driven at bayonet point into the stockades. And in the chill of the drizzling rain on an October morning I saw them loaded like cattle or sheep into 645 wagons and started towards the west.

One can never forget the sadness and solemnity of that morning. Chief John Ross led in prayer and when the bugle sounded and the wagons started rolling many of the children rose to their feet and waved their hands goodbye to their mountain homes, knowing they were leaving them forever. Many of these helpless people did not have blankets and many of them had been driven from home barefooted.

On the morning of November 7th we encountered a terrific sleet and snow storm with freezing temperatures and from that day until we reached the end of the fateful journey . . . the sufferings of the Cherokees were awful. The trail of the exiles was a trail of death. They had to sleep in the wagons and on the ground without fire. And I have known as many as twenty-two of them die in one night of pneumonia due to ill treatment, cold and exposure . . .

At this time in 1890 we are too near the removal of the Cherokee for our young people to fully understand the enormity of the crime that was committed against a helpless race, truth is the facts are being concealed from the young people of today . . .

. . . Murder is murder whether committed by the villain skulking in the dark or by uniformed men stepping to the strains of martial music. Murder is murder and somebody must answer, somebody must explain the streams of blood that flowed in the Indian country in the summer of 1838. Somebody must explain the 4,000 silent graves that mark the trail of the Cherokee to their exile. I wish I could forget it all, but the picture of 645 wagons lumbering over the frozen ground with their cargo of suffering humanity still lingers in my memory.

Let the historian of a future day tell the sad story with its sighs its tears and dying groans. Let the great Judge of all the earth weigh our actions and reward us accordingly to our work.

Children – thus ends my promised birthday story. This December the 11th 1890.

Figure 6.19

Such a list can then be used as the basis for discussion and to raise initial interest. Where do we get these images of Native Americans from? How true are they? What impression do they give? (But see the comment on page 101 on the need to avoid reinforcing negative images.)

2. Most descriptions of Native American struggles in the nineteenth century were written by whites. It is important, however, to understand also how things appeared from a Native American perspective. The following questions for pupils involve small group discussion arising out of the two passages 'Native American Voices' and 'The Trail of Tears' (see Figures 6.18. and 6.19). Each may well require some introduction and explanation by the teacher.

Individually
- Imagine that these events have happened to *you*. Write down three words to describe how you would have felt about them.
- Think about what this might have made you feel like doing.
- Now write down three things you might do as a result.

In Your Group
- Make a list of all the words describing your feelings.
- How many words in this list come more than once? What kind of feelings are they?
- How are the other feelings different from each other?
- Make a list of all the things your group thinks they might do and choose one or two as the best ideas.

Figure 6.20

The Class

Groups take it in turn to report back to the whole class on how they feel about their situation and what ideas for action they have chosen.

3. Copies are needed of the eight fact cards and their accompanying questions shown under 'Native Americans Today' (Figure 6.21). Each set of cards should be kept in an envelope. Children work in groups of five with the following instructions:

- In your group take it in turn to read out the fact cards.
- The information you are reading out is about *you*. How does it *feel*?
- What will you *do* about it?
- Discuss this within the group.
- Each fact card also has a question on it. Take it in turns to say what you think some of the answers might be to each question.
- Make a list (one person can do this) of all the possible answers that you can think of to each question.
- Plan what you will do now to improve your situation in the 1980s.
- Each group reports on their decision to the whole class.
- Look again at the fact cards and write about the main problems Native Americans have to face today. Do not forget to take into account what you have learnt about Native American history.

DISCUSSION

Further development of the activities described above should focus on what has been learnt about stereotyping, prejudice and discrimination, and questions of minority rights. There is also plenty of scope for exploring values and beliefs, unequal distribution of power, and interdependence between people and their environment.

FOLLOW-UP

The slide–tape set *Chief Seattle's Testimony*[7] provides an interesting nineteenth-century statement of the Native American world view which is also remarkably prophetic.

Native Americans today

1. *Income*
In a year you earn less than half the amount that white Americans earn.
Question: Why might this be the case?

2. *Land*
At present your people are fighting a big court case to gain compensation for lost lands.
Question: How might your lands have been 'lost' in the first place?

3. *Employment*
40% of your people are unemployed.
Question: How will this affect your everyday life?

4. *School*
42% of children drop out of school.
Question: Why do you think they do this?

5. *Health*
You have a life expectancy of only forty-two years compared with seventy years for white Americans.
Question: What might be some reasons for this?

6. *Mining*
Several large mining companies are planning to dig up much of your land for coal and uranium.
Question: Do you think they should be allowed to do this?

7. *Nature*
You are sad at the way in which white people often pollute and damage the environment.
Question: How many ways can you think of in which this happens?

8. *Prejudice*
In many of your dealings with white people you have met with unkindness and prejudice.
Question: Why do you think this is?

Figure 6.21

Studying other worlds: one teacher's account

The main approach taken throughout the year was learning through activities, some specially devised, in which the children when working in small groups had to discuss and co-operate with each other. In fact most of the work set was primarily concerned with developing the children's linguistic and social skills.

Linguistic and social skills

In the first unit of work, which focussed on the idea of uniqueness, there was plenty of opportunity for talking and working together. We began by asking and answering the question 'Who am I?' This initially caused some difficulty as the children tended to think in terms of 'I have . . .' After this the children interviewed each other in pairs. This in turn caused them to think about their attitudes, their feelings and how these affected their behaviour. They completed their own attitudes chart by answering the questions 'What do I feel about . . .?' 'What action do I take?'

I thought it was important that the children should begin to understand what was meant by attitude, as this idea was fundamental to the whole project. Continuing with the theme, 'We are unique', the children made their own personal life lines, which then prompted the question 'What is life for?' Working in groups the children had to put in order of importance some suggested answers. In order to do this they needed to sort out their values and ideas and defend them. I hoped that this activity would make the children aware of the fact that different people do find different things important – an idea which was further developed later in the project.

Religious education

Another area of the curriculum which was approached through this world studies work was that of religious education. For example, it is only a short step from thinking about ancient Egyptian beliefs, and their concern about life after death, to thinking about the question, 'Is there life after death? And how does this question relate to us today?' The question involved the children in a discussion about different beliefs and customs to do with death.

Moving away from questions of perhaps a spiritual nature the project provided ample scope for finding out about other religions. In particular a study of Islam was made. We started with the life of Mohammed and saw how, with the conversion of the Bedouin nomads, Islam expanded beyond the Arabian borders. We concluded our study with finding out about the Muslims' religious pilgrimage to Mecca, the Hajj. This work was particularly popular with the Muslim children in the class, some of whom commented 'I liked the Bedouin work because I found out more about deserts, about their lives and more about Islam.' 'I liked the work about the rise of Islam because I like to learn about the prophet Mohammed.'

Geography and history

Throughout the project certain themes recurred; a geographical one was that of environment. Very early in the course the children studied their own environment. Simple mapping skills were encouraged, when drawing their own neighbourhood maps, and then the children mapped their own homes on a large scale map of St Pauls. The work on 'homes around the world' also mirrored this idea of environment. Pictures of homes from around the world were laid out along the corridor. The children walked along and had to select their own ideal home and then explain why. Many of the Asian children chose a picture of a home in Pakistan, more for reasons of place than because of the building. In many of the pictures the structure of the building quite often was a reflection of the environment, and so again the children's attention was focussed on this theme. At a later stage in the project, environmental factors were studied as one of the main causes and consequences for people migrating or settling. Many of the topics developed from this unit of work were geographical or historical in essence. It was in the way they were developed or approached via a world studies perspective that they were transformed into something more challenging and creative than they might have been before.

For example, a historical topic on the great river valley civilisations began along fairly traditional lines by studying Egypt. To find out what the children already knew, the word Egypt was brainstormed. Ideas collected on the blackboard formed the basis of any questions the children wanted to ask, and find out about. Personal research was followed by a visit to the Egyptian department in the Bristol Museum. Information about the Sumerian civilisation was obtained mainly by listening to the *Man* radio programme, while deductions about the Indus Valley civilisation were made from a large historical picture. All the information was recorded on a matrix comparing the three civilisations. It was at this point that the work took a less traditional line. From thinking about the *past* the children changed direction and thought about the *future*. Re-using the main ideas employed in comparing the ancient civilisations, the children in small groups had to construct their own imaginary future civilisation. They enjoyed every moment. The work was popular with every one in the class. Enthusiastic comments were made. In this way a traditional topic was transformed and enlivened.

A study of the slave trade also contained moral and political ideas that broadened the childrens' knowledge and understanding. The children had to prepare speeches in support of, or against, slavery in which they had to consider the viewpoints of the plantation owner, the slave trader and the abolitionist. One child decided that slavery was such an abomination that he completely refused to consider it from a slave owner's point of view. Nevertheless, speeches were completed and then argued out in a thoughtful if also often rather boisterous parliament session held in class. The Speaker of the House was kept very busy maintaining order!

Conclusions

Overall I feel that the work stimulated by world studies spanned the whole curriculum enabling every child to find something that appealed particularly to them. For me, success was reflected in two unconnected events. The first one was the smile of recognition that crossed the face of one of my most unlikely pupils when the first Vietnamese child to come to our school was made welcome in assembly. It was a smile that showed she connected the work we had done on Vietnam with this new pupil. The second was a comment made by a child who found me after school one evening and enquired whether I was doing world studies with my new class. He hoped I was, for he said 'It was good. We really did learn a lot of things.'

Elaine Hicks, a teacher in Bristol

Myths and Facts

PURPOSE

To encourage critical questioning of popular opinions which may, in fact, be based on misinformation.

PREPARATION

Pupils will each need a copy of the statements shown in Figure 6.22 for the first activities, and a passage similar to the one in Figure 6.23 for the remainder.[8]

PROCEDURE

1. Pupils individually read the statements and note down their own responses to them. In particular they consider whether the statements are true or false, and why. Then in small groups they share their responses to see if, through discussion and argument, they are able to arrive at a group consensus.

The teacher reads the statements to the class. Then buzz groups are formed, i.e. pupils already sitting close to each other, in threes of fours, have two or three minutes to discuss a question given to them. Such questions might be:

Which statements are true/false?
How do you know? How do you decide?
What evidence is there for your answer?
Who do you think might have made this statement?

Pupils are then given the correct answers to the statements and discuss these also in their buzz groups.

While buzz groups are brief and formed from people immediately adjacent to each other, the above questions can also be profitably considered in more formal small discussion groups.

A further development of these activities can be for pupils to monitor the local and popular press, not forgetting the letters columns, looking for similar statements. These can be brought to the class and investigated.

2. Each pupil, or small group, is given a short passage such as the one in Figure 6.23 with some words missing (those in brackets, for example). They have to think up the best possible word to go in each gap. When they have finished, the teacher provides the missing words from the original text so that the two versions can be compared.

The missing words can be those which most invite discussion or, more simply, the gaps can be at regular intervals: every tenth word, for example. The advantage of this is that some gaps will be easily filled and an initial sense of self-confidence given.

Figure 6.22 (sources: *Some People Will Believe Anything!*, Commission for Racial Equality, 5th edition, no date; Tierney, J. (ed.), *Race, Migration and Schooling*, Holt, 1982, Chapter 3)

Four common myths

1. Most immigrants are black people.

- More people have come into the UK from the European Community (excluding Ireland) than from India, Sri Lanka and Bangladesh combined.
- The biggest group of foreign-born residents from any one country are those born in the Irish Republic.

2. There wasn't immigration in the past.

- Britain has traditionally taken many groups who were facing starvation or persecution in their own country.
- Over the last century the major groups have been Irish, Jews, Poles.

3. Immigration is making Britain overcrowded.

- Since 1964 more people have left the UK each year than have entered.
- The Netherlands, Belgium and West Germany all have more people per square kilometre than the UK.

4. There are nearly as many black people in this country as there are whites.

- The latest estimate (1983) is 2 million or 4% of the total population.
- 40% of black people in Britain were born here.

◇

As British as the next person

He tried to get back to his [book], but he couldn't concentrate on it. Why were they always on about [immigration] anyway? They were always making laws and regulations about it. Once someone had asked Mr Andrews how many black immigrants there were in Britain, and the teacher had said about [three] per cent. Delroy had been [amazed] that the number was so small. 'What are they so [scared] for then?' he had asked. Because everyone did seem to be [scared]. Everyone seemed to be terrified that there were going to be [riots] and [violence] all over the place if they let any more immigrants in. Every time anything happened it was [blared] out on television and there were huge [headlines] on the front pages of the [newspapers]. It didn't make [sense].

People sometimes called him an [immigrant], but he had been born here. He was as British as the next man.

Figure 6.23 (source: Jones, Rhodri, *Delroy is Here*, University Tutorial Press, 842 Yeovil Road, Slough ISBN 0 7231 0850 1 educational edition)

Figure 6.24 (source: *New Internationalist*, No. 128, October 1983)

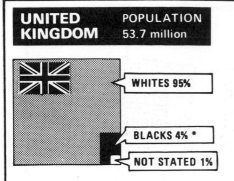

UNITED KINGDOM — POPULATION 53.7 million

WHITES 95%

BLACKS 4% *

NOT STATED 1%

JOBS   Employment ladder

Blacks are almost twice as likely to be unemployed, and their job levels are substantially lower than those of whites.

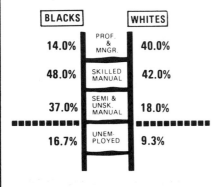

BLACKS		WHITES
14.0%	PROF. & MNGR.	40.0%
48.0%	SKILLED MANUAL	42.0%
37.0%	SEMI & UNSK. MANUAL	18.0%
16.7%	UNEM-PLOYED	9.3%

*The term 'black' refers to people of both Asian and Afro-Caribbean origin.

INCOME
16% of blacks compared with 9% of whites, live 'in poverty' according to the Townsend Report (1979).

RACIAL DISCRIMINATION
According to the Commission for Racial Equality, 50% of British employers discriminate against black applicants.

VIOLENCE
A Home Office study *Racial Attacks* (1981) found that black people were 50-60 times more likely than whites to be victims.

EARNINGS
Because their job levels are lower, black workers earn less than whites for the same working hours. A 1979 survey of unemployed men showed these patterns.

Level of last job	Weekly take-home pay	
	WHITES	BLACKS
Non-manual	£62.7	£48.2
Skilled manual	£69.0	£59.6
semi-skilled man	£57.3	£58.9
Unskilled manual	£50.8	£60.1

Black unskilled workers earned more than whites because they did more shift work.

EDUCATION
National statistics have not been collected since 1973. A survey of London primary schoolchildren in 1971 found that black children were performing at least *one year* behind their white classmates. West Indian children lagged well behind Asians.

HEALTH
There are no detailed national statistics on the health of black people in Britain.

HOUSING
Two-thirds of Britain's black population live in major urban areas like London, Manchester, Bradford, Leeds, Leicester or Birmingham. They tend to rent or buy old, sub-standard housing in run-down, inner city areas.

Household amenities:

HOUSEHOLDS LACKING THEIR OWN BATH HOT WATER AND INSIDE WC.

West Indian	33%
Pakistani)	
Bangladeshi)	57%
Indian	35%
African/Asian	31%
Gen. Population	17.9%

LAW
No figures yet available for proportion of black population in prison.

Sources: **Unemployment and Racial Minorities,** *by David Smith, 1981*
Poverty in the United Kingdom, *by Peter Townsend, 1979*
Racial Disadvantage in Britain, *by David Smith, 1977*
Labour Force Survey, *Office of Population, Censuses and Surveys*
Annual Report 1982, *Commission of Racial Equality,*

VARIATIONS

The following tasks can be carried out on the passage in Figure 6.23.

- Give a title to the passage, or choose a phrase from it to act as the title.
- Pick out the five most important or difficult words in the passage.
- Write down three questions you would like answered as a result of reading the passage.
- Draw a picture to show what the passage is about.
- Write one sentence to summarise the passage.

DISCUSSION

Pupils can be asked to find out the meaning of the word 'myth'. The following questions can then be used to prompt discussion: Can pupils think of any examples of prejudiced behaviour against other people? Are they themselves on the receiving end of prejudice? What does it feel like? How does prejudice turn into discrimination? Which newspapers and television programmes help to perpetuate or reduce such thinking? Do they know of any countries where discrimination is or was carried out officially? (Some examples are the Soviet Union, the United States in the 1950s, South Africa.)

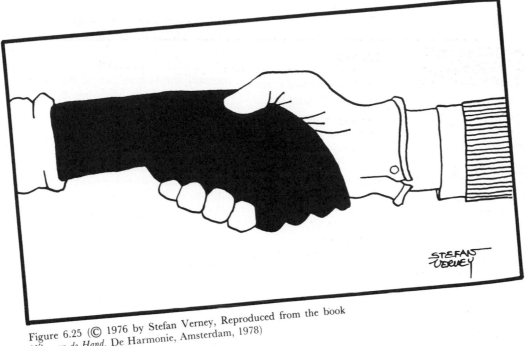

Figure 6.25 (© 1976 by Stefan Verney, Reproduced from the book *Niks aan de Hand*, De Harmonie, Amsterdam, 1978)

Starting Points

● Radio Programmes

The teacher makes a recording of a relevant radio programme and plays it to the class. Pupils are then asked in groups to jot down as many questions as they can think of . . . who, what, how, why, when, and so on. They speculate about the answers and decide on some areas to investigate more fully.

● Newsboard

Pupils monitor the news over a period of time. Each week they fill in what they consider to be the most important information and issues on a newsboard and add illustrations. This is sited prominently in the school foyer.

● The News

Pupils watch recordings of *John Craven's Newsround* or the national news for a set period. They note down which places and countries are mentioned and how often. They mark this information on a map of the world and discuss what they know about these places. Why are some places mentioned more than others?

● Bias

Pupils use a simple checklist for examining their textbooks and library books. They want to see how fairly other countries and peoples are portrayed and whether the materials are biased in any way.

● Local Exchange

Two classes in two nearby schools take part in a series of exchange visits. One school might be multicultural and in an inner-city area. The other might be all-white and in the suburbs, or rural. The pupils take it in turn to act as hosts and to entertain their guests with dancing, drama, storytelling, cooking and so on.

● Stories

Pupils read and listen to a wide range of folk tales and contemporary stories from other countries and cultures. They use books published in other countries as well as those published in Britain.

129

School Policy

A working party of teachers is set up to produce an anti-racism policy for the school. This encompasses all areas of school life. It is amended as a result of discussion with parents, the staff as a whole and with pupils before it becomes official. Before being appointed, all new teachers are asked to read it and commit themselves generally to supporting it.

Artefacts

Pupils are introduced to a wide range of objects used in everyday activities in another country. They then have first-hand evidence of another culture which they can see, hear, touch, smell and taste.

Penfriend

Pupils imagine that their penfriend in Bangladesh has written to say that he/she will be coming to live in England next year. From a selection of newspapers or newscuttings, they choose some items to show what life in England is like.

Futures

Having studied life in a country or culture other than their own pupils consider what things will be like there in fifty years time. How different will it be and who will have influenced changes the most? Will they be for better or worse? Who will have benefited most/least?

Selected Resources

T: for the use of teachers
P: for the use of pupils

Discrimination and Racism

Bayfield, Tony, *Churban; The Murder of the Jews of Europe*, available from Michael Goulston Foundation, 8 Manchester Square, London, W1. (T) Compiled around contemporary documents, this book considers the inevitable question: how did ordinary people in Germany stand by and let the genocide take place?

Desai, Anita, *The Peacock Garden*, Heinemann, 1979. (A cheap edition is also available from Soma Books.) (P) The troubled time of partition is related through one Muslim family who refuse to leave what has suddenly become the Hindu part of the Punjab, and hide out in the garden of the Mosque. Age eight and over.

File, Nigel and Power, Chris, *Black Settlers in Britain: 1555–1958*, Heinemann Educational, 1981. (T) Using contemporary documents, the authors show how considerable has been the black presence in Britain and their contribution to their country of settlement, notwithstanding the racism encountered from the start.

Institute of Race Relations, *Roots of Racism, Patterns of Racism*, both 1982, available from 247 Pentonville Road, London, N1. (T/P) A splendid study of slavery for classroom use, indicating how the dehumanising of slaves as a justification of their exploitation extended to a justification of colonialism, and finally of racism.

Levoy, Myron, *Alan and Naomi*, Bodley Head, 1977. (T/P) Two Jewish children in New York 1944; Alan is coerced by his parents into helping the war-shattered Naomi and learns to care deeply about her. A sad haunting novel that could be read aloud to children younger than the thirteen plus range for whom it may have been intended.

Richter, Hans Peter, *Friederich*, Longman, 1971. (P) Germany 1925–42, seen through the eyes of a growing boy. He accepts unquestioningly the indignities and finally atrocities that pile up against his neighbour – and erstwhile friend – the Jewish Friederich. A most moving book for age ten and over.

Smucker, Barbara, *Underground to Canada*, Penguin, 1978. (P) The 'underground railway' served by black and white anti-slavery Americans ran from Mississipi to Lake Ontario. This book tells the story of twelve year old Julily and her friend Lisa, who make the journey to freedom. Age nine and over.

Strands series, A. & C. Black. (P) Attractive colour picture books about children from ethnic minority cultures who live in Britain. Examples: *Pavan is a Sikh*, *Gypsy Family*, *A Welsh Mining Village*.

Taylor, Mildred, D., *Roll of Thunder, Hear My Cry*, Gollancz, 1980. (T/P) Compelling novel about Cassie and her farming family in the American South. Thomas Tallis school (ILEA) has produced a booklet of information support, should teachers use this book as a classroom project, but it also makes a marvellous private read for age eleven and over. Sequel: *Let The Circle Be Unbroken*, Gollancz.

Western, John, *Outcast Cape Town*, Allen & Unwin, 1981. (T) A profound – and readable – analysis of apartheid: its historical evolvement, ideology and how it affects the lives of South Africans.

Learning About Other Countries

Beans series, A. & C. Black. (P) Attractive colour picture books about individual people in other lands. Especially recommended: *Pakistani Village, Chun Ling in China, Sri Lanka, Village in Egypt*; whereas *Zambia* and *Mexico* should be used with care.

Bennet, Oliva, Patterns of Living Series Macmillan. (P) Rather than dividing the world up geographically, this series presents a world perspective through colour photo-books on: *City Life, Family Life, Village Life, Working Life, Food for Life* and *Learning in Life*.

Bernheim, Marc and Evelyn, *In Africa*, Lutterworth, 1974. (P) Impressive black and white photographs and simple text that depict Africa as a vast continent with a complete range of lifestyles, from the most traditional to the most sophisticated and westernised.

Cooper, Susan, *Jethro and The Jumbie*, Chatto, 1980. (P) Fine writer and illustrator have collaborated to evoke a magical book, set in the Caribbean, but with an appeal that should cross cultures, and a skilful use of dialect. The Jumbie helps Jethro to get what he wants from his brother: a trip sea-fishing. Eight to twelve years.

Hicks, David, W., *Minorities: A Teacher's Resource Book for the Multi-ethnic Curriculum*, Heinemann, 1981. (T) A readable resource book on most aspects of minority/majority issues which attempts to relate these to multicultural issues in Britain.

Hodge, Merle, *Crick Crack Monkey*, Heinemann Educational, 1981. (P) Primary and secondary school in Trinidad seen through the eyes of a lively pupil, though not written specially for children. Eleven year olds and over will find this story delightful and gain many insights.

How They Live Now series, Lutterworth, 1980. (P) *Ravi of India, Kiku of Japan, Rashid of Saudi Arabia, Dimitra of the Greek Islands.* Better than most 'Children of Other Lands' series, offering real understanding of the characters depicted. Enjoyable reading and accessible classroom material.

Humphris, Frank, *The story of the Indians of the Western Plains*, Ladybird, 1973. (P) *Battle of the Little Big Horn: Custer's Last Stand*, Ladybird, 1976. (P) These two narrative accounts for children of how Europeans treated the American Indians are informative and sensitive.

Lindsay, Zaidee, *India*, and *West Indies*, A. & C. Black, 1978. (P) The texts are likely to need further informational support, but the illustrations, by children of the countries, are delightful evocations of their world.

Luling, Virginia, Surviving Peoples series, MacDonald Educational, 1979–81. (T/P) *Aborigines, Eskimos, Indians of the North American Plains.* A worthy attempt to avoid a Eurocentric view of 'exotic' peoples, and the pictures are splendid.

Young World Books, *Cuba: An Anthology For Young People* (c/o Liberation), 1983. (T/P) A good counter image of Cuba to that presented by the West: a mix of poetry, prose and information for age twelve and over.

Too Much and Too Little

Campaign Co-op, *The World in Your Coffee Cup: How the Rich Get Richer and The Poor Get Poorer on the Coffee You Drink*, available from 35 Cowley Road, Oxford. (T/P) A provocative and informative booklet that could be effectively used in class.

Foreman, Michael, *War and Peas*, Hamish Hamilton, 1974. (P) King Lion's people don't have enough to eat, so appeal for help to their overstocked – and overweight – neighbouring kingdom, who retaliate by mobilising and invading King Lion's country. Only the happy ending matches the colour picture book format.

George, Susan, *How the Other Half Dies: The Real Reasons For World Hunger*, Penguin, 1979. (T) Exploding the myth, George shows that it is not too many people for too few resources that causes world hunger, but inequitable shares. The final chapter, 'What can I do?' suggests: 'study the rich and powerful, not the poor and powerless'.

Harrison, Paul, *The Third World Tomorrow: Report From The Battlefront in The War Against Poverty*, Penguin, 1980. (T) Self-help and mutual help, traditional in the 'third world', were largely destroyed by the colonisers. Ways of restoring them and of developing health education and population control education and economics are explored by this self-described 'part-time peasant'.

Richardson, Robin, *Progress and Poverty*, Nelson, 1977. (T/P) Inequalities in food, wealth, education, etc. are imaginatively exposed for children. Many suggestions for classroom work.

Williams, Jay, *The Practical Princess and other Liberating Fairy Tales*, Chatto, 1979. (P) Elegant presentation, good stories, successful overturning of the passive – beautiful – helpless 'heroines' of most European folk tales. Age nine and over.

7. The World Tomorrow

Introduction

Thinking About the Future

All education springs from images of the future and all education creates images of the future. Thus all education, whether so intended or not, is a preparation for the future. Unless we understand the future for which we are preparing we may do tragic damage to those we teach. Unless we understand the powerful psychological role played by images of the future in motivating – or de-motivating – the learner, we cannot effectively overhaul our schools, colleges or universities, no matter what innovations we introduce.[1]

Thinking about the future is an essential and exciting aspect of world studies. Children in school now will, after all, spend most of their lives in the next century, and the world of their adulthood is already being shaped by the events and trends of the 1980s. They need, in addition to learning about world society as it is today, to begin to explore where the world might be heading and to identify the main influences on its future, and their own. They need to think about the way they would *like* things to be in the future, and to learn how to become involved in making such visions a reality. They need to do all this, not only for their own self-fulfilment, but also in order to become informed and responsible citizens. Without such forethought, the problems of scarcity, inequality, injustice and violence which at present beset the world may become even more intractable.

For adults, nearly every action of our lives presumes the existence of a tomorrow. Virtually everything we do or think is based on assumptions, often unconscious, about the future. Yet, in most schools, teaching and learning remains almost entirely concerned with the past and the present. Schooling often seems to reinforce the status quo rather than ask challenging questions about where we are being taken. Perhaps this is in part because, in the world at large, change seems to be becoming ever more rapid and uncontrollable, and to be lead-

Figure 7.1

ing us in directions which do not always inspire confidence in those who control it. The most natural response for many is not to think about the future, and to shield pupils from such concerns.

But, even if we do think about it and try to introduce a future element into the curriculum, there are problems of approach. In particular, how do we study the future without reinforcing a possible sense of unease and powerlessness? How can we teach about something which is, by definition, unknown, with no 'right' answers?[2]

The activities in this chapter show some of the ways in which teachers are finding practical answers to these questions.

Alternative Futures

People tend to think about futures in two main ways. Perhaps the most common way is to make forecasts based on existing trends in population growth, economic development, depletion of resources and so on. This is the future as it is *expected* to be if no action is taken to change it.

Alternatively one may look at one's own community or the world as a whole and consider what it *ought* to be like. Inventing futures in this way involves not only defining what sort of future we would *like* but also exploring what steps are necessary to reach that preferred future.

Visions of the future are often influenced by differing attitudes towards technological change. Thus some will see modern technology as providing freedom from work leading to increased opportunities for leisure for all. On the other hand, others may see the same technology as generally socially damaging, leading to recurrent and possibly unresolvable political and ecological crises.

Probably the most useful way of looking at alternative futures is to group them under the three following headings.

- *Possible futures* are all the futures that *might* conceivably come about. These range from the most likely to the most improbable. Thinking about them involves imaginative exploration of a variety of possibilities.
- *Probable futures* are those which are *likely* to come about. Thinking about them involves projecting trends, for example about industrialisation or the arms race, and making forecasts or predictions about what is expected to happen.
- *Preferable futures* are those which we feel *should* come about. Thinking about them involves envisaging what a just and peaceful community or world would look like and the steps needed to achieve this. It inescapably includes reflecting on, challenging and clarifying one's own values and priorities.

With the awareness that the future is not fixed and unchangeable comes the realisation that we all have *some* choice about the kind of future that we would like. An important purpose of exploring 'the world tomorrow' is thus to help children understand, cope with, and influence change as it affects their lives and neighbourhood.

A summary of current views[3] about probable and preferable futures would suggest that most people incline towards one of the following broad viewpoints.

- *Business as usual*: the future will be very much like today with similar national and global problems being handled much as they are today.
- *Disaster*: poverty, pollution, crime and war will increase, perhaps leading to nuclear war or some kind of global breakdown.
- *Authoritarian control*: basic freedoms will be restricted by increasingly authoritarian governments in order to conserve resources and ensure order.
- *Hyper-expansionist*: accelerated industrial, technological and scientific expansion is the only practical solution to current problems.
- *Ecological*: the need is for a major change in direction, for decentralisation and balance within and between ourselves, for partnership between humankind and nature in a peaceful and just world.

- *Socialist democracy*: the capitalist system is unstable, and the cause of many of the world's problems. Only when socialism replaces it will these be resolved and justice established.

The trouble with our time is that the future is not what it used to be.

Paul Valery

Today, as never before, we have the opportunity to take hold of our destiny. We are at last free for the task of growing up as a species. But growing up is not comfortable; it is accompanied by stresses and strains.

L. S. Stavrianos

To take a step into the future we need to shift our weight to the opposite foot.

William Irwin Thompson

We can only pay our debt to the past by putting the future in debt to ourselves.

John Buchan

If the quality of life for the majority of us is not to deteriorate, far reaching changes in human behaviour must occur in the years immediately ahead.

Lester R. Brown

The real problem is to sort out the values that motivate our social and individual behaviour, to analyse them clearly and profoundly, to uncover the conflicts between them, and then to choose, as consciously as we know how, which one to give precedence.

Alvin Toffler

The real future is no mechanical continuation of the present, which can be projected by a simple curve on a graph. From moment to moment the inertia of the past may be altered by new factors springing from both inside and outside the human personality.

Lewis Mumford

Just take a superficial look at history and see whether the course of future events would not have been better perceived in broad outline if more study had been devoted to the future itself.

Fred Polak

Figure 7.2 (source: these quotations are the chapter openings from Fitch, R. M., and Svengalis, C. M., *Futures Unlimited: Teaching about Worlds to Come*, National Council for the Social Studies, Washington, 1979)

Children and the Future

Children themselves, not surprisingly, are very interested in the future. One class of eight to nine year olds in Avon compiled a list of all the questions they would like to ask about the future. Among the questions were:

> What will happen in the future?
> How old will we be in the year 2000?
> Will we die?
> How big is the future?
> Will schools change?
> Will clocks tick faster?
> Will dinosaurs ever come back?
> Will it be an adventure?

In defining what is meant by 'future' some seven to nine year olds in Oxford wrote:[4]

- Something after. Something else.
- When you think of things that you want to happen to you when you grow up.
- Time ahead or time to come or even something to happen that has not happened.
- I think the future will be a ball of fire.
- The future is what you keep in your mind.
- A new world.

Each child's private image of the future shapes her or his development in numerous ways. It is in turn itself shaped largely by external influences. Questions such as 'What do you want to be when you grow up?' encourage children to consider 'anticipated selves'. Both parents and teachers have future images of their children which they convey powerfully to them. One example of this is the effect of teacher expectation (future) on pupil's performance (present).

Children also receive strong messages about what the future can be expected to be like via television programmes, advertising and adolescent culture. To a large extent these managed images give rise to a fantasy world which is further developed by video and computer games and popular films. This 'hyper-expansionist' future is received enthusiastically by many young people who perhaps see it as a compensation for some of the de-humanising aspects of their own lives.

In What Will the World be Like? The focus is on the concept of change and thinking about ways in which the future seems likely to develop. It is about 'probable' futures. In What Should the World be Like? the emphasis moves to 'preferable' futures. The activities enable children to explore their own feelings about the future, both in relation to the local community and the wider world. Making Changes then looks at ways in which people, including children, can make decisions about the future they would like and participate responsibly in changing the world around them.

Figure 7.3 (source: Richardson, R., *Fighting for Freedom*, World Studies Series, Nelson, 1978, p. 23. Copyright World Council of Churches)

134

What Will the World be Like?
My Future

To help children reflect on their past and their future, and in so doing to think about the idea of change.

Pupils each need a large piece of paper, A4 size or larger with a line ruled across it lengthwise, and coloured pens or pencils.

1. The teacher explains to the children that they are each going to be drawing a timeline. This is simply a line drawn to a suitable scale on which one marks events that have occurred in the past and ones which are likely to occur in the future. The charts they will be making should be colourful and lively, with explanation and humour as they see fit.

2. Pupils are asked to divide their line into four equal parts and to mark the left end of the line with their date of birth, then go across marking each division with 10, 20, 30, 40, to show the decades up to their fortieth birthday.

3. They mark in the main personal events in their life so far: for example, their birth, those of their brothers and sisters, moving house, going to school.

4. They then compare their lives in small groups. How do their lives differ so far? How are they similar? What events are seen as important and why?

5. It is suggested to them that today can be looked at as 'the first day of the rest of your life'. Whatever they have or have not done so far, the rest of all their lives is still in the future, a future which starts now. They are to think carefully about what they consider is *likely* to happen to them in the future, for example, changing schools, leaving school, different kinds of work, waged or unwaged, unemployment, marriage, children, and so on up to the age of forty, and add these to the chart.

It will be interesting to compare their views of the future. What are the differences, and why have these occurred? Are there noticeable differences between the projected future of boys and girls? A second stage is to consider what evidence, if any, they have used to forecast the future. Or is it all speculation? Can one actually predict what will happen?

Pupils can also draw timelines for the whole of their lives. These can include the main anticipated milestones up to, say, 2060, and can include retirement and even death.

A timeline can be drawn marked off in decades (1970, 1980, 1990, and so on) and the dates of actual events up to the present written in. Children are asked to note or draw events of national and/or global significance, which they think will occur. As before, differences and similarities can be discussd, and finally any match or mismatch between these timelines and the personal ones described above can be considered.

Pupils can take a news story, or perhaps an event that obviously relates to everyday life, such as a quarrel between two people or two families, and draw a timeline showing the events in the past which might have led to the current story. The timeline can then be continued into the future, as pupils speculate about what might happen in the years ahead. In the case of a quarrel, the future might include the steps involved in resolving the particular conflict peacefully.

Figure 7.4 (source: *Times Educational Supplement*, 19 June 1983, p. 21)

What Will the World be Like?
Making Forecasts 1

PURPOSE

To encourage pupils to reflect on their own personal plans, hopes, fears and expectations for the future, and to investigate the ways in which their own lives affect and are affected by events and places in other parts of the world.[5]

PREPARATION

Each pupil needs to be given a copy – as large as possible – of the first chart in Figure 7.5, or to draw one for themselves.

PROCEDURE

The teacher introduces pupils to the chart and talks with them about what they might put in some of the boxes in response to the question 'What do you think will happen in the future?' The task is for them, individually or in pairs, to write or draw something in some or all of the boxes.

Pupils can then present some of their forecasts to the class. It is probably best to concentrate on one line or one box at a time: to ask, for example, for forecasts relating to the world at large, or to next week, or to the local area next year. Wherever possible these should be compared and contrasted and the connections made between the boxes. For example, what happens in the neighbourhood next week could affect individual class members next year; what happens in the world as a whole in the pupils' lifetimes (twenty years from now) could, conceivably, be influenced by what happens in our country this week. An overall list can then be made to demonstrate the range of expectations of the class members.

VARIATIONS

Further horizontal columns can be added, for example: my family, my school.

The exercise can be repeated on a second copy of the chart using the question 'How would you *like* things to be?', and the results of the two charts compared.

The media can serve as the basis for completing the chart. A news bulletin can be taped and replayed so that the class can fill in each item. Or pupils can work, with any necessary explanation and help, from one issue of a local or national newspaper. How far does either source refer, explicitly or implicitly, to the future, to the wider world beyond one's own country, to individual people's lives?

Futures chart 1

Time ——————————————————→

Space	This week	Next week	Next year	My lifetime	My children's lifetime
Myself					
My locality					
My country					
The world					

Futures chart 2

	Event	Why does this event seem likely to happen?	What might stop this event from happening?
Local			
National			
Global			

Figure 7.5

138

What Will the World be Like?
Making Forecasts 2

PURPOSE

To help pupils reflect on some of the problems involved in considering the future and to understand that all trends and events can be influenced by human action.

PREPARATION

Copies of the second chart in Figure 7.5 will be needed. Sets of cuttings from the local or national press will also be useful. It will help if the class has already carried out the previous activity on forecasting.

PROCEDURE

Pupils work in small groups. Each group is provided with a copy of the chart and a set of twelve or fifteen newspaper cuttings taken from the local or national press, which should be explained if necessary. The cuttings are used to stimulate thinking generally, and to prompt ideas for forecasting.

The task now is to forecast events within, say, the next month at local, national and international levels, and to produce one or more reasons why each might happen. Pupils should think, too, about what might happen to change each forecast, either as a result of accident or human intervention. All of this should be entered on the chart. The different forecasts can then be presented to the whole class.

DISCUSSION

Quite young children can profitably do this exercise, although the sophistication of the thinking will vary according to the children's capabilities. What is important is that they understand that the future at all levels *is there to be made*. What are the implications of this for them now, and in the next few years?

FOLLOW-UP

A further stage can be to display all or some of the forecasts and to see during the coming month which actually were accurate, with the children monitoring the news to check this. At the end of the month the forecasts which didn't come about are looked at and some of the possible reasons for this are considered.

VARIATION

Pupils can be asked to forecast, from the standpoint of people at a particular time in the past, what might happen in the coming twenty or fifty years. What did actually happen? For example, how far could their grandparents have foreseen at the end of the second world war the major changes that have taken place since then? How far did they in fact foresee them?

The shape of things to come...

Just 1,000 years ago human beings were an insignificant species on this planet: only a quarter of a billion people, barely into the Iron Age, spread thinly across the earth – and subject to nature's whims. Today that species has increased more than fifteen-fold and its power has increased to immense proportions. The human race has made the world produce more, has covered it with cities, is felling its forests and consuming its oil. From being at Nature's mercy we now have the power to determine our own future. But this new power brings with it tremendous and unprecedented responsibilities. It is now up to us to shape our own future.

FEEDING THE TEN BILLION

If current trends continue food production will keep pace with population growth. But feeding the world's hungry depends on better distribution of production, not just higher yields.

Annual per capita grain consumption in kilograms

	1975	2000	% increase
WORLD (average)	402	571	42
Africa & Middle East	190	194	2
Asia & Oceania	193	222	15
Latin America	238	283	19
USSR & E. Europe	783	965	23
W. Europe	443	582	31
USA	748	1,183	58

Source: The Global 2000 Report

Projected global grain yield (in metric tonnes per hectare)

Source: Global 2000

THE TIME BOMB

Inequality fuels unrest within countries. Untrammelled growth leads to competition and conflict between nations. Both mean increased military expenditure. Today the world has approximately:

● 50,000 nuclear weapons
● 25 million regular armed forces

There are twice as many people in military occupations as there are doctors, nurses and teachers in the world.

Military expenditure in US $ (billion)

Developing world
Industrialised world

1960 1965 1970 1975 1979

Source: World Military and Social expenditures 1981, by Ruth Leger Sivard

FOR RICHER, FOR POORER

The rich will get richer, and the poor will get slightly richer too. But if the division of the world's wealth remains the same as today, when world population stabilises the Third World will have 90% of the world's people and only 20% of the world's wealth.

Per capita Gross National Product
(US $ corrected for inflation)

	1973	1985	2000	% increase
WORLD	1,473	1,841	2,311	57
Industrialised countries	4,325	5,901	8,485	96
Developing countries	382	501	587	54
Bangladesh	111	118	120	8
USA	7,066	9,756	14,212	101
USSR	2,618	3,286	4,459	70
China	306	384	540	76

FIELDS OF CONCRETE

By the year 2000 three-quarters of people in the North and half of people in the South will be living in cities. Urban growth in the North is fuelled by investment in industry. In the South people flock to cities to escape poverty in the countryside. By the year 2000 eight of the ten biggest cities will be in the Third World.

GIANT CITIES (over 5m people)

□ = Rich world   ■ = Poor world

1950   1980   2000

Photo : ILO

POPULATION COUNTDOWN

Population growth is already slowing down. By the year 2110 global population is predicted to stabilise at around ten and a half billion.

Average annual increase in world population (millions)

1950 1960 1970 1980 1990 2000 2010 2020 2030

Source: UN Population Division

LIMITS TO GROWTH

The earth's resources are running out . . .

. . . OIL If exponential increases in oil consumption continue the wells will be dry by 2025.

. . . URANIUM The costs of extracting the earth's diminishing uranium deposits will become almost prohibitive by 2050

. . . TREES 5.6 million hectares of forest are being felled annually – an area the size of Sri Lanka

. . . DESERTS 19 per cent of the earth's surface is threatened with desertification

. . . POLLUTION Between 1978 and 2000 the amount of carbon dioxide in the atmosphere will have increased by 15 per cent.

Conserving the earth's resources means an 'energy transition' from non-renewable to renewable sources. Whether or not we continue to devour the earth's resources depends on who controls them and the price tag we put on them.

Figure 7.6 (source: *New Internationalist*, July 1982)

What Should the World be Like?
Mental Maps

PURPOSE

To provide an opportunity for children to express and communicate graphically their mental images of the world. They can in this way begin to clarify their own ideas and look more closely at those of others.

PREPARATION

None necessary, although one or two examples of children's work such as those shown in Figures 7.7 and 7.8 can be provided as stimuli. The mental maps may be of a geographical nature or be more freely expressive and symbolic: there is no limit to the possibilities.

PROCEDURE

The children are asked to draw one of the following:

- Our school as we'd like it to be
- Our neighbourhood as we'd like it to be
- Our country as we'd like it to be
- Our world as we'd like it to be

Figure 7.7 (Sarah Taylor)

Figure 7.8 (Lorraine Schneider, for Another Mother for Peace)

They should write as few words as possible, allowing the pictures to speak for themselves.

DISCUSSION

An important part of this activity is to translate the pictures into words. Encourage the children first to explain to each other, in pairs or small groups, what their picture means. The next stage is for each to explain *why* they have chosen this view of the future. What do they like about it? How do these reason differ from those of others? Can we learn anything from this about peoples' values, i.e. why people think different things are important in life?

VARIATION

Children can be asked to draw their school, neighbourhood, country, or world as they would *least* like to see it. A discussion of the reasons behind their worst possible futures will also help to highlight and clarify children's hopes and fears.

What Should the World be Like?
Arming the World

PURPOSE

To consider in outline (*a*) the developing sophistication and destructive potential of weapons over time and (*b*) some alternatives to the continuing arms race.[6]

PREPARATION

Sets of the pictures shown in Figure 7.9 are needed (cut up into separate pieces). Each set of nine pictures needs an additional three blanks. Each set can be stored in its own individual envelope.

PROCEDURE

Pupils work in small groups. Each member of the group is dealt one or more of the pictures, face down. They describe, in turn, what is in their picture(s), without showing it to the rest of the group. Next the group decides, as a whole and still without looking, what pattern or sequence the pictures are to be put in and these are placed on the table, face up, in the agreed order or pattern. The group then reviews its decisions and alters the position of the pictures as it feels necessary. The final stage is for the group to discuss and agree on what pictures should go on the three blank slips to illustrate future steps in halting the arms race. Members of the group draw these and position them with the other slips.

Figure 7.9 Arming the world (source: *An Approach to Peace Education*, UNICEF School Series Pack No. 6. Drawing by John Wyatt Nelson)

143

Behind the War Machine
A CONSUMER'S GUIDE

History's most costly arms race is making the world poorer, not safer. Here are some examples of the resources used by the war machine:

MONEY

Global military spending, now running at well over $1 million per minute, topped the $600 billion mark in 1981 – equivalent to $110 for every man, woman and child on earth. (By comparison, only 6 cents per capita were spent on international peace-keeping efforts.) Worldwide military expenditure averages $19,300 per soldier – compared with public education expenditure of $380 per school-age child.

Developing countries have more than trebled their share of global military spending during the past two decades.

Source: Sivard, World Military and Social Expenditure 1982

Distribution of World Military Expenditure 1960 and 1980
(percent, 1980 constant prices)

1960 TOTAL $ US 260 billion
- USA & USSR 63.7%
- 'Other Warsaw Pact and Nato countries' 21.7%
- Other developed * 10.1%
- Developing 4.5%

1980 TOTAL $ US 550 billion
- 48%
- 21%
- 16%
- 15%

* Other developed countries incude China, Japan, Israel and South Africa

Source: Sanger, Safe and Sound, 1982

PEOPLE

- **500,000** scientists researching military projects
- **5 million** civilians working in industrial jobs indirectly supported by military expenditure
- **5 million** civilians producing weapons and other military equipment
- **4 million** civilians working in government defence departments
- **10 million** people in para-military forces (police, frontier guards etc)
- **25 million** people enlisted in regular armed forces

This adds up to:

49.5 million people engaged in military activities worldwide.

Source: UN, Disarmament and Development, 1982

RAW MATERIALS

The military machine consumes large slices of the world's raw materials:
- **5–6 per cent** of oil consumption
- **6–7 per cent of aluminium, nickel and zinc**
- **11 per cent of copper** Military consumption of aluminium, copper, nickel and platinum is greater than the demand for those minerals for all purposes in the *whole* of Africa, Asia (including China) and Latin America.

Source: UN, Disarmament and Development, 1982

RESEARCH

Military objectives are by far the single most important purpose of research and development. One in every five scientists worldwide is engaged in military work. In 1980 global expenditure on military research was a staggering $35 billion – a quarter of the world total of $150 billion and more than the *total* amount spent on energy, health, pollution control and agriculture.

The average military product is 20 times as research-intensive as the average civil product. Countries investing heavily in military research have lower rates of industrial growth than those concentrating on civil research.

	Military R&D as percent of total R & D (1975)	Growth rate in industrial productivity (1973–77)
United States	30	1.3
Britain	30	0.2
France	19	2.1
F. R. Germany	7	3.5
Japan	0.6	5.8

Source: Sanger, Safe and Sound, 1982

TRADE

The growth of military exports to Third World countries has far outstripped the growth of total world trade since 1970. Third World countries now account for two thirds of the international arms trade, which was worth $35 billion in 1981.

In the period 1979–81 the Soviet Union overtook the United States as the leading exporter of major weapons, but the US has more customers – 67 countries compared with the Russians' 28. Other major arms exporters include France, Italy and the UK. Some Third World countries such as Brazil and Israel have also started exporting domestically-produced weapons.

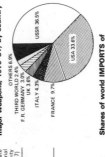

Shares of world EXPORTS of major weapons, 1979–81, by country
- USSR 36.5%
- USA 33.6%
- FRANCE 9.7%
- ITALY 4.3%
- UK 3.6%
- F. R. GERMANY 3.0%
- THIRD WORLD 2.4%
- OTHERS 6.9%

Shares of world IMPORTS of major weapons, 1979–81, by region
- INDUSTRIALISED COUNTRIES 37.8%
- MIDDLE EAST 27.3%
- NORTH AFRICA 9.2%
- FAR EAST 8.3%
- SOUTH AMERICA 6.2%
- SOUTH ASIA 4.9%
- SUB-SAHARAN AFRICA 4.8%
- CENTRAL AMERICA 1.5%

Source: SIPRI Yearbook 1982

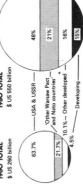

Source: Sivard

SINCE 1960 AT LEAST 10,700,000 PEOPLE HAVE DIED IN 65 WARS FOUGHT ON THE TERRITORY OF 49 COUNTRIES – A RATE OF 1,330 WAR DEAD EVERY DAY FOR THE PAST 22 YEARS.

Illustration : Clive Offley

Figure 7.10 (source: *New Internationalist*, March 1983; illustration Clive Offley)

Initially discussion can focus on how each group arranged the slips and why. A natural next step is to look at how weapons have evolved over the centuries, followed perhaps by discussion on the hazards of modern weapons. Comparisons of costs can then be referred to: for example, for the cost of one modern tank 1000 school classrooms could be built; basic pharmacies could be provided in 40 000 villages for the cost of one jet fighter. How would the children like arms expenditure to be redirected, if at all? Finally, groups should explain their own three future pictures to the rest of the class and explain how they see these steps changing current trends.

What Should the World be Like?
Projects for a Better World

PURPOSE

To enable pupils to reflect on their own values and priorities for their world and to consider some practical ways in which individuals and groups can try to influence change.[7]

PREPARATION

Some hypothetical projects for change are described in Figure 7.11 Pupils each need a copy of these or a similar set, real or imaginary. The descriptions provided will need to be fully discussed and explained for younger children, and perhaps simplified.

PROCEDURE

Pupils work first as individuals or in pairs. They are asked to imagine that they have units of money which must be distributed between some or all of the projects. As there is not enough to support all four the question is: which should be supported and to what extent? They may give less than the amount asked for as long as they can offer good reasons for doing this. After ten minutes or so, they form small groups of five or six and agree as a group on how the money should be distributed. The groups then announce their decisions and the reasons for them to the whole class, and the total amount allocated to each project is worked out.

DISCUSSION

Follow-up discussion is likely to concentrate mainly on the reasons which pupils give for their decisions. What factors do they take into account? Why? Are some world problems more important than others? Does it make sense to work on one or two in isolation from the others? What *are* some effective ways of changing things?

145

Projects for change

Planet Earth bus
We are a group of actors who travel round the country in a double-decker bus, trying to make people understand why so many people in the world are poor and what they and we can do about this. We give talks, sing, show films, put on plays in schools, offices, the street – wherever we can. A very good film has just been made which gives examples of how ordinary people in different countries are working together to help overcome poverty. We need fifty units to buy it.

Do-it-yourself farm
We live and work on a small farm where people who don't have a job can come to learn how to grow their own food, keep animals and do basic do-it-yourself work, making and repairing. The idea is to give them practical help in living on very little money. More and more people want to come to the farm and we urgently need thirty units to buy tools for them to use: spades, forks, hammers and saws especially.

Advertising peace
Our small group all used to have jobs in advertising. We think the most important thing we can do is to tell people the facts about the arms race and war and the need to make peace, so we now spend our time designing and printing large posters and try to get them bought and displayed in towns all round the country. Our latest poster has these words: 'In the world as a whole, more money is spent on weapons and soldiers than on health and education together. What are *you* doing about it?' But we have run out of money. We urgently need forty-five units to send letters to all our contacts asking them to order the poster.

Future home
We are doing up an old terraced house in the middle of our town to show how the houses of ordinary families can save energy and avoid pollution. Our house shows ways of getting heat and light from the sun, re-using things which are usually thrown away, insulating the walls and roof cheaply, and much more. The house is now nearly finished and many people are visiting us. For everyone to get the message, we need to make an exhibition explaining what we are doing and why, and what others can do too. For this we are asking for thirty-five units.

Figure 7.11

The class can be split into five groups. Four of them each take a project, either one of those described here, or a real one they know of, or one which they have chosen themselves, together with a written request for money. The role of each of these four groups is to try to ensure that their project gets the money it needs. The fifth group is the 'grants committee': it has control over how the one hundred available units are allocated.

The first step is for each group to work out the arguments needed to support *their* project. They list these and decide who will present their case. The grants committee meanwhile makes a list of the questions which they will want to ask about each project in order to decide how the money should be allocated. Secondly, the project groups present their cases in turn and answer questions from the grants committee. Thirdly, the grants committee discusses, in the hearing of all, which projects should be supported and with how much money, and announces its decisions.

FOLLOW-UP

Many organisations concerned with world issues have to make decisions about which projects and which kinds of work are to be supported. Pupils could send for the annual reports of, for example, Oxfam, Christian Aid, Friends of the Earth, Campaign Against the Arms Trade, War on Want, Help the Aged, Shelter, and examine the way in which the money available is spent. Is this how the pupils themselves would allocate the money?

What Should the World be Like?
A New Society

PURPOSE

To explore issues relating to equality and justice.

PREPARATION

A set of ideas for discussion on issues such as those shown below is needed. These can be used as they stand or adapted according to the age and interests of the pupils.

PROCEDURE

The teacher describes to the class the following imaginary situation:

It is the year 2423. You are among the passengers on board a spaceship travelling to another planet. The aim is to set up a new society which will be an example to people on Earth.

During the journey you are to plan with your fellow passengers the kind of new society which you and they are going to set up together on the planet.

There are all sorts of things which need deciding. Decisions need to be made about the following.

- *Justice*: how will you make sure that some people don't get more money, food and clothing than they need, and leave others without enough to live on?
- *Order*: how will you make sure that some people do not take advantage of others either by stealing or hurting them?
- *Politics*: how are things to be decided – by everyone, by an elected group, by the wisest, or by the strongest?
- *Education*: how are children to learn about themselves, their society, their history, themselves?
- *Male and female*: should there be any differences between what men and women are allowed to do?
- *The good life*: how are people to have a satisfying life, one which is enjoyable and worthwhile?

It is a good idea for the teacher first to discuss some of the possibilities under each heading with the class as a whole. Then pupils work in small groups. Each group is given one of the above issues to work on for, say, half an hour. Finally, they should, in turn, present their preferred solutions to the class, perhaps in graphic or dramatic form.

DISCUSSION

The class as a whole will want to express their feelings about some of the solutions suggested and perhaps modify these if they feel improvements can be made, particularly where the solutions are in conflict.

An important next step is to look at how things are organised in our own country, and on the planet as a whole. Are some of the issues (for example, order) dealt with satisfactorily *within* some countries but not between them? How does the children's own schooling compare with their preferred solution for education? What is their idea of a worthwhile 'good' life?

VARIATIONS

A more complex version of this activity is to give each group all six issues to tackle. What would a society look like which incorporated all their preferred solutions?

The children can be asked to design a spaceship which will take them on a long journey in space. What would it, and they, need to survive? They can choose whatever they like to take with them as the spaceship is extremely large. However, they cannot get more supplies once the journey has started. In Figure 7.12 a teacher describes how a similar project worked in practice.

Mothership Earth [planning a journey to the stars]

The children worked in pairs and reported back to the group. Questions came from other children, 'What about dead people?' 'What about sewage? . . . Can't afford to throw it away!' Back to the design . . . 'Can we take a forest?' 'How can we recycle water?' 'We'd better take some of every type of animal and plant.'

Gradually they were inventing a closed ecosystem of increasing complexity. We need plants to give oxygen, water to grow the plants — oxygen cycle, water cycle — weather, recycling systems, conservation of raw materials, skilled people to help keep us healthy and safe, an education system so that the next generation knows how to control the space-ships, a non-polluting transport system to get around, shelters, food cycles, decay and growth . . . It was several days before the children realised:

'Hey, we've invented the Earth!'

It came like a revelation! They had had a glimpse of the whole system, of where everything fitted in place, of the inter-dependence, the smallness and delicacy of our little world. They understood that they were in control and could destroy the whole thing very quickly by upsetting the balances. We called our invention: Mothership Earth. And then it took off!

Attitudes were changing.

Children wrote letters to the Prime Minister, to the Queen, and to Jimmy Savile, asking them to use their influence to help save the natural world. We started a magazine called *Friends* to start educating the rest of the community. We worked with the county and district councils, and conservancy organisa-tions, to obtain the wood adjacent to the school as a nature reserve to be managed by the school. We cleared rubbish, trimmed ivy, watched the County Tree Team fell the dead elms. We made video-tape programmes and presented a Christmas show on 'How to save the world' . . .

The whole school became involved in different aspects of the project which seemed to colour every dimension of school life.

Bob Hart, Headteacher, the Pines School, Hertford

Figure 7.12

Figure 7.13 (source: New Internationalist, *Peace Pack*, 1983)

149

Making Changes
Using and Re-using

PURPOSE

To consider the idea of recycling as one way of conserving environmental resources.

PREPARATION

A blank class chart, similar to the one in Figure 7.14 will be useful. Detailed arrangements for handling materials will need to be made in the later stages.

PROCEDURE

The teacher makes a list with the class of the most common items that are regularly thrown away at home. The class then works in small groups. Each group selects one item so that the main items on the list are as far as possible covered. They are then (*a*) to brainstorm (see page 79) all the possible ways in which this item could be re-used and (*b*) to select the one or two ideas which they think are the most practical and useful. A large class chart can then be filled in as the groups present their findings with, no doubt, additional thoughts from the teacher.

The next stage consists of action in some form, and the discussion and process of decision making is of central importance. One possibility is for the children to bring in certain items such as paper bags or egg boxes to be taken to local shops for re-use, or large empty tins to be turned into wastepaper bins by covering and decorating them.

Another is for each pupil to make a copy of the class chart, show it to their parents, and see what changes might make sense at home. They could make a conservation diary and talk in class from time to time about the changes that have been made. The children should also find out what local facilities there are for recycling: for example, bottle banks, wastepaper collections.

A third possibility is to investigate how the waste from the school could be re-used and recycled, and then implement changes.

DISCUSSION

Whichever course of action is decided on, it clearly needs to be accompanied by ample discussion on why re-using and recycling is important on a global as well as a local scale. Basic reasons include the approaching exhaustion of some raw materials, the pressure that wasteful use of them puts on the price for those who urgently need them, and pollution of the environment.

Using things again: our class chart

Waste	New uses
Food	Use for compost
Milk cartons and yogurt pots	Grow seeds, pot plants
Detergent bottles	Cut in half and invert to make paint containers
Plastic and paper bags	Take back to the shop for re-use
Large tin cans	Cover and paint to use as wastepaper bins
Stamps	Give to charity shops
Envelopes	Re-use with economy labels
Paper	Use for papier mâché modelling, insulation, polishing mirrors; roll up tightly and burn in grate
Egg boxes	Take back to the shop; use as painting trays; attach to walls as sound proofing; use for model making
Glass bottles and jars	Use for storing things, home-made jam; give to bottle bank
Clothes	Give to a jumble sale; use to make a sponsored patchwork quilt; use to stuff cushions

Figure 7.14

FOLLOW-UP

A recycling centre can be started, or one item (say, newspapers) can be selected which the class will regularly collect and pass on to an organisation such as Friends of the Earth.

The class can investigate how the local council disposes of waste, and ask them in what ways they are actively involved in recycling.

The headteacher can be invited to be interviewed by the class about this issue. Could the school change, for example, to using recycled paper?

The class can interview someone from Friends of the Earth about the World Conservation Strategy and world resources generally.

Making Changes
In the Making

For pupils to meet and talk to people who have deliberately changed their lifestyles as a result of involvement with a project based on co-operation and a particular vision of the future.

If it is possible to arrange a visit to a project, urban or rural, then it is important that the teacher knows exactly what to expect. This is best established by visiting the project oneself sometime beforehand. Project literature, if available, can then be obtained and used, or developed, as a resource for the class. Larger projects may be specifically geared to educational visits: for example, the Centre for Alternative Technology in Wales, or City Farms (see Figures 7.15 and 7.16). Others may need clarification from the teacher about their, and pupils', hopes and expectations.

Details of various co-operative projects can be found in magazines such as *Undercurrents* and *Peace News* or the community and alternative press.[8]

Figure 7.15

City Farms and Community Garden Projects in Great Britain
(March 1984)

North East
Bradford City Farm
City Farm Byker, Newcastle on Tyne
Idlethorpe City Farm, Bradford
Meanwood Valley Urban Farm, Leeds
Southwick Village Farm, Sunderland

North
Clayton City Farm, Manchester
Darnall Community Farm, Sheffield
Furness Improvement & Development Organisation, Halifax
Heeley City Farm, Sheffield
Reddish City Farm, Manchester

North West
Diggers Environmental Project, Liverpool
Rice Lane City Farm, Liverpool

Midlands
Bulwell Urban Farm, Nottingham
Coventry City Farm

Newparks Adventure Playground, Leicester
Stonebridge City Farm, Nottingham

West Midlands
Caldmore Urban Farm, Walsall
Hawbush City Farm, Brierley Hill
Hockley Port City Farm, Birmingham
Holy Trinity Farm, Birmingham
Paper Mill Farm, Redditch
Telford City Farm
Woodgate Valley Farm, Birmingham

South West
Bath City Farm
Hartcliffe Community Farm, Bristol
Millbrook City Farm, Southampton
St Werburghs City Farm, Bristol
Windmill Hill City Farm, Bristol

London
Adelaide Road Community Gardens
Culpeper Community Garden, Islington
Deen City Farm, Mitcham
Elm Farm, Battersea
Hackney City Farm

Holly Street Adventure Playground
Kentish Town City Farm
Markfield Project, Tottenham
Newham Allotments, Stratford
Oasis Community Garden, Wandsworth
People's Farm, Dalston
Sunnyside Gardens, Dalston
Tottenham Farm
Vauxhall City Farm

South East
Brent City Farm
Cambridge City Farm
Reading City Farm
Thameside Park, Dagenham
Wellgate Community Farm, Romford

Scotland
Balbirnie Community Farm, Glenrothes
Gorgie City Farm, Edinburgh
Inverclyde Project
Knowetop City Farm, Dumbarton
Lamont City Farm, Erskine
Possil City Farm, Glasgow

Wales
Cardiff City Farm
Quarry City Farm, Newport

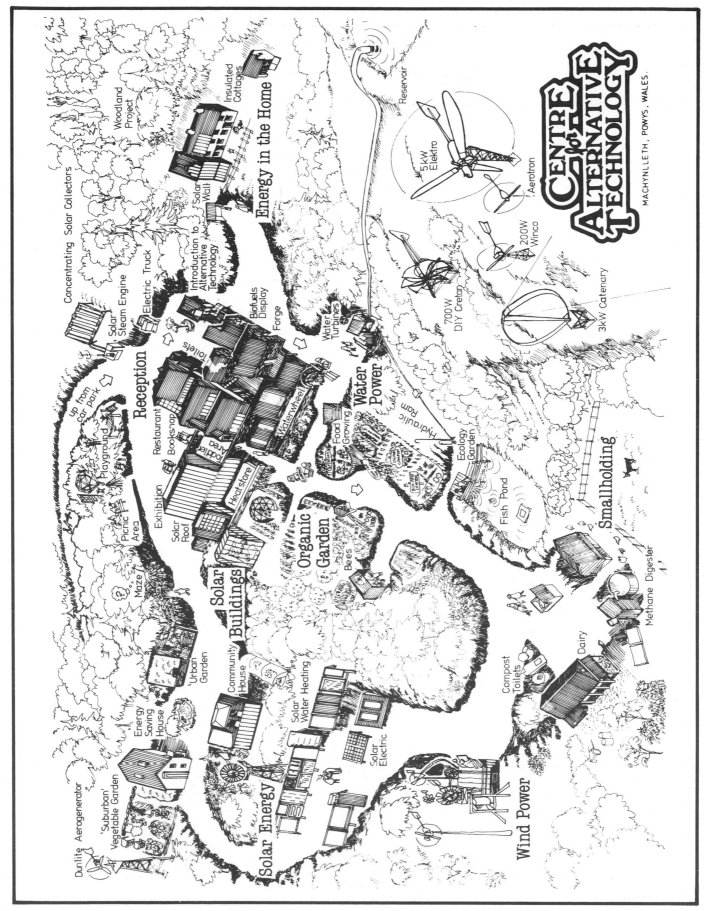

Figure 7.16

153

The following checklist will be useful in planning:

- What is there of real interest for pupils to see?
- What is there for pupils to handle?
- Are there any skills that pupils can learn?
- How can the adult vision be clearly interpreted for pupils?
- Who is best able to communicate this to pupils?
- What exactly will pupils do while they are there?
- What can pupils do later on returning to school?
- In what ways can pupils stay involved in the project?

PROCEDURE

This will vary depending on the particular project being studied. Some examples of projects are shown. They demonstrate that everyday life can be different. Both relationships and structures can be transformed. World studies must embody vision and give hope, showing how things can be changed.

Making Changes
Action for Change

PURPOSE

To enable pupils to plan and take a responsible part in action for change in their own locality, thus giving them some small experience of influencing the future.

PREPARATION

Various, depending on events and issues occurring in the local community and in the news. Certainly the teacher will need to obtain as much background information as possible, and in a variety of forms, for his or her own use and for the pupils.

PROCEDURE

Pupils carry out a survey of facilities in their local neighbourhood for the elderly or the disabled. Maps can be drawn, interviews carried out, requirements identified and proposals drawn up. Pupils' findings can then be used in a variety of ways. For example, once a lack of facilities for the disabled has been identified, both the local paper and the local council can be approached. The pupils' work can thus make a contribution towards positive change in the local community.

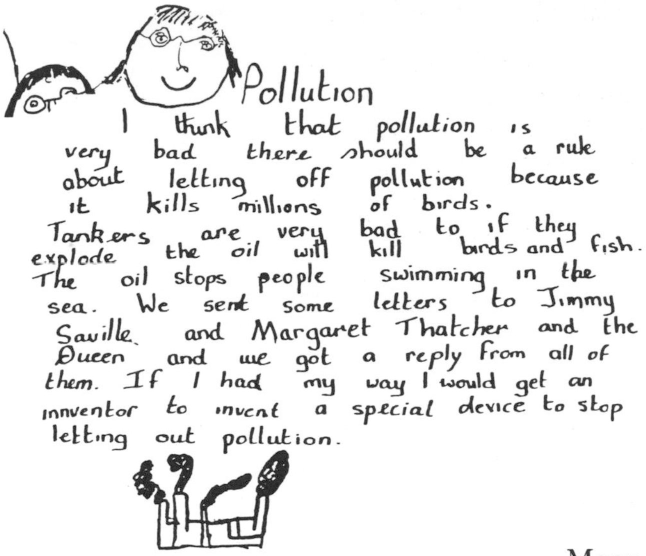

Pollution

I think that pollution is very bad there should be a rule about letting off pollution because it kills millions of birds. Tankers are very bad to if they explode the oil will kill birds and fish. The oil stops people swimming in the sea. We sent some letters to Jimmy Saville and Margaret Thatcher and the Queen and we got a reply from all of them. If I had my way I would get an innventor to invent a special device to stop letting out pollution.

Figure 7.17

If racial attacks or racial discrimination are a feature of the local community, then this is also something that pupils could monitor both by keeping a file of relevant articles from the local press and by interviewing those who have suffered. Discussion in school should arise from, or could lead to, an overall policy to counter racism. Teachers will find Chapter 6 in *Multicultural Education*, on 'Race in children's experience', useful here (see page 13).

Many events and issues that are of interest locally offer an opportunity for pupil involvement. Cues can be taken from local papers. There may be issues to do with factory closure, urban redevelopment, road schemes, use of waste ground, conservation, vandalism, traffic flow, and so on. What do local people think? Who is saying what? What particular interests do individuals and groups have? What information is missing that could be relatively easily obtained by the class? What part, if any, can the pupils play in the debate? Self-confidence, social and political skills, experience of democracy in action, all these can come from being involved in action for change.

Letters are a very useful and effective form of action. They can be written with effect to the local press, and to local councillors and organisations asking for some course of action to be considered. They are also one way in which pupils can begin to exercise influence on the world at large. Letters to the local Westminster or European MP, if written carefully and with evident thought, are likely to evoke a response, which will in turn maintain and stimulate the interest of the children.

One teacher here has started a Conservation Unit arising out of a topic on the changing environment of the school. The Unit is composed of kids who are getting up a petition to be presented personally to the chairman of governors who is also a councillor. They will show him alternative plans for one particular area which they have drawn up themselves. We must try and build the real world into what goes on here — to explore the possible areas of social and political involvement in a non-threatening way, as this class is doing.

155

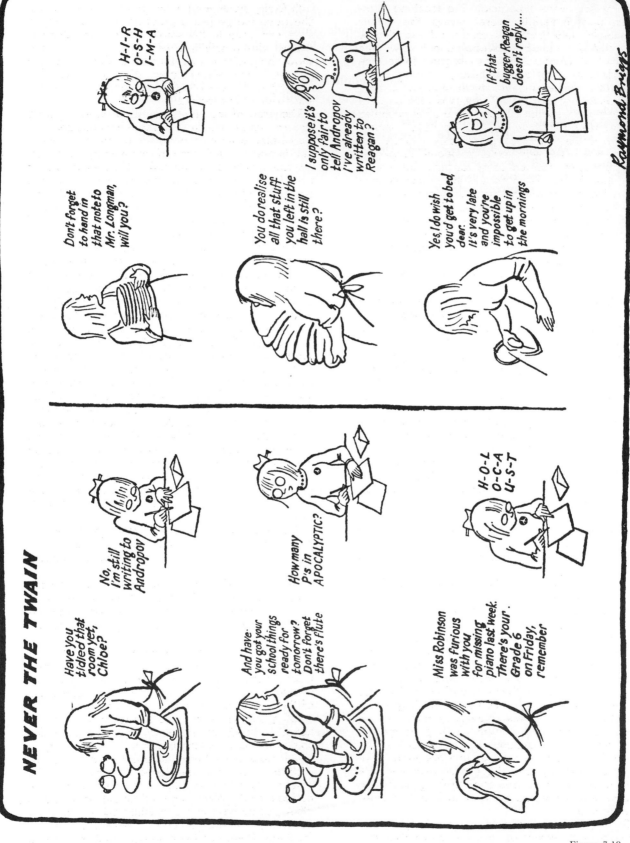

Figure 7.18

156

Making world studies come alive

My initial attempts to encourage co-operation, problem solving and to explain what interdependence meant, were superficial. The teaching strategies and materials were giving the pupils admittedly useful, but still second hand, experiences as is most often the case in schools and there was the danger that world studies was just going to become a variation on geography or history.

World studies for me implies an important change in position and attitudes. There is a real physical distance gap between ourselves and other countries which makes it difficult even for adults to comprehend world events. One pupil aptly summed the situation up in this way. 'When someone I know gets hurt I get upset and feel sorry for them, but when I hear that thousands of people in another country are dying of starvation I just say that's a shame, because I don't know those people.'

Then, quite by chance, the class saw a television programme about the deforestation of the Amazon, which caught their imagination and started a very lively class discussion.

'If they keep cutting down the trees we won't have any oxygen.'

'If they don't cut down the trees there won't be anywhere for the people to grow their food.'

'There won't be any animals and the world would be horrible without plants and trees.'

The solutions which the children offered were both sensitive and imaginative. It became clear that they wanted to do something practical which they felt would help towards solving the problem. Someone suggested planting our own forest and stocking it with wild animals, along the lines of a big game park. This suggestion was modified and the class decided that it would be a good idea to build some form of nature reserve. I posed several questions which made them check their initial headlong enthusiasm and involved them in the practical necessities of planning.

'Where is the nature reserve going to be?'

'Is the site you have chosen suitable for a nature reserve?'

'Who must you ask permission from before you can start?'

'If you don't know whether the site is suitable or not, who do you ask?'

'What equipment will you need?'

'What plans have you for the site?'

Choosing the site provided a very useful range of experiences. I deliberately set out as the devil's advocate: every time a site was proposed I pointed out all the difficulties. The children became quite annoyed but, gradually, they started looking for sites which overcame my objections, until finally the corner of the playing field well away from most of the school activities was chosen. Getting permission was simpler. Throughout, the headmistress has given the project full support and has made sure that the necessary funds have been available. We have also had the co-operation of the ground-staff and neighbours whose gardens back on to the nature reserve.

To keep the enthusiasm alive, we quickly planted some trees. It became apparent to the children that we needed a variety of tools, equipment, plants and expertise. Although we could have bought the necessary equipment and struggled by, learning as we went, I wanted the children to experience the problems of seeking resources when supplies are short.

Then I was very fortunate in meeting a worker on a local conservation project who was able to help with tools, plants, and many practical suggestions. She gave the project a great boost by showing a slide sequence to the whole school, and demonstrated what possibilities were open to us. After the show, the pupils in my class each designed a nature reserve in the selected area. We held a planning meeting and eventually the best features of the designs were incorporated.

The area of the reserve is about three hundred square metres. Within this area it was decided that we wanted a wide range of shrubs and trees, three ponds and a marsh area, a tree nursery, and various features which would make suitable habitats for a variety of plants and creatures. By foraging and approaching builder's merchants, timber yards and the Forestry Commission, we were able to obtain most of the materials we needed for the construction of ponds, steps and fences.

There were two problems which needed consideration. The first was labour for the heavier work, the second was the perennial problem of vandalism in the after school hours. A teacher at the local secondary comprehensive school had already agreed to send some sixth form pupils from his photography course to make a continuous record of progress. It seemed a useful exercise to ask him if he could also supply some labour, particularly if those concerned were liable to be those who might also be responsible for some of the vandalism. He was very willing for some of his fifth form boys to become involved. These boys have proved a great help. The work could hardly have been done without them. A very good relationship has been built up between the older pupils and my class. They have all worked on the project co-operatively and have developed considerable pride in the work they have done. It has been very gratifying to see the older pupils take charge and direct the efforts of the younger children.

'Come on, young 'uns, take these posts over to that corner. I'll bring the hammer and wire.'

'You kids tip this earth on the pile once the buckets are full.'

This relationship had never been established between the two schools before. It seems now to be gathering momentum. Recently my class wrote inviting the pupils from the secondary school to our Christmas play.

The nature reserve is a continually growing project. At present, alongside the three ponds and marsh area, there are more than fifty trees growing, and soon a beech hedge is to be planted along two of the sides. For the future, it is proposed that a weather station be built and bird tables and nesting boxes installed, with pupils taking responsibility for some parts and making use of the whole facility.

My class have benefited greatly from this approach. They have developed an interest in the natural world and through this, I believe, a more caring attitude. When I now talk about the problems other people have in organisation and in obtaining necessary materials, it certainly has more meaning for them. There has been no overnight conversion, no sudden illumination. What has happened is that there has been a slight change of attitude, which has given a concrete and meaningful starting point from which to encourage a realistic study of the world and its peoples.

Steve Barnes, a teacher in Bristol

Starting Points

> ## Thinking globally, acting locally
>
> One cannot live in the world; that is one cannot become, in the easy, generalising sense with which the phrase is commonly used, a 'world citizen'. There can be no such thing as a 'global village'. No matter how much one may love the world as a whole, one can live fully in it only by living responsibly in some small part of it. Where we live and who we live there with define the terms of our relationship to the world and to humanity.
>
> Wendell Berry, *The Unsettling of America*, Sierra Club Books, 1977. Copyright © 1977 by Wendell Berry

● Marooned

Pupils imagine that they have been marooned on a desert island for the last twenty-five years and have just been rescued. How might they respond when confronted with civilisation in the 1980s?

● Daily Life

Pupils describe how they envisage, and how they would like, the following to be in twenty-five to fifty years time: families, homes, transport, jobs, entertainment, food.

● Newspaper

Pupils make a *Future Times* newspaper. It should cover local and global news. They agree on a date wtenty or more years in the future. They write reports describing what is happening in the world at that time.

● Technology 1

Children are asked to imagine that the supply of electricity in our society has suddenly and indefinitely been cut off. They list all the things they would no longer be able to use and discuss how they would live.

● Technology 2

Children consider various technological developments (for example, cars, drugs, *Concorde*, television, nuclear power, etc.) and the problems which these have been designed to solve. They then look at the problems which these developments have in turn created. They weigh up the various pros and cons, remembering that preferable futures may involve rejection of some of today's trends.

● Time Machine 1

Pupils role-play a time traveller who has arrived in their town from the future. What might her feelings be and how might she try to explain where she has come from?

● Time Machine 2

Pupils design a time machine and decide where they would like to go to in the future and to what moment in time. They describe what they find. What would they take with them to show to people as typical of life in the 1980s?

● Extra-Sensory Perception

Pupils imagine a future in which they have developed powers of extra-sensory perception such as telepathy. What might be some of the advantages of this? They discuss and write about the most positive way of using such powers.

● National Park

Pupils find out about the nearest National Park to their school. What problems does it face and what plans are there for its future? They look, for example, at numbers of visitors, amount of traffic, pollution, damage to the countryside.

Predictions

Pupils keep a class scrapbook of predictions made about the future in newspapers, comics, books. On the opposite page could be class comments about the predictions.

Endangered Species

Pupils find out about an endangered species such as whales. In what ways do humans threaten animals? Pupils can also find out about threats to animals in this country: for example, experiments on animals, factory farming. Why are some people vegetarian? Should there be rights for animals as well as people?

Basic Needs 1

Pupils imagine they are planning a long journey in a spaceship. They make a list of everything they would like to take with them under two headings: 'Things we need to survive' and 'Things it would be nice to have'. They compare their list with that of a friend and draw up a single list with the same two headings. A class list can also be made.

The idea of the earth as a spaceship can then be introduced. What sort of life support system does it have? It it possible for everyone in the world to have all the items of the list? If not, who should have what? (Some of the suggestions in A New Society (pages 147–8) are relevant here.)

Basic Needs 2

Pupils draw a picture of themselves in their favourite room at home, with all their favourite belongings around them. If there was a sudden flood and they could save only three things, which would they choose? Would they mind doing without the rest? What do they think of as luxuries, and what as necessities for a happy life? They can finish the exercise by crossing out all the items they have decided not to save. Or, alternatively, all the items can be cut out and two class collages made, one consisting of the things saved, and the other consisting of items abandoned to the 'flood'.

Pollution

Pupils investigate a local example of pollution. This might be of a river, the air or the land, or to do with noise. They take photographs and interview local people about their feelings. They draw a timeline (see page 135) to show how and when the problem began and put on it several ways (good and bad) in which it might be resolved. Pupils write to the local newspaper with their suggestions for improving the situation.

Selected Resources

T: for the use of teachers
P: for the use of pupils

Changing the World

Christopher, John, *White Mountains*, trilogy, Hamlyn, 1976. (P) Set in the future, a future where the docility of all humans is ensured by 'capping'. Inevitably, a small resistance group is formed; the choices are clearly expressed in an exciting narrative for ten year olds and over.

Diagram Group, *Earthship*, Longman, 1980. (P) The situation on Earth is seen here from a positively Galactic perspective! Attractive and informative on such topics as geology, civilisations, conservation, energy and space.

Gatland, Kenneth and Jefferis, David, *The World of The Future*, Usborne, 1976. (P) A compendium of *Robots*, *Future Cities* and *Star Travel*: a sci-fi glossy that may stimulate students to consider the implications of technology on *their* adult lives. It may be worth pointing out that this book still projects a world controlled by white men.

Gibson, T., *Education for Neighbourhood Change*, School of Education, University of Nottingham, 1980. (T) A pack which explores priorities for planning in the local neighbourhood.

Gribbin, J., *Future Worlds*, Abacus, 1979. (T) An interesting and readable overview of recent thinking about alternative futures involving a range of forecasts and scenarios.

Leguin, Ursula, *Wizard of Earthsea*, Penguin, 1977. (P) Science-fiction trilogy set in the imaginary world of Earthsea, where an arrogant young wizard battles with an evil power.

Lester, Julius, *Long Journey Home*, Penguin, 1977. (P) Short stories about the black people in America who put an end to slavery, which can be used in class, or read by age eleven and over.

MacShane, Denis, *Using the Media: How to Deal With The Press, Television and Radio*, Pluto, 1979. (T) A handbook aimed simply at informing individuals and groups who have a case to put over, how to do so most effectively through the media.

Norton, Michael, *Planning Your Environment: A School and Community Kit*, 1976, available from Community Service Volunteers, 237 Pentonville Road, N1. (T) Aimed at providing schools with information about the local environment, how it works and who controls it, and how things can be changed. Lively project suggestions.

Summers, Stamford, *Wacky and His Fuddlejig*, 1981 available from New York Arts in Context, 484 West 43rd Street, 24.0 New York City, NY 10036, USA. (P) The toy that Santa delivers to the child who's got everything becomes the rage for the following year, so Wacky's set up with a home industry!

Youth Environmental Action, *Up Your Street*, available from 173 Archway Road, London, N6. (T) Group and individual action for young people on conservation: nature, trees, food, energy, recycling, transport, pollution.

Saving the World: Ecology

Conservation series, Ladybird. (P) *Disappearing Mammals*, by John Leigh-Pemberton, 1973, describes some of the species threatened, and the causes. *Energy* by Nigel Dudley, 1981. Energy sources simply explained and some of the future problems considered.

Croall, Stephen and Rankin, William, *Ecology for Beginners*, Writers & Readers, 1981. (T) Comic book treatment of humanity's destruction of our planet and the inequalities in the world, that extend even to erosion.

Friends of the Earth, *What on Earth are We Doing at Home?* Birmingham, 1979. (T) Explains how ordinary life at home affects the environment and suggests ways in which harmful effects can be minimised. Covers food, clothes, aerosols, paper, etc.

Keen, D. H. and Simmonds, G. E., *What on Earth are We Doing?* Ladybird, 1976. (P) The familiar Ladybird format flits through significant issues: noise and other pollution are better dealt with than hunger which is still related to the population explosion.

Richardson, Robin, *Caring For The Planet*, Nelson, 1977. (T/P) Sets out to educate children about the actions of governments and individuals in relation to conservation, energy, ecology.

Watson, James, *Talking in Whispers*, Gollancz, 1983. (P) An Amnesty International perspective is brought to this political thriller based on fact. Set in Chile in the near future, it is a story about oppression and the courage of the three young people who stand up against it. For age twelve and over.

Saving the World: Peace or War?

Benson, B., *The Peace Book*, Jonathan Cape, 1980. (T/P) A small boy visits the presidents of the world's superpowers and persuades them to disarm. Visual and very engaging.

Briggs, R., *When the Wind Blows*, Penguin, 1982. (P) This is not a pleasant book – but, having read it, teaching peace studies may take on a new meaning. It's a comic book account of a retired couple who survive the nuclear bomb in their fall-out shelter, but, confused by memories of the second world war, soon emerge onto the destroyed surface. While their dialogue remains deliberately banal and unaware, the pictures portray their deterioration.

Children of Hiroshima, Children of Hiroshima Publishing Committee, 1981. (P) An anthology of translated essays of these children, written six years after the bomb dropped.

Coerr, Eleanor, *Sadaka and the One Thousand Paper Cranes*, Hodder, 1983. (P) Aged two when the bomb dropped on Hiroshima, Sadaka is an athlete until, at ten, leukemia strikes. A touching novel.

Kidron, Michael and Smith, Dan, *The War Atlas: Armed Conflict, Armed Peace*, Pan, 1983. (T) Vivid, attractive pictures and language, showing who benefits from arms and arms dealing – and that it is we, the individual people, who have everything to lose.

Maruki, Toshi, *The Hiroshima Story*, A. & C. Black, 1983. (P) Told through the experience of a little girl who was seven at the time. Though the language is simple enough for nine year olds and over, the reality is brought powerfully home. The final message is that 'our suffering was no accident. Without your will to prevent it, it could happen again.'

Noble, Dave, *The War and Peace Book*, Writers & Readers, 1977. (T/P) 'It is quite untrue that if one wishes for peace, one should prepare for war, but if one wishes for peace, one should understand war.' Good information, much of it pictorial, on the arms race and outcomes.

Nottingham Education Committee, *Report on the Development of a Curriculum for Peace Education*, Nottinghamshire County Council, County Hall, Nottingham. (T) Practical suggestions and strategies for teachers.

Peace Pack, available from New Internationalist, Freepost, Oxford OXI 2BR. (T) Includes posters, a 'finger on the button' game, wallchart of nuclear states, booklets of facts and argument, captioned photographs for an exhibition.

United Nations Association of Great Britain and Northern Ireland: *Peaceworking; A Campaigning Handbook*, 1982, available from 3 Whitehall Court, London SWIA 2EL. (T/P) Practical details of how groups can organise and campaign for change.

PART THREE

In-service
Ideas

8. Teachers Together

The Whole School

In Part 2 of this book ideas have been presented which show how world studies can relate to daily classroom work. A world dimension in pupil learning can be achieved by a gentle broadening of the curriculum to include the sorts of ideas and issues referred to in earlier chapters.

This final part of the book is concerned with a consideration of how as teachers we can work towards a more world-focussed curriculum in our schools. It is important to emphasise again that world studies is also concerned with the way that children learn. The classroom activities described present learning as an active and dynamic process characterised by a high degree of pupil activity and interaction. Such an approach to teaching and learning should be part of the repertoire of methods whatever the curriculum area. This chapter will offer strategies for bringing world studies into the curriculum decision making of schools and suggest in-service ideas designed to help teachers develop their own skills and qualities.

It is important to remember that innovation in schools is a complex and sometimes painful process. Success depends very much on a high degree of organisational awareness among staff and a climate of relationships which facilitates professional discussion of curriculum and teaching styles.[1] In primary schools scale post holders are all concerned to represent their own particular areas of responsibility and, because so little time is available for the staff to meet together, curriculum development has to be selective, with a major innovation taking up to a year to plan and anything up to four years to implement fully. In secondary schools, with subject departments, cross-curriculum developments are problematic and innovation may need to focus within a department or seek to develop alongside new thrusts in tutorial work or personal and social education.

Planning Workshops and Courses

In the whole process of change towards a more world-orientated school, carefully planned meetings and discussion are crucial as a means of introducing new ideas and exploring their implications. Such discussion needs to take place not only through day-to-day conversation but also in specifically planned workshops and courses for staff.

The Schools Council/Rowntree project *World Studies 8–13* developed a model for such in-service meetings which puts a high priority on co-operation and practical involvement and makes extensive use of small-group work. The model suggests that an in-service meeting or course should have four main stages, as shown in Figure 8.1.

Climate	Enquiry	Debate	Action
•Affirming	•Experiencing	•Arguing	•Planning
•Trusting	•Studying	•Evaluating	•Resourcing
•Questioning	•Experimenting	•Agreeing	•Teaching

Figure 8.1 The life cycle of a course

Climate

Initially an appropriate climate needs to be established, namely one which involves giving security and support to participants yet also challenges them. For this to happen it is important that, at the start of a course, teachers:

- get to know and develop some confidence in each other;
- recognise the value of their own and others' skills, experience and uncertainties;
- get an overall idea of the world studies field;
- realise that world studies is controversial;
- know that they themselves will be able to contribute later to the course.

It is important to note that an introductory lecture does not help in setting such a climate. While it may be useful later to give an idea of the world studies field as a whole, its effect at the start of a meeting is to devalue the knowledge and experience which participants bring, and prevent them from meeting each other in anything other than a superficial way.

Activities such as the following can be used to achieve the above ends:

Participants are asked to find a partner. For four minutes one person listens to the other talking, *uninterrupted*, about 'Who I am and what I'm hoping for from this course.' Then the process is reversed. Notes may be made if this is helpful.

Then, in a small group of four or six, each person introduces their partner to the others. While this is happening one person lists the various hopes and expectations of the group on a large sheet of paper. This is put up on the wall as a focus for reflection during the session and for the remainder of the course.

After this, one can use a discussion activity such as the one on page 165–7. A further activity, which enables questions to be raised, is Staffroom Comments on pages 168–9, or alternatively this activity can be used later, in the debate stage.

Enquiry

The second phase is enquiry. Here participants look in detail at certain aspects of world studies, through case studies of school practice presented by teachers, and take part in some selected classroom activities. Both approaches should lead to discussion on implications for the participants' own school situation.

The simplest approach here is to use classroom activities drawn from Part 2 of this book. Some particularly useful ones are: The World in our Newspapers (pages 49–53); Co-operative Shapes (pages 74–6); Using Photographs (pages 104–6); Arming the World (pages 142–3); My Future (pages 135–6); Interviewing People (pages 48–9).

Participating in these activities prompts discussion and an interest in trying them out in school, a process which is enhanced by the fact that this has been a shared experience. It can also lead to a closer study of what one is trying to achieve in world studies in the school as a whole. The teachers'

activities Objectives Across the Curriculum and Using Concepts (pages 169–73) can be helpful here.

Ideas and arguments such as those put forward in Part 1 of this book need at this point to be drawn in and made explicit. While, in the first stage of a course, theory is certainly referred to and acknowledged, towards the end of the second stage it needs to be explicitly examined so that practice is set in, and arises out of, a clear pedagogical framework.

Debate

The third stage, debate, is crucial for exploring some of the issues surrounding world studies. The extent to which this occurs will depend on the participants themselves and their willingness to voice strong feelings and views as they reflect on the course so far. These issues may include those to do with bias and indoctrination (Is there such a thing as a balanced view? Should all perspectives be given equal emphasis?), political education (Is world studies inevitably political? What difference does a teacher's political standpoint make?), race (Should we teach about racism if there does not appear to be evidence of it among our pupils? Should we adopt an anti-racist stance in school?) and problems of learning itself (How can children be helped to cope with ideas such as conflict and interdependence? Should world studies be a separate topic or course rather than, or as well as, being built into existing schemes of work as a dimension?) Two useful ways of raising issues such as these, in addition to the activity Staffroom Comment, are to interview a teacher with substantial experience of world studies and also to review resources in the manner suggested on page 176.

To give participants a clear sense of direction it is important that such questioning and exploration of issues be drawn together and some general principles established. These can be embodied in a joint statement or declaration, but they can also be expressed visually or through drama. A useful activity for this process is Working Towards Consensus, on page 173.

Action

In the fourth stage, action, plans need to be laid for future work in school. Whether or not the teachers are from the same school, it is a good idea if they can co-operate in this process and also meet from time to time after the course to review progress. If they know this in advance, it is likely to engender a sense of mutual accountability and ensure that the plans are realistic. Practical Next Steps, on page 174, suggests two ways in which participants can draw up individual proposals for the future.

With the planning of further meetings comes the possibility that the linear stages in Figure 8.1 should perhaps be seen more as a spiral, a process which is continually repeated as teachers deepen and extend their understanding of, and involvement in, world studies.[2]

A possible programme for a day course is shown in Figure 8.2. Its constituent parts could also provide a programme for a school working party. The rest of this chapter contains detailed suggestions for organising in-service meetings and finishes with a case study of how one school began to develop a world studies curriculum.

Programme

Time	Activity	Group
9.30	**Welcome:** and introduction to the day	*LEA Adviser*
9.40	**Introductions:** to each other (see page 162)	*Small groups*
10.00	**What and why?:** a look at some methods and objectives (see page 165). (i) Selecting and ranking brief descriptions of some typical world studies activities (ii) Looking at some of these activities in the context of world studies objectives	*Small groups*
11.00	Coffee	
11.15	**Classroom activities:** involvement in and discussion of two activities	*Small groups*
12.30	**Viewpoints:** reflection and discussion in one group on the use of these and other classroom activities	*Whole group*
1.00	Lunch	
2.00	**The whole school:** exploring the implications of world studies for the curriculum and organisation of the school (see page 169)	*Small groups*
2.45	**Doubts and queries:** discussion of some of the issues raised by world studies (see page 168)	*Small groups*
3.15	Tea	
3.30	**Resources:** reviewing and evaluating materials (see page 176)	*Small groups*
4.00	**Looking forward:** considering and planning and next steps (see page 174)	*Whole group*
4.30	Finish	

Figure 8.2 A possible programme for an initial day course

Some In-Service Approaches
Methods and Objectives

PURPOSE ⟩ To relate some typical classroom activities in world studies to appropriate objectives.

PREPARATION ⟩ The classroom activities listed in Figure 8.3 need to be reproduced so that there is a set of fifteen slips of paper for every two participants. They are best stored in individual envelopes, each set of slips held by a paper clip. The objectives chart set out in Figure 8.4 also needs to be available in the same numbers, together with the set of objectives, listed on page 25.

PROCEDURE ⟩ **1.** People sit in groups of six and work initially in pairs. They are asked to sort the slips of paper into three piles: (*a*) those activities they would *like* to try as soon as possible; (*b*) those they *might* be willing to try and (*c*) those they would *not* wish to try. Each pile should be in order of preference. New ideas should be written on spare slips of paper and included. After 10–15 minutes each pair registers their choice on a master chart displayed on the wall. Each pair then explains their responses to their small group. If time permits, a plenary discussion can follow on the choices of the group as a whole and on the criteria for making such choices.

2. There are many reasons for choosing certain activities rather than others: for example, time, energy, pupils, resources available. The key question is: What are the main elements of a world dimension which should figure in the curriculum for my pupils? Participants are referred to the suggested set of objectives on page 25 of this book. They receive copies of the objectives form (Figure 8.4) and it is pointed out that each of the listed objectives headings is elaborated further in the book. They are asked, in the same pairs as before, to place the three activities they would most like to try in the spaces marked on the form. They should then go down the list putting a tick if they feel a particular objective would be fully achieved, a question mark if it would be partially achieved and a cross if it is not relevant to the activity. If they disagree with any objectives, these should be amended as desired. New objectives can of course be written in. There is also space on the form for any additional written comments.

After 15 or 20 minutes the whole group can exchange views on the objectives – which additions have people made, which have been crossed out? – and on possible ways in which they can be used as a practical aid to planning and teaching.

Some classroom activities

The World in Our Town
Pupils study their local area, including shops, firms, and current issues and events. They also look at how things have changed in the past. They then make a town trail which draws out the links with other countries.

Global Cake
Pupils take part in a simulation exercise to do with food and trade. In groups they represent the main continents or countries and have a chance to experience the frustrations of 'underdevelopment' and the meaning of interdependence.

Solving Conflicts
Pupils focus on a real or imaginary problem, perhaps between members of the class. They listen to various points of view, list as many solutions as they can, discuss the various possibilities and finally select one which they feel is best.

Images
Pupils in pairs select three photographs which they think are typical of a particular country. They describe these to another pair, negotiate a joint selection and discuss these with the whole class.

School Exchange
Pupils in a rural school and pupils in an inner city school visit each other regularly, each providing a welcome and some entertainment when playing host.

Our Town in A.D. 2010
Pupils create models, pictures, written descriptions of what their local area will be like in the year 2010. They discuss differences between what they would like to happen and what they think will happen among themselves and with a local planning officer.

Studying Conflicts
Pupils observe younger children over a period of time and note down the causes of any conflicts, how they are resolved and their consequences. The pupils then discuss these in class, searching for similarities, and look for parallels with conflicts in the wider world.

Presenting an Issue
Groups of pupils collect all news items referring to a chosen issue over a period – for example, the arms race, world development, human rights – and make a scrapbook. They then make a display for the school, do a simulated TV report or prepare a quiz for other groups.

Time-machine
Pupils design a time-machine and decide when and where to go. Which typical artefacts do they take with them to illustrate life in the 1980s? They describe their journeys.

Questions
Pupils compile a book of questions about the future. They discuss and research possible answers.

Co-operative Games
Pupils take part in a series of carefully planned activities designed to develop their ability to work effectively together on common tasks.

Radio News
Pupils listen to the news on Radio 1 or 2 each morning, discuss one item and mark on a world map the places concerned.

Ranking Newscuttings
Pupils rank a set of nine newspapers cuttings in response to these instructions: 'You are writing a letter to a penfriend in a distant country. Which of these will you enclose to show the world as seen in your country?'

A Filmstrip Bulletin
Pupils in small groups choose twelve from a collection of twenty copies of photographs of a local or school event. They arrange these in a sequence and write a soundtrack from different points of view to accompany them. Each group then presents a brief 'filmstrip' to the class.

Before and After
Pupils write, draw and say all they know about a country or culture before a topic or course begins. They do so again at the end, and compare the two pieces of work.

Figure 8.3

Activities

Objectives

1 Ourselves and others

2 Rich and poor

3 Peace and conflict

4 Our environment

5 The world tomorrow

6 Human dignity

7 Curiosity

8 Appreciation of other cultures

9 Empathy

10 Justice and fairness

11 Enquiry

12 Communication skills

13 Grasping concepts

14 Critical thinking

15 Political skills

Figure 8.4 Objectives and activities

167

Staffroom Comment

PURPOSE

To enable some possible staffroom reactions to world studies to be aired and responses considered, and for the teachers' own doubts to be discussed.

PREPARATION

A set of nine comments such as those shown in Figure 8.5 needs to be available on separate slips of paper, for every two participants.

Overheard

Old-fashioned geography
We have just got used to the idea of using the local environment and now they want us to go back to old-fashioned geography? What has happened to children learning from first-hand experience?

Race
There is no racism in this school. A lot of teaching about race and culture is at best irrelevant and at worst could actually create the problems it is supposed to resolve.

Resources
The trouble is there aren't any decent resources.

Our country first
I can see it might be important to do projects about other countries in multicultural schools but my class are all British and they should learn about their own country first.

Political issues
Once you start bringing political issues into education there's no knowing where it will stop.

Explaining complex problems
It's all very well relating classroom work to what children see on television but how do you explain complex political problems or terrorism to young children? They love violence anyway.

Why worry children
Why worry children about world problems at this stage? They will have time enough later to come to terms with those.

Secondary level
The primary curriculum is crowded enough without adding to it subjects which are best left to secondary level.

Commitment
If you teach about world issues in the typically 'balanced' liberal way you are in effect reinforcing the unjust status quo. World studies teachers need to be committed to radical change, in the classroom and outside.

Figure 8.5

PROCEDURE

Participants work in pairs with between six and twelve 'overheard' comments on separate slips of paper. They have to rank them (see page 90) in the order in which such comments are most commonly heard and need answering.

VARIATION

Alternatively the slips can be sorted into three piles as in the previous activity, Methods and Objectives. In this case the criteria would be (*a*) very important; (*b*) fairly important; (*c*) not important. As each pair finishes, a note can be made of their first three choices and this information transferred to a master chart. Pairs then come together in small groups to show and explain their choices to each other.

FOLLOW-UP

There can be a discussion of the practical questions which the anecdotes raise: If you were in the staffroom when that comment was made, what would you do or say?

The group can phrase three questions arising from discussion of the comments, which people hope will be answered or clarified in this meeting or later.

Objectives across the Curriculum

PURPOSE

To look at the practical implications for the curriculum of world studies objectives (see Chapter 3).

PREPARATION

Copies of Figure 8.6 or 8.7 are needed for each participant, together with the description of the world studies objectives on page 25.

PROCEDURE

Participants are asked to fill in all or part of the matrix indicating which objective is relevant to which area of the curriculum or school organisation, using the following code:

3   *definitely* relevant
2   *probably* relevant
1   *possibly* relevant

Note. It is best to focus on a few objectives, or areas of the curriculum, at any one time.

Ideally this activity should be done before a planning meeting so that a summary of the completed charts can be produced. Alternatively ratings can be assessed rapidly on the spot. Either way the outcome needs to be considered, differences aired and suggestions discussed. Once it has become clear which objectives are considered most relevant it is important to focus on the practical implications. This is best done in small groups, perhaps based on age ranges or subject specialisms. The proposals put forward by these groups can then be considered by the staff as a whole.

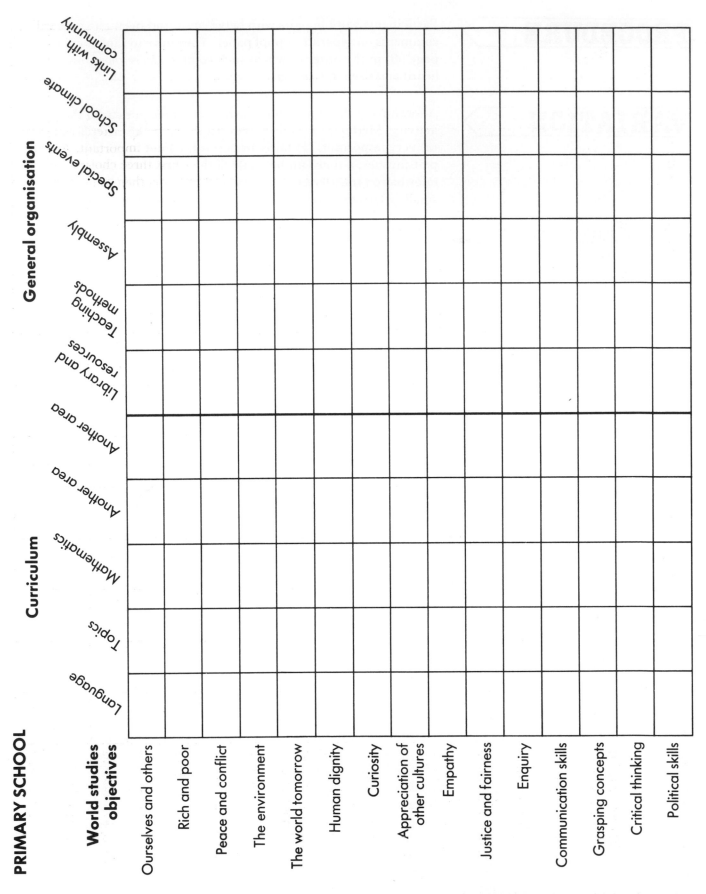

Figure 8.6 World studies objectives and the primary school

SECONDARY SCHOOL

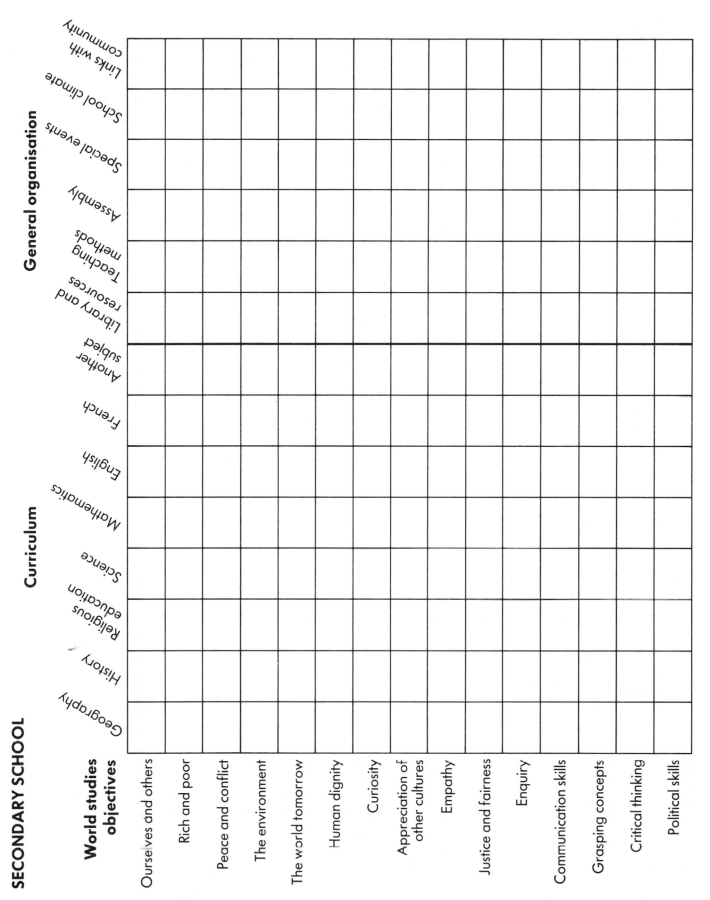

Figure 8.7 World studies objectives and the secondary school

Using Concepts

PURPOSE
To look at some key concepts in world studies and their place in the broader curriculum. The session involves exploring the use of concepts and discussing practical examples.

PREPARATION
Course members are asked in advance to read through and reflect on the concepts set out on page 30. Each pair of participants needs a large sheet of paper and a set of ten slips of paper, on each of which is written one of the ten concepts.

PROCEDURE
Participants work in pairs. The task is to arrange the slips of paper in an agreed pattern or flow chart that draws out connections and interrelationships in accordance with their own particular ideas and priorities. The slips are laid on a large sheet of paper and then stuck down. Participants should add arrows, boxes and pictures to explain their chart. They may also discard, rephrase or add to the concepts.

When each pair has finished, they come together in groups of six to eight, and explain their charts to each other. The exercise may finish at this point or it can continue in two possible ways.

Participants can look at a course or topic currently being taught by one or more teachers and at some of the books and materials being used on it. Does it embody any of these concepts? If so, are pupils likely to begin to understand some of these concepts as a result of it?

Each participant can work with a partner concerned with a similar age range. They choose two concepts whose practical implications they would like to explore further. Then they take a topic which they would like to plan, and write down all the teaching ideas and content which could illustrate the two chosen concepts.

FOLLOW-UP
The chart on page 173 can be used to match the teaching activities in this book to particular concepts.

A further stage is to explore the importance of the world studies key concepts across the whole curriculum with a view, perhaps, to establishing an agreed policy. In many schools the possibilities can be assessed by using a chart such as that shown in Figure 8.8. Teachers are asked to list the topic or course they are planning to teach next and indicate with a tick the major concepts which they will be focussing on. They continue to fill this in over the year and to try to ensure equal emphasis on all the major concepts.

An alternative to this essentially topic-based or course-based approach is a more explicitly concept-based framework. Here two or three of the likely ten concepts are agreed as the foundation of work

World studies key concepts

Topic or course	Causes and consequences	Communication	Conflict	Co-operation	Distribution of power	Fairness	Interdependence	Similarities and differences	Social change	Values and beliefs

Figure 8.8 World studies key concepts

in any one class or year, with the aim of covering a set of key concepts over a year, or a pupil's school career. Such a framework, while it may seem initially somewhat abstract, does give individual teachers a good deal of freedom over the content of lessons.

Working Towards Consensus

PURPOSE To enable participants to think about the underlying principles of world studies and to draw up an agreed statement about them.

PREPARATION Each participant needs four blank cards or slips of paper.

PROCEDURE Each person, in a small group, is given four cards or slips of paper. On each of them they write a sentence, the beginning of which is the same for everyone. Examples of opening phrases are:

- When planning a course or topic relevant to world studies we should . . .
- When drawing up a school policy for world studies we should . . .
- If world studies is to take root in schools we should . . .

The cards for each group are then collected in by one member, shuffled and dealt out again, three to each person, with the remainder placed face up on the table. Next, each person looks at their cards and discards, face up on the table, any which (*a*) they have themselves written, or (*b*) they do not fully agree with. They also pick up any cards which they feel in agreement with, provided they did not write these themselves. This process continues until everyone has three or four cards which represent the best set they can find.

Then in twos and threes people show their cards to each other and draft a composite text. Finally the small group draws up an overall agreed statement for presentation to the whole meeting.

VARIATION

Instead of drawing up composite statements participants can be asked, in their groups, to arrange the cards on a large sheet of paper in a suitably annotated flow chart or any pattern they wish.

Practical Next Steps

PURPOSE

To enable teachers to explain and discuss their plans relating to world studies once the course has finished, and to consider ways of keeping in touch and supporting each other.

PREPARATION

Forms for making detailed planning notes may need to be available for each course member (see Figure 8.9). Teachers should already have give some thought to their own future plans relating to world studies.

PROCEDURE

Whatever form world studies will take in a particular school – as a dimension added to existing schemes of work or a distinct subject, course or topic – its introduction requires detailed planning and support.
1. Participants form small groups according to their future plans. Course members take it in turn to describe their plans, or simply, at this stage, their hopes. At its broadest this discussion can be about: How will my teaching or my school be different as a result of this in-service course?

174

<table>
<tr><td colspan="2">**_Practical next steps_**</td></tr>
<tr><td>_Title_</td></tr>
<tr><td>_Class_</td></tr>
<tr><td>_Time available_</td></tr>
<tr><td>_Particular objectives_</td></tr>
<tr><td>_Concepts to develop_</td></tr>
<tr><td>_Content_</td></tr>
<tr><td>_Methods_</td></tr>
<tr><td>_Resources available_</td></tr>
<tr><td>_Resources needed_</td></tr>
<tr><td>_Other ideas & requirements_</td></tr>
</table>

Figure 8.9

2. Participants make notes individually about their plans. This is both for their own use and for the co-ordinator or course leader, who may wish, by agreement, to take copies of these notes and circulate them to the whole group as an important step in sharing future plans.

3. The session can end with teachers making arrangements for future meetings of their group. If the course is to achieve its full potential it is important that the teachers continue to meet periodically – perhaps monthly, or every half-term – to exchange experiences, discuss successes and failures and offer support to each other. It is also important that this commitment has a definite end-point, perhaps two terms on from the end of the initial course. An alternative and more open-ended way of considering the future is to use a chart such as the one shown in Figure 8.10. If some of the participants will be continuing to work closely together after the course, a composite chart can be drawn up, changing the wording to 'we . . .'.

Future plans

	Within the next two weeks	Within the next two months	Within the next six months
I shall myself . . .			
I shall join with others to . . .			
Ideally I would like to . . .			
Problems I foresee are . . .			

Figure 8.10

Reviewing Resources

PURPOSE To review some of the materials used in school in the context of the need for a world dimension.

PREPARATION Collect together some of the books and packs most used in the school or department. Copies of the checklist shown in Figure 8.11 will be needed for each participant.

PROCEDURE In pairs colleagues study closely two or three books to see the extent to which they avoid the distortions listed in the checklist and incorporate the positive qualities. Then pairs join together to form small groups to discuss their findings. The final stage, clearly, is to discuss what action, if any, needs to be taken as a result of the exercise.

Graffiti Wall

PURPOSE To provide an effective and humorous way for participants to express their feelings on a course.

PREPARATION A large sheet of paper is put up for the day, or at each session, and divided up into bricks. The titles of the different sessions are written up on the wall. Brick-sized slips of paper are laid by the wall.

PROCEDURE Participants write comments as they wish on the slips of paper provided and stick them on the wall under the appropriate heading (see Figure 8.12). Such comments provide invaluable feedback to course organisers and can also be typed up and given back to participants as a record of the group's responses to their world studies course.

Reviewing resources: a checklist

Some distortions

1. *Our country: right or wrong*
Do the materials suggest uncritically that 'our' country is more civilised, peace-loving, tolerant than others? Or that another country is utterly evil?

2. *Isolation*
Do the materials imply that people and countries are isolated self-contained entities with no binding economic or cultural links with the wider world? Do they ignore the fact of interdependence?

3. *Sex stereotyping*
Do the materials imply that male and female roles are universal or unchangeable? Do they imply that men are superior to women?

4. *Race and prejudice*
Do the materials exaggerate the uniformity of any particular racial group and its distinctiveness from others? Do they imply that one group is superior to others?

5. *Technological fantasy*
Do the materials imply that the world's major problems can be solved exclusively by further developing industry and technology, irrespective of the widening gap between rich and poor and the finite nature of the environment and the world's resources?

Positive qualities

1. *Multicultural life*
Do the materials feature people from different countries and cultures going about everyday pursuits such as working, going to school, shopping? Are they shown as decision-making self-respecting people with whom children can identify?

2. *Conflict*
Do the materials deal honestly with tensions and conflicts and examine the different perceptions of participants in them? Is it shown that there are a variety of ways of resolving conflict?

3. *Peace*
Do the materials deal with issues relating to justice and peace? Are examples given of co-operation and fairness in practice?

4. *Environment*
Do the materials draw attention to the vulnerable nature of the earth's environment and ecology, and describe protective measures which are and could be taken? Do they question why the environment is under threat?

5. *Futures*
Do the materials contain a future dimension? Whatever their theme, do they help children to explore different futures, both probable and preferable?

Figure 8.11

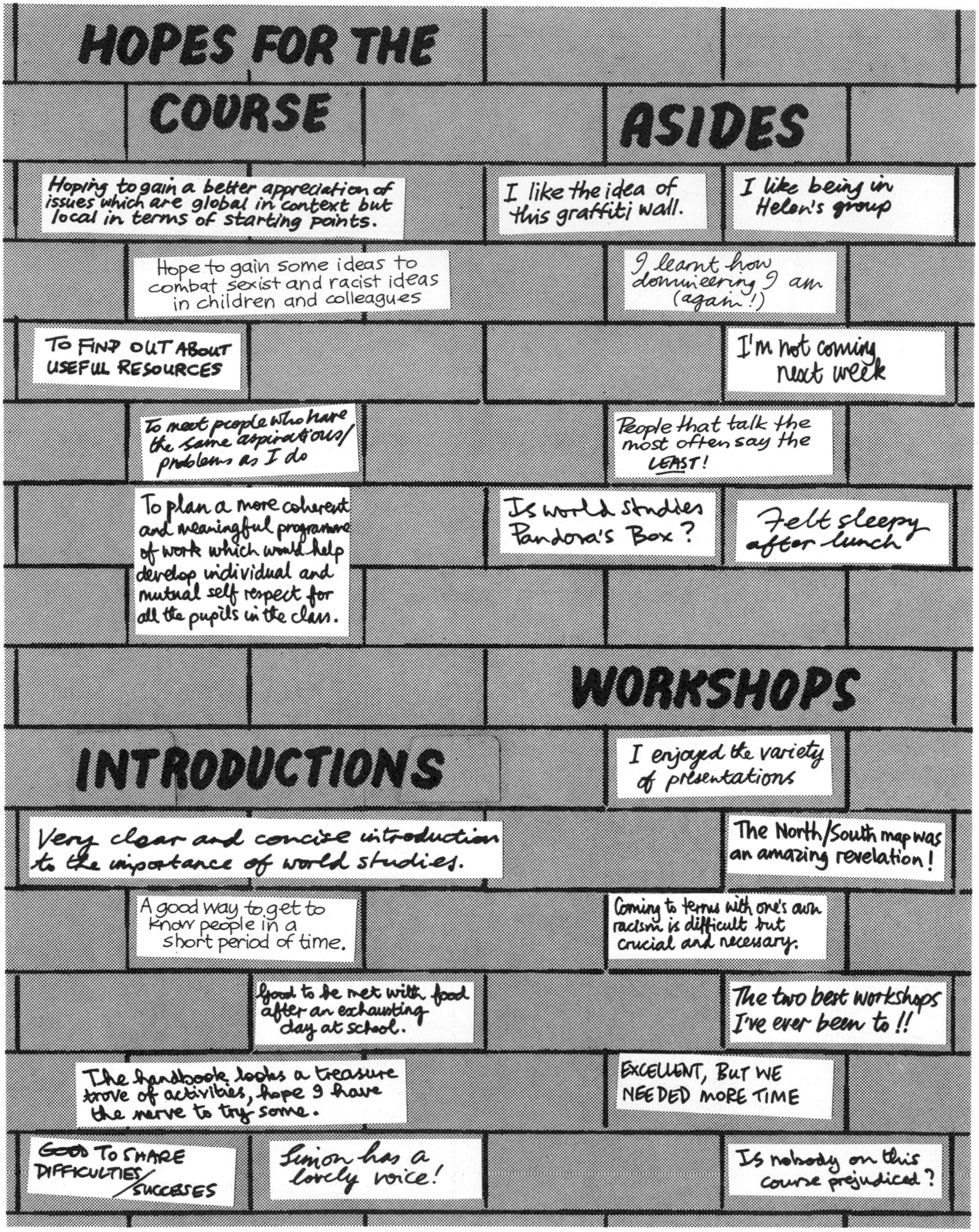

HOPES FOR THE COURSE

Hoping to gain a better appreciation of issues which are global in context but local in terms of starting points.

Hope to gain some ideas to combat sexist and racist ideas in children and colleagues

TO FIND OUT ABOUT USEFUL RESOURCES

To meet people who have the same aspirations/ problems as I do

To plan a more coherent and meaningful programme of work which would help develop individual and mutual self respect for all the pupils in the class.

ASIDES

I like the idea of this graffiti wall.

I like being in Helen's group

I learnt how domineering I am (again!)

I'm not coming next week

People that talk the most often say the LEAST!

Is world studies Pandora's Box?

Felt sleepy after lunch

WORKSHOPS

INTRODUCTIONS

Very clear and concise introduction to the importance of world studies.

A good way to get to know people in a short period of time.

good to be met with food after an exhausting day at school.

The handbook looks a treasure trove of activities, hope I have the nerve to try some.

GOOD TO SHARE DIFFICULTIES/ SUCCESSES

Simon has a lovely voice!

I enjoyed the variety of presentations

The North/South map was an amazing revelation!

Coming to terms with one's own racism is difficult but crucial and necessary.

The two best workshops I've ever been to !!

EXCELLENT, BUT WE NEEDED MORE TIME

Is nobody on this course prejudiced?

Figure 8.12 Graffiti wall

A School Case Study

Each school finds its own way towards a world dimension. At Sefton Park Junior School in Avon two teachers attended an in-service course organised by the *World Studies 8–13* project. One of the teachers, Nick Clough, writes the following description of how the staff subsequently set out to draw up a humanities policy which incorporated a world dimension. The school itself is near the centre of Bristol. It has a mixed intake, 18% of which is from ethnic minority groups.

Stage 1

The infants and junior schools spent an in-service day with two Local Education Authority (LEA) Humanities Advisers discussing the Avon LEA guidelines 'Geography and History in the Primary School'. During this day it was, among other things, possible to make some analysis of what we already did as a staff and come to a common understanding about the objectives described in the guidelines.

Stage 2

The junior school staff planned to mount an exhibition of work on the theme 'People and Places' to be presented some five months after this in-service day. The teachers organised exhibits of resources and of children's work resulting from the in-service day or from the world studies course. Among the aims of the exhibition were the following.

- To provide an incentive for us to question our objectives and co-ordinate our thinking in this area of the curriculum.
- To provide a framework in which we can test the value and viability of these objectives.
- To provide opportunities for children to share their experiences with each other and to be actively involved in explaining work to their parents.
- To provide an opportunity for parents to discover what we are trying to achieve and to invite feedback from them.
- To involve parents, teachers and pupils in a live multicultural event.

Stage 3

Teachers were asked to describe the content of what they intended to study with their classes in the form of a flow diagram. The content was then regrouped according to the objectives. A combination of the world studies objectives and the objectives described in 'Geography and History in the Primary School' was used. It was planned that the children's work should be presented under the appropriate objectives headings with explanatory notes written by teachers (see Figure 8.13).

Forecast/record sheet

Knowledge
Own self/family
Own society/culture
Own societies/cultures
Local environments
Distant environments
Things in common
Geometry of landscapes
Recent history (regressive)
Past times
Linear history
Futures
Trade/development
Peace/conflict

Skills
Use of evidence
Chronology
Empathy
Maps
Reasoning
Social skills
Political skills
Co-operation

Attitudes
Self-respect
Curiosity
Critical approach to information
Appreciation of other societies
Justice/fairness
Open mindedness

Concepts
Interrelationships/interdependence
Similarities/differences
Social change
Causes/consequences
Values/beliefs
Fairness
Communication
Conflict
Co-operation

NB On the actual forms, space is left below each heading for teachers' notes.

Figure 8.13

Stage 4

Exhibitions of work and of the resources used were mounted for an open evening and complemented by a number of live events. There was a performance of a traditional Ghanaian story accompanied by Ghanaian dancing and drumming (by the children). Bush Telegraph Theatre in Education Company organised co-operative games with another group of children. There were displays of Caribbean cookery and hair plaiting. Ekome Arts Dance Company and the Ujamaa Players (from Ghana) also performed. Staff from the local City Farm, a resource much used by the school, set up a stall to explain its developments and the opportunities it offered.

Stage 5

As parents went round the exhibition they were given written explanations of the teaching objectives. In some cases children acted as guides to the parents. The parents were also given a checklist of objectives and asked to identify those which *they* thought were most valuable. the results of this questionnaire were later analysed and it was found that those objectives relating to the development of children's attitudes scored highest.

> **Objectives: the parents' priorities**
>
> Objectives preferred by parents of pupils at Sefton Park Junior School, Avon, following an exhibition of world studies work in the school. (NB The headings ranked below were those given to the written explanations of teaching objectives.)
>
> 1. Openmindedness
> 2. Justice and fairness
> 3. Own society and culture
> 4. Other societies and cultures
> 5. Expression
> 6. Appreciation of other cultures
> 7. Enquiry
> 8. Co-operation
> 9. Critical approach to information
> 10. Environment
> 11. Curiosity
> 12. Positive self-image
> 13. Empathy
> 14. Things in common
> 15. Migration
> 16. Trade and development
> 17. Exploration
> 18. Mapping skills

Concepts

Topics	Interdependence	Similarities and differences	Social change	Causes and consequences	Values and beliefs	Fairness	Communication	Conflict	Co-operation
Mammals				✓	✓	✓		✓	
British society	✓					✓	✓		
Farming	✓	✓	✓	✓	✓	✓	✓		✓
How we used to live		✓	✓	✓	✓	✓	✓	✓	✓
Our homes/community		✓	✓	✓		✓			
North America			✓	✓	✓	✓		✓	
Ships/exploration		✓	✓				✓		✓
Homes	✓					✓			

Figure 8.14

Stage 6

The information in Figure 8.14 summarises the concepts used in a term's topic work across the whole school. It was taken from record sheets filled in by members of staff. Similar tables were drawn up to show what objectives for knowledge, skills and attitudes were used. At present our humanities curriculum is still very much in mid-development. It is hoped that the structure of the forecast/record sheets will provide us with a common purpose, maintain our direction and yet allow enough freedom for individual teachers to be able to meet the varying needs of the children in their classes and to be able to develop their own approaches. As we develop methods and resources it may be possible to select particular approaches for particular age ranges so that we may be confident that children will experience a balanced humanities curriculum as they pass through the school. The essential key to any future developments will be to keep discussion alive. It is inescapable that the implications of world studies go beyond a restructuring of the declared curriculum. Any curriculum development which involves looking at relationships, problem solving, decision making and fairness is bound to encompass aspects of the 'Hidden Curriculum'. It becomes increasingly clear that the core of the curriculum lies not in *what* we do, but in the *way* that things are done.

Further Reading

Richardson, R., Flood, M. and Fisher, S., *Debate and Decision: Schools in a World of Change*, World Studies Project of the One World Trust, 1979.

Richardson, R. (ed.) 'In-service education', *The New Era*, Vol. 59, No. 6, 1978.

Davies, M., *Social Responsibility in a Challenged World: A Description and Evaluation of a Weekend Workshop for Teachers*, Kingston Teachers Centre, 1979.

Ruddock, J., *Making the Most of the Short In-service Course*, Schools Council Working Paper 71, Methuen Educational, 1981.

Sinclair, S., *Learning about Africa: Dilemmas, Approaches, Resources: An account and evaluation of an in-service course.* Development Education Centre, 1979, available from Gillet Centre, Selly Oak Colleges, Bristol Road, Birmingham B29 6LE.

Braun, D. and Sinclair, S., *Birmingham and the Wider World – A Report on an In-service Course.* Development Education Centre, Birmingham, 1979 (address above).

Morrison, I., *Multi-Ethnic Education: Changes and Choices, A Conference Report*, Lewisham Teachers Centre, 1981.

Figure 8.15 (Len Munnik)

Appendix 1
Important Sources of Support

Organisations

Centre for Peace Studies
  St Martin's College, Lancaster LA1 3JD (0524 37698)
Centre for World Development Education
  128 Buckingham Palace Road, London SW1W 9SH (01 730 8332/3)
Christian Aid
  PO Box No. 1, London SW9 8BH (01 733 5500)
Council for Education in World Citizenship
  19–21 Tudor Street, London EC4Y 0DJ (01 353 3353)
Council for Environmental Education
  University of Reading, London Road, Reading RG1 5AQ (0734 875234 ext. 218)
Commonwealth Institute
  Kensington High Street, London W8 6NQ (01 602 3252)
International and Multicultural Education Project
  Jordanhill College of Education, Glasgow G13 1PP (041 959 1232)
National Association of Development Education Centres
  128 Buckingham Palace Road, London SW1W 9SH (01 730 0972)
National Association of Multiracial Education
  PO Box 9, Walsall, West Midlands WS1 3SF (0922 646183)
One World Trust
  24 Palace Chambers, Bridge Street, London SW1A 2JT (01 930 7661)
Oxfam
  274 Banbury Road, Oxford OX2 7D2 (0865 56777)
World Studies Teacher Training Centre
  York University, York YO1 5DD (0904 59861 ext. 453)

Periodicals

Action for Development
  Centre for World Development Education, 128 Buckingham Palace Road, London SW1W 9SH
Bulletin of Environmental Education
  Streetwork Ltd, c/o TCPA, 17 Carlton House Terrace, London SW1Y 5AS
Development Forum
  Development Forum General Education, DESI, C-527, United Nations, 1211 Geneva, Switzerland
Future Studies Centre Newsletter
  Birmingham Settlement, 318 Summer Lane, Birmingham B19 3RL
Multiracial Education
  Andrew Dorn, CRE, Elliott House, 10/12 Allington Street, London SW1E 5EH
Multiracial Teaching
  Trentham Books, 30 Wenger Crescent, Trentham, Stoke-on-Trent ST4 8LE
New Equals
  Commission for Racial Equality, Elliott House, 10/12 Allington Street, London SW1E 5EH
New Internationalist
  42 Hythe Bridge Street, Oxford OX1 2EP
Peace Education Newsletter
  37 Heights Lane, Bradford BD9 6JA
Peace News
  8 Elm Avenue, Nottingham 3
Turning Point Newsletter
  Spring Cottage, 9 New Road, Ironbridge, Shropshire TF8 7AU
World Studies Journal
  World Studies Teacher Training Centre, York University, York YO1 5DD

Appendix 2
World Studies 8–13: Co-ordinators and Contacts

The *World Studies 8–13* project has built up a network of LEA co-ordinators and contacts. This list indicates who to contact if you want to find out more about what is happening in your area.

Avon
Rex Beddis
  Senior Adviser, Education Department, PO Box 57, Avon House North, St James Barton, Bristol BS99 7EB (0272 290777)

Bradford
Barbara Davy
  Advisory Service, Provincial House, Tyrrel Street, Bradford BD1 1NP (0274 729577)

Bedfordshire
John Huckle
  Head of Geography, Bedford College of Higher Education, Polhill Avenue, Bedford MK41 9EA (0234 51671)

Berkshire
Robin Richardson
  Adviser for Multicultural Education, Education Department, Shire Hall, Shinfield Park, Reading (0734 875444)

Birmingham
David Flint and Peter Rogers
  Newman College,
  Birmingham B32 3NT
  (021 476 1181)

Brent
Islay Doncaster
  Adviser, Education Department, PO Box 1, Chesterfield House 9 Park Lane, Wembley, Middlesex HA9 7RW (01 903 1400)

Buckinghamshire
Peter Wenham
  Senior Adviser, Education Department, County Hall, Aylesbury, Bucks. (0296 5000)

Derbyshire
Pat Whitaker
  Adviser, Area Education Office, 16 St Mary's Gate, Derby DE1 3NN (0332 40251)

Devon
Roger Horth
  Adviser, East Devon Education Offices, Morwenstow, 7 Barnfield Crescent, Exeter EX1 1SU (0392 77977)

Dudley
Ian Cleland
  Adviser, Education Offices, 2 St James's Road, Dudley (089 428 55433)

Durham
Peter Livesey
  Adviser, Education Centre, Front Street, Stanley, Co. Durham DH9 0ST (0207 30521)

Hampshire
John Poxon
  King Alfred's College, Winchester SO22 4NR (0962 62281)

Haringey
Ann Baker
  Haringey Teachers' Centre, 336 Philip Lane, Tottenham, London N15 4AB (01 808 0771)

Hertfordshire
Colin Harris
  Adviser, Education Department, County Hall, Hertford SG13 8DF (0992 54242)

Inner London
Aileen McKenzie
  Ujaama Centre, 14 Brixton Road, London SW9 (01 582 2068)

Manchester
Miriam Steiner
  Manchester Urban Studies Centre, 328–30 Deansgate, Manchester M3 4FN (061 832 559)

Newcastle
Cliff Winlow
  Adviser, Pendower Hall, Teachers' Centre, West Road, Newcastle-upon-Tyne NE15 6PP (0632 743620)

Newham
Lesley Hagon
  Multicultural Support Team, Newham Jusenice Education Centre, New City Road, London E13 9PY (01 472 9635)

Norfolk
Ralph Jones
  16 The Close, Roydon, Diss, Norfolk

Oxfordshire
Cathy Holden
  Bishop Kirk Middle School, Middle Way, Oxford OX2 7LQ

Rochdale
Richard Bramwell
    Adviser, Education & Training Centre, Hind Hill Street, Heywood, Lancs OL10 1AH (0706 624 923)
Sheffield
Di Durie
    Lowfield Multicultural Centre, Lowfield Junior School, London Road, Sheffield S2 4NJ (0742 52501)
Somerset
John Burns
    Danesfield School, Williton, Somerset
Walsall
Keith Allison
    Education Department, Civic Centre, Darwall Street, Walsall WS1 1DQ (0922 21244)
Waltham Forest
Kathy Wiltshire
    West Indian Supplementary Service, Kirkdale Centre, Kirkdale Road, London E11 (01 556 0406)

Warwickshire
Peter Birch
    Adviser, County Education Department, 22 Northgate Street, Warwicks. CV34 4SR (0926 493431)
Julie Bradley
    Warwickshire World Studies Centre, 32a Bath Street, Leamington Spa, Warwicks CU31 3AE. (0926 26476)
West Glamorgan
Vivian Thomas
    Adviser, District Education Office, Princess House, Princess Way, Swansea SA1 4PD (0792 42024)
Wiltshire
John Fisher
    Adviser, Educational Department, Sanford House, Sanford Street, Swindon, Wilts. SN1 10H (0793 33531)
Wolverhampton
Gordon Boon
    Adviser, Education Department, Beckminister House, Birches Barn Road, Wolverhampton WV3 7BJ (0902 337244)

Appendix 3

The One World Trust

The One World Trust was set up in 1952 by the all-party Parliamentary Group for World Government at Westminster. In the 1950s and 1960s the Trust sponsored several projects, for example on history syllabuses in different parts of the world and on teaching about world community. From 1973 to 1980 Robin Richardson directed the Trust's World Studies Project which focussed on the secondary curriculum. Simon Fisher became Field Officer for the project in 1979 and subsequently its Director. From 1980 to 1983 he co-directed *World Studies 8–13* for the Trust. Further details of the Trust's work are available from: The Secretary, One World Trust, 24 Palace Chambers, Bridge Street, London SW1A 2JT.

The Centre for Peace Studies

The Centre for Peace Studies was established in 1980 to provide a national advice and information service on all issues relating to education for peace. Its first venture was co-directing *World Studies 8–13* (1980–3). The Centre has a particular interest in education for peace, world studies and multicultural education, and provides in-service training in all of these fields. Consultancy work is also carried out for LEAs planning guidelines or working parties on education for peace. Various Occasional Papers of specific interest to teachers appear periodically. For further details of the Centre's work write to: The Information Officer, Centre for Peace Studies, St Martin's College, Lancaster LA1 3JD.

Notes

Chapter 1

1. This fable by Robin Richardson is taken, slightly adapted, from *Change and Choice: Britain in an Interdependent World*, a study pack published by CWDE, 128 Buckingham Palace Road, London SW1W 9SH.
2. This account was inspired by a longer passage in Anderson, Lee, *Schooling and Citizenship in a Global Age: An Exploration of the Meaning and Significance of Global Education*, Mid-America Program for Global Perspectives in Education, Indiana University, 1979.
3. The situation faced by Native Americans today is detailed in Wilson, James, *The Original Americans: U.S. Indians*, Minority Rights Group Report No. 31, 1980.
4. Described by Norman Myers in 'What gets the chop when the axe falls?', *The Guardian*, 10 December 1981.
5. Contributed by Robin Richardson.
6. *The Global Cake* forms part of a pack called *The People GRID*, published by Oxfam and Cockpit Arts Workshop, 1977.
7. See page 00 for further information.
8. See Milner, D., *Children and Race: Ten Years On*, Ward Lock Educational, 1983, Chapter 5, and Heater, D. W., *World Studies: Education for International Understanding in Britain*, Harrap, 1980, Chapter 4.
9. See Tolley, H., *Children and War: Political Socialisation to International Conflict*, Teachers College Press, New York, 1973.
10. See Carnie, J. M., 'Children's attitudes to other nationalities' in *New Movements in the Study and Teaching of Geography*, Temple Smith, 1972.
11. The text of this is quoted in full in Heater, D., *World Studies: Education for International Understanding in Britain*, Harrap, 1980.
12. See Bowles, T. S., *Survey of Attitudes Towards Overseas Development*, HMSO, 1978.
13. See for example Hicks, D., 'World studies and education for peace' in Keeble, R. (ed.), *The Dove in the Classroom*, (forthcoming).
14. Further information on these can be obtained from the Project Director, Jordanhill College of Education, Glasgow, G13 1PP.

Chapter 2

1. Hall, David, 'World studies: their place and emphasis', Geography Extra, *Times Educational Supplement*, 3 December 1982.

2. Roszak, Theodore, in 'School: letting go, letting grow', Chapter 7 of *Person/Planet*, Granada, 1981.
3. Slightly adapted from Postman, N. and Weingartner, C., *Teaching as a Subversive Activity*, Penguin, 1971.
4. Galton, M., Simon, B. and Croll, P., *Inside the Primary Classroom*, Routledge & Kegan Paul, 1980.
5. Wren, B., *Education for Justice*, SCM Press, 1977. page 22.
6. Raths, L. E., Harmin, M. and Simon, S. B., *Values and Teaching: Working with Values in the Classroom*, Merrill, 1966.
7. Mike Rathbone, 'Learning to question', *Junior Education*, July 1982.
8. *Primary Education in England: A survey by HMI*, HMSO, 1978.

Chapter 3

1. See, for example, Bono, E. (ed.), *The Cort Thinking Lessons*, Pergamon Press, 1982 and Stevens, O., *Children Talking Politics: Political Learning in Childhood*, Martin Robertson, 1982.
2. Ted Wragg's 'Personal Column' in *Times Educational Supplement*, 11 June 1982.
3. As suggested by Robin Richardson in *Learning for Change in World Society*, World Studies Project of the One World Trust, 1979, page 109.
4. For a detailed discussion of the use of concepts see the publications of the Schools Council History, Geography, Social Science Project, especially *Curriculum Planning in History, Geography and Social Science 8–13*, and Blyth, A. *et al.*, *Teaching for Concepts*, Collins/ESL, Bristol.
5. Wren, B., *Education for Justice*, SCM Press, 1977.
6. Raven, J., 'Bringing Education back into schools', Chapter 9 in Burgess, T. and Adam, E. (eds.), *Outcomes of Education*, Macmillan, 1980.

Chapter 5

1. Several of these activities have been adapted from Prutzman, P., Burger, M. L., Bodenhamer, G. and Stern, L., *The Friendly Classroom for a Small Planet* (see Selected Resources on page 98).
2. For more discussion of this see Oakley, A., *Subject Women*, Fontana, 1982.
3. Whyte, J., *Beyond the Wendy House*, Schools Council, 1983.

4. Adapted from a checklist published by the Equal Opportunities Commission.

5. This activity is taken from Richardson, R., *Learning for Change in World Society*, World Studies Project of the One World Trust, 1979 (second edition).

6. Some of the suggestions made here are adapted from *Doing Things in and About the Home: Photographs and Activities About Work, Play and Equality*, Serawood House, 1983 (see Selected Resources on page 99).

7. This information is contained in *Subject Women*, pages 111–12 (see note 2 above).

Chapter 6

1. See Carnie, J., 'Children's attitudes to other nationalities', Chapter 10 in Graves, N. (ed.), *New Movements in the Study and Teaching of Geography*, Temple Smith, 1972.

2. See for example Institute of Race Relations, *Roots of Racism* and *Patterns of Racism*, available from 247/9 Pentonville Road, London N1 9NGY.

3. Bowles, T. S., *Survey of Attitudes Towards Overseas Development*, HMSO, 1978.

4. Clark, B. (ed.), *The Changing World and The Primary Classroom*, Centre for World Development Education, 1979,

5. Roberts, J., *From Massacres to Mining: The Colonization of Aboriginal Australia*, War on Want, 1978.

6. Available from Council on Interracial Books for Children, 1841 Broadway, New York 10023–7648.

7. *Chief Seattle's Testimony*, Slide/tape set, United Society for the Propagation of the Gospel.

8. Some of the approaches suggested here are adapted from *Discussion in Small Groups: Exercises, Activities, Approaches*, a booklet compiled by the Teaching and Support Service, West Berkshire.

Chapter 7

1. Toffler, A., *Learning for Tomorrow: The Role of the Future in Education*, Vintage Books/Random House, New York, 1974.

2. Much of the inspiration for this chapter came from Fitch, R. M. and Svengalis, C. M., *Futures Unlimited: Teaching About Worlds to Come*, National Council for the Social Studies, Washington DC, 1979.

3. The first five scenarios are based on Robertson, J., *The Sane Alternative: A Choice of Futures*, 1983, available from 9 New Road, Ironbridge, Shropshire TF8 7AU.

4. Nicholson, S., *No Vanished Futures*, Open University, 1978.

5. This activity is adapted from one which is described in Richardson, R., *Learning for Change in World Society*, World Studies Project of the One World Trust, 1979 (second edition).

6. This style of activity and many others are described in Byrne, D. and Dixon, S., *Communication Games*, NFER, 1979.

7. See note 5 above.

8. *Undercurrents*, 27 Clerkenwell Close, London EC1R OAT; *Peace News*, 8 Elm Avenue, Nottingham 3.

Chapter 8

1. There are two books which consider the whole process of curriculum development and decision making in primary schools. In Whitaker, Patrick, *The Primary Head*, Heinemann Educational, 1983, this process is considered from the Head's point of view. In the chapter on 'Curriculum Planning', world studies is used as an example of the planning process and there are helpful suggestions for whole school decision making. In Waters, Derek, *Responsibility and Promotion in the Primary School*, Heinemann Educational, 1983, the process is looked at from the scale post holders' point of view, and consideration given to the sorts of skills needed by those exercising curriculum leadership.

2. Further discussion by Robin Richardson on some of these ideas can be found in *Learning for Change in World Society*, World Studies Project of the One World Trust, pages 122–3 of the 1979 edition, and at greater length in an article which appeared in UNESCO's *Prospects*, Vol. 9, No. 2, 1979, pages 184–96. Richardson, R., Flood, M. and Fisher, S., *Debate and Decision: Schools in a World of Change*, World Studies Project of the One World Trust, 1980, provided inspiration for this chapter and contains more examples of in-service activities based on this style of approach.

"Finally, Mr Hicks, and purely as a matter of interest, what colour are you?"